Contents

1 All About Cornwall — 2

2 East Cornwall — 16

3 North Cornwall and Bodmin Moor — 30

4 The South Coast — 46

5 The Far West — 62

Resources — 78

Index — 79

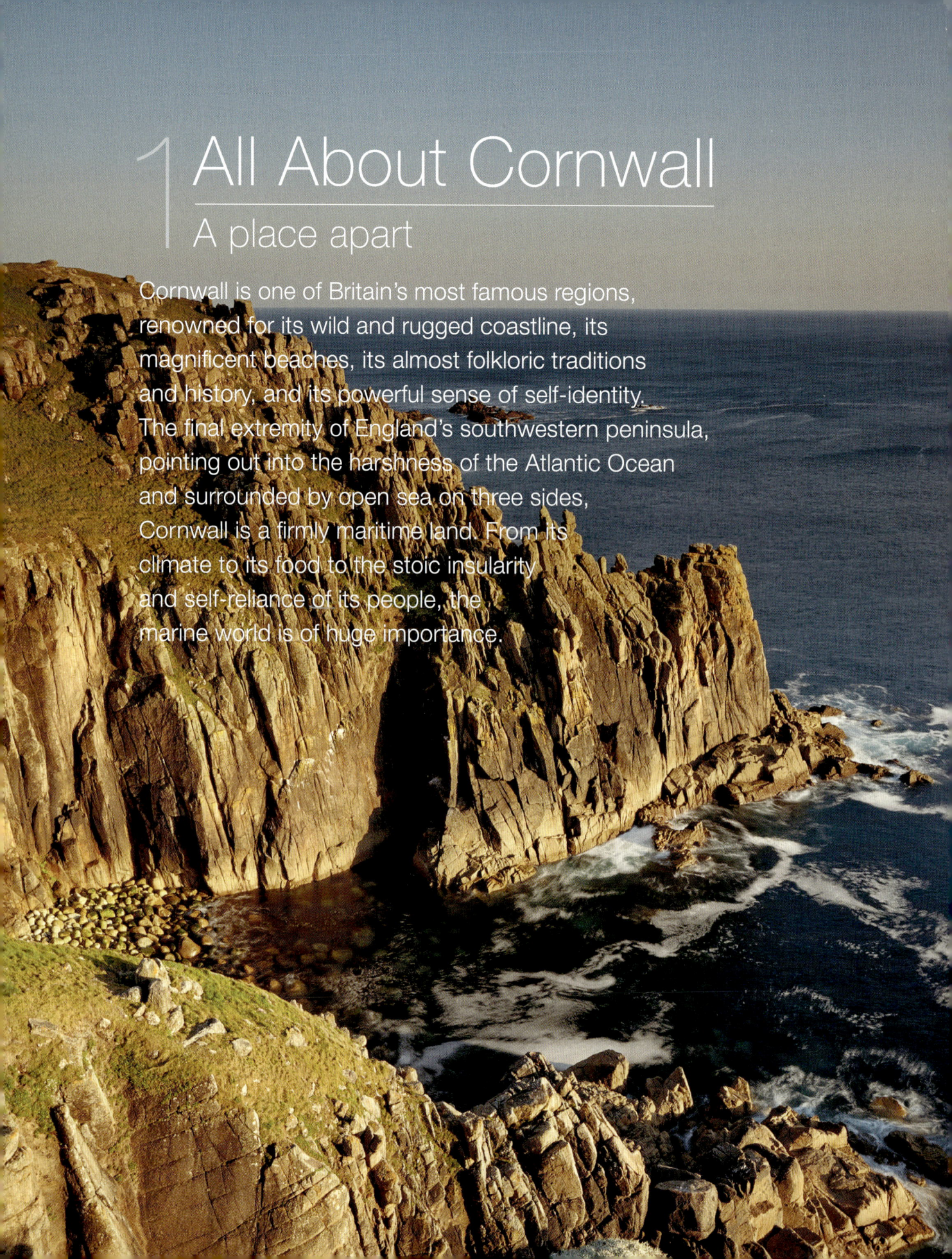

1 All About Cornwall
A place apart

Cornwall is one of Britain's most famous regions, renowned for its wild and rugged coastline, its magnificent beaches, its almost folkloric traditions and history, and its powerful sense of self-identity. The final extremity of England's southwestern peninsula, pointing out into the harshness of the Atlantic Ocean and surrounded by open sea on three sides, Cornwall is a firmly maritime land. From its climate to its food to the stoic insularity and self-reliance of its people, the marine world is of huge importance.

All About Cornwall

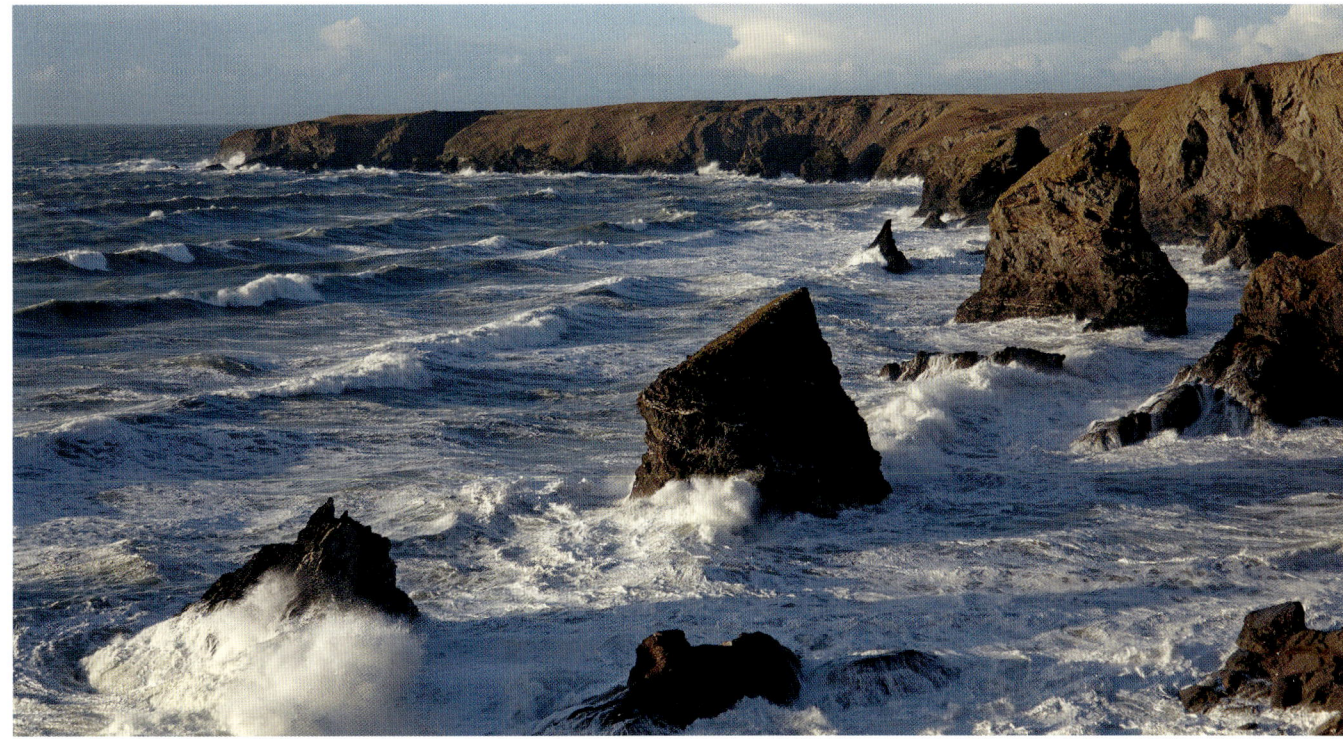

Left: The rugged granite cliffs of Gwennap Head glow in evening sunlight. Despite being a relatively unknown place, it is actually one of Cornwall's most important headlands, the very spot where the Atlantic north coast meets the English Channel south coast, in a sharp right-angle turn.

Above: Cornwall is famous for its rugged coastal views, especially along its northern, Atlantic coastline. In this case the rocks of Bedruthan Steps seen just after a storm has passed through, really encapsulate Cornwall's wildness.

Quite apart from the sea, however, another huge influence on Cornwall has been historically its remarkable industrial heritage. Its prowess in tin and copper mining put Cornwall firmly in the vanguard of the world's 18th and 19th century Industrial Revolution. Today the remains of that past era provide one of Cornwall's greatest icons: hundreds of crumbling mine ruins, whose characteristic outlines provide a quintessential Cornish stamp to many landscapes, from hilltops to dramatic coastal cliffs.

One of the UK's Celtic areas, the Cornish proudly uphold their traditions as evidence of their distinct identity, reviving the nearly-defunct Cornish Gaelic language, just about everywhere flying the black-and-white flag of St Piran, the patron-saint of Cornwall, and in the process gaining recognition as a minority people.

Today, it is, of course, the region's coastal scenery that makes it famous, the long golden beaches, superb surf, excellent seafood, and impossibly quaint ancient fishing harbours, drawing in huge numbers of visitors from across the UK and Europe. Some of the main attractions, such as Newquay's Fistral Beach, and the coastal towns of Padstow and St Ives, can become impossibly crowded in mid-summer, but this lasts for just a few weeks each year, and anyway beyond these few places there is plenty of space for everyone. All that is needed is the willingness to just get out there and explore Cornwall's multitude of treasures.

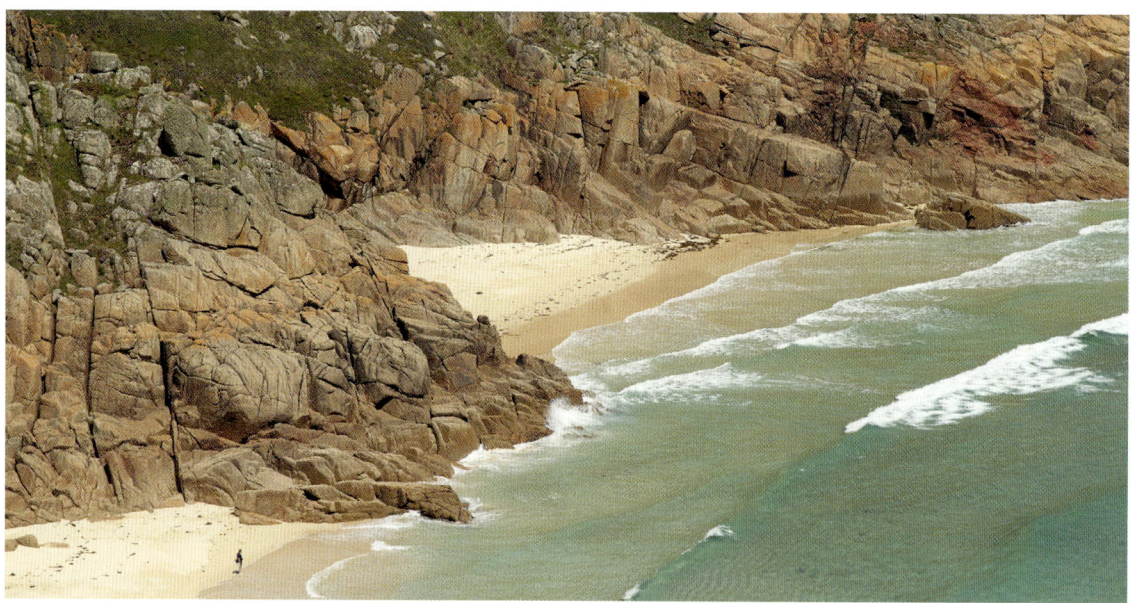

Above: One of the hallmarks of the Cornish coast is its golden sandy beaches, in this instance at Porthcurno, near Land's End.

A maritime land

The final promontary of England's southwest peninsula, Cornwall is a highly maritime land, bordered by the Atlantic Ocean to the north and west, and by the English Channel to the south. Its 3563 sq km (1376 sq miles) is mostly quite rugged, with a spine of hills running along much of its length, the highest of which consist of Bodmin Moor in the northeast. These are areas rich in granite, with its western limit in the Isles of Scilly, a stunningly beautiful cluster of islands about 45 km (28 miles) off Cornwall's western tip. It is on Bodmin Moor that Cornwall's highest points occur, at Rough Tor (400m/1312ft) and Brown Willy (420m/1378ft), both in the heart of the moor's wildest area, site of blanket bogs, marshes and rough grassland.

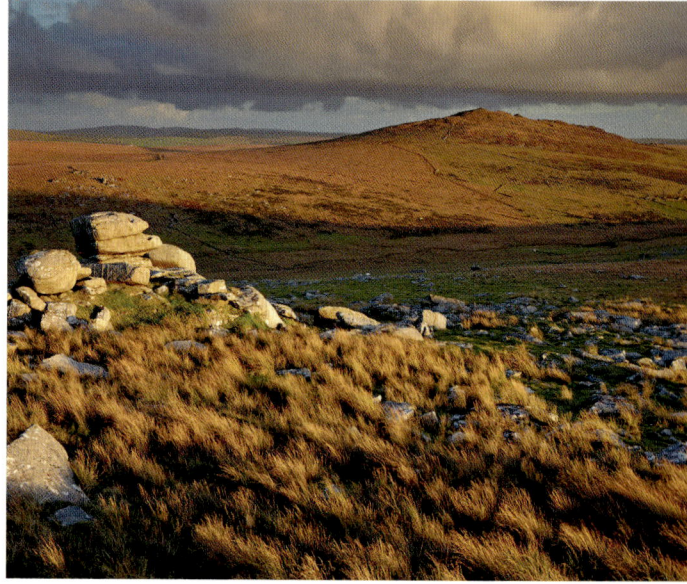

Above: An autumnal view from Rough Tor towards Brown Willy, Cornwall's highest point, and wildest part of Bodmin Moor.

To the east, Cornwall borders with the county of Devon, the boundary marked along most of its length by the River Tamar, a designation established as long ago as 936 by the Anglo-Saxon King Athelstan. This river rises in hilly farmland not far from Bude in north Cornwall, before winding its way through deep, remote and densely wooded valleys almost devoid of significant towns, before joining the sea on the south coast beside the Devonian city of Plymouth.

The Tamar is not the only river along this south coast. Firstly, there is the lovely Lynher River, which flows down from Bodmin Moor, draining much of

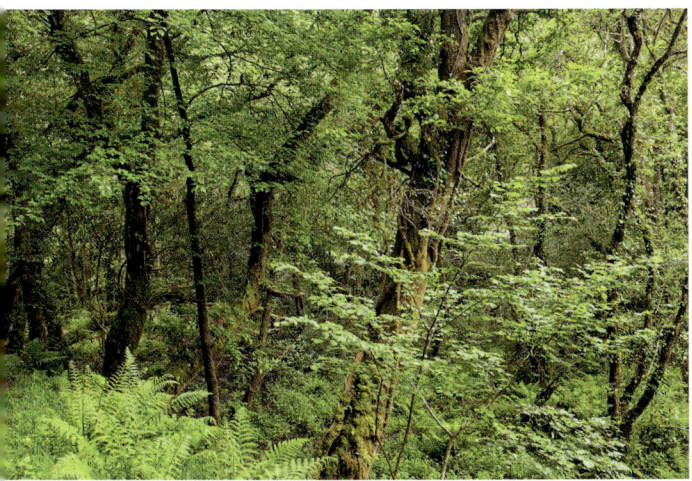

Above: Beautiful Cardinham Woods, near Bodmin, is one of the best known of the woodlands that nestle in the shelter of deep valleys, particularly on the southern side of Bodmin Moor.

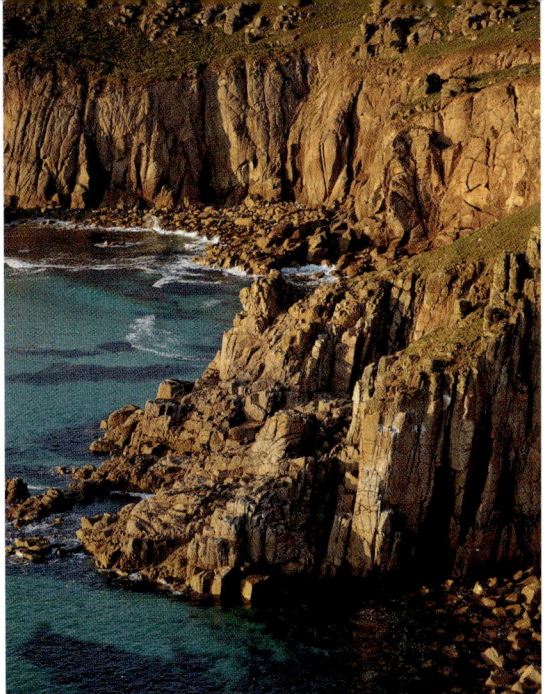

Above: The rugged granite cliffs of Gwennap Head, a few miles from Land's End.

east Cornwall before joining the Tamar shortly before it reaches the sea. Further west are the Looe and Fowey Rivers, both of which also rise on Bodmin Moor, while further west again are the Fal and Helford Rivers, both joining the sea near Falmouth and renowned for their shellfish.

While the southern side of Cornwall has a relatively gentle and largely agricultural landscape of rolling hills, the northern side is mostly wild and rugged, exposed as it is to the Atlantic storms. The only river of any size to reach the sea on this coast is the Camel, which flows down from Bodmin Moor to join the sea in a beautiful estuary at Padstow. Apart from this, the north coast consists of alternating high cliffs and spectacular sandy beaches, site of most of the county's major surfing venues, including Newquay, Bude, Hayle and Sennen.

The landscape of Cornwall's two western peninsulas – the Lizard and Penwith – is mostly quite rugged and windswept. Here are some of the county's most spectacular cliffs and most iconic views, including Land's End, St Michael's Mount and the cliffs of Treen and Logan Rock. It also has one of the UK's most magnificent beaches, at Hayle, backed by a vast expanse of dunes.

Finally, there are the lovely Isles of Scilly, a cluster of 200 islands, surrounded by the Atlantic. All quite low-lying, only five of the islands are inhabited. Most of the main islands encircle a large 'lagoon', whose waters are quite shallow and whose shores are lined with magnificent sandy beaches.

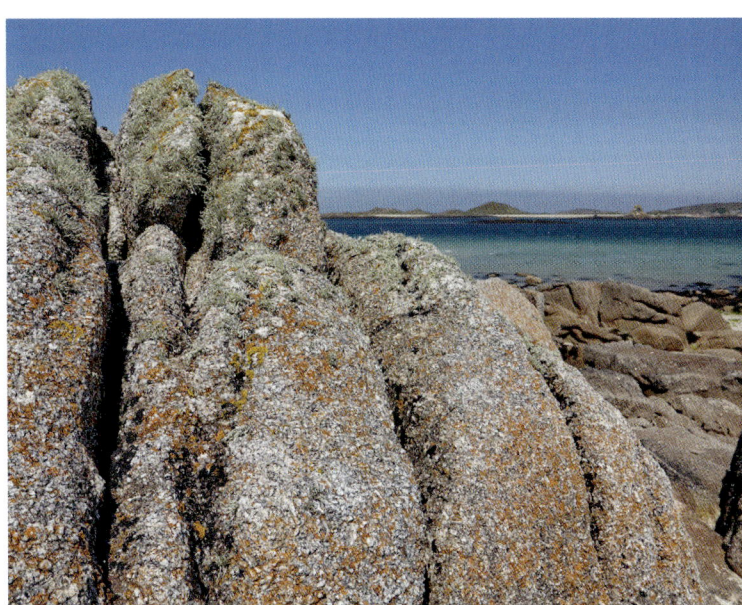

Above: A beautiful lichen-covered granite boulder along the shore in Pentle Bay, on the island of Tresco, is typical of the Isles of Scilly.

Beautiful Cornwall: A Portrait of a County

Wildlife and the natural environment

Cornwall's maritime air controls its climate, providing cooler weather in summer than many parts of the UK, but significantly warmer in winter, leaving much of it largely free of snow and frost. That should result in a lush vegetation, but the high winds and salt-laden air work against this, limiting growth, particularly on the exposed hills and clifftops, and restricting dense woodlands to just the most sheltered valleys.

As a result, much of Cornwall's natural beauty is quite stark, hillsides often populated largely by stunted, wind-gnarled hawthorns and tough grasses. Clifftops are covered at most with low-growing scrub, but more usually with simply heather, gorse, a few hardy grasses and – in early summer at least – a plethora of magnificent flowers. These include such beauties as thrift, yellow kidney vetch, sea campion and bird's-foot trefoil, to name just a

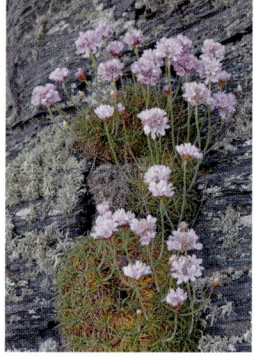

Above: Thrift, or sea pink, is found right along Cornwall's coast, especially on the rugged and exposed clifftops.

Above: The brilliant yellows of kidney vetch in full bloom in early summer, on the cliffs above Boscastle.

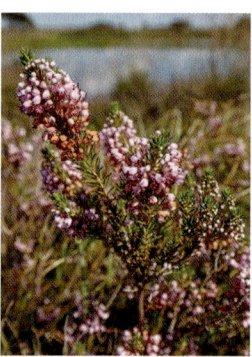

Above: Cornish heath is quite a rare heather that in Cornwall grows only on the Lizard peninsula.

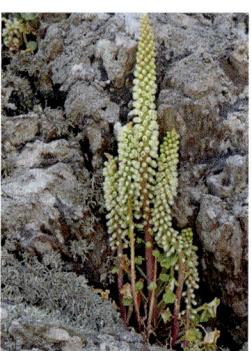

Above: Wall pennywort is extremely common in Cornwall, growing out of walls and bare rocks.

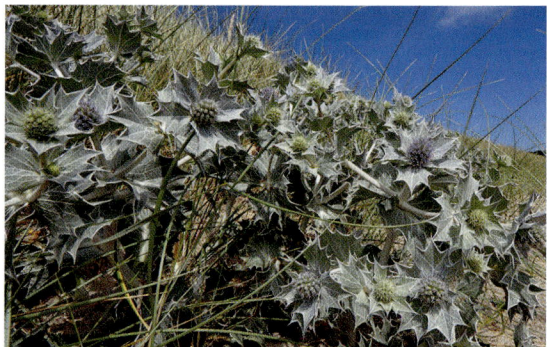

Above: Sea holly can sometimes be found growing on the seaward side of dunes and is quite unmistakable.

few. Heathers consist mostly of ling (or true heather) and bell heather, while in addition the Lizard peninsula is one of only two homes in the UK to the lovely Cornish heath.

Inland, the few woodlands are home to many of the usual species of southwest England, including oaks, beech and ash trees, plus at ground level bluebells, wood anemones and southern marsh orchids. In terms of animals, well known mammals include roe and fallow deer, badgers, rabbits and the occasional hare, with otters living along just about all the rivers and streams.

Along much of the coast, such mammals are hard to come by, but instead birds of prey are easily seen, including buzzards, peregrine falcons and kestrels. The chough, an emblem of Cornwall, has recently made a comeback to the cliffs after an absence of many years. Often mixed in with crows and difficult to distinguish at a distance, the chough can be identified by its bright orange bill and legs.

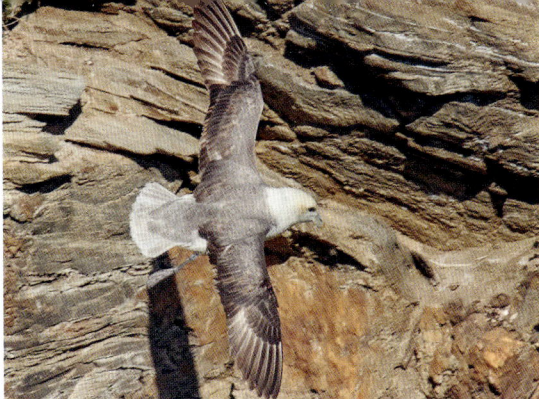
Above: The fulmar is quite common along Cornwall's coasts. Resembling a gull, it is actually a member of the albatross family.

Above: The kestrel is frequently seen along Cornwall's coasts, especially along the remoter cliffs.

The heathlands and dunes are home to a wide array of smaller animals, such as adders and lizards, and there is quite a wealth of butterfly species – particularly on the Lizard peninsula – including peacock, pearl-bordered fritillary, painted lady, wall brown, tortoiseshell and several species of blue.

The quiet river estuaries provide shelter and feeding grounds for many thousands of ducks, geese and wading birds, particularly in winter. Most commonly seen are wigeon, pochard, shovelers, herons, godwits, curlews, dunlin and redshanks, though there are many more.

It is for the marine wildlife that Cornwall is justifiably well known. The most frequently seen marine birds include of course various gulls, plus turnstones, cormorants, shags, fulmars and gannets. Charismatic puffins, along with guillemots and razorbills, can be seen nesting in the Scillies during summer.

The most commonly seen marine mammal is the grey seal, frequently visible in the water or hauled out on rocks. The common seal (aka the harbour seal) can also be seen from time to time, though it is much less common here. Dolphins and basking sharks are frequently seen around Cornwall's coast, though usually a little further offshore, and in deeper waters whales ares spotted from time to time.

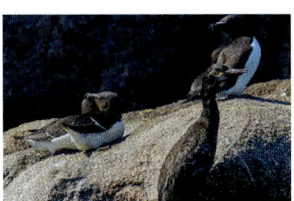
Above: Razorbills are a common sight in the Scillies during early summer, while shags (single bird on the right) are common throughout the year.

All this natural beauty and wildlife make Cornwall an important place for conservation. Large parts of the coastline, as well as Bodmin Moor and a number of other inland sites, have multiple layers of protection. A third of the county is incorporated into what until late 2023 was known as the Cornwall Area of Outstanding Natural Beauty (AONB), but which is now known as Cornwall National Landscape. There is also a long string of Sites of Special Scientific Interest (SSSIs), as well as a plethora of nature reserves, including several Ramsar sites (protected wetlands of international importance), marine conservation zones, special protection areas and special areas of conservation.

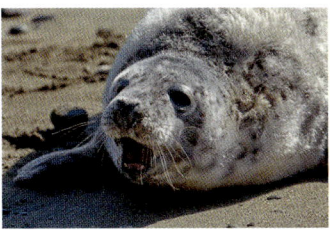
Above: A grey seal pup in a remote cove on Cornwall's south coast.

Beautiful Cornwall: A Portrait of a County

A way of life

Being Cornish, or even just living in Cornwall, usually comes with a certain amount of local pride and/or kudos, at the very least a warm glow resulting from the belief by outsiders that a Cornish lifestyle is automatically associated with outdoor ruggedness, self-reliant independence, a constantly bronzed skin and tousled hair, and regular doses of surfing. Needless to say, although there is a certain amount of truth in at least some of this, daily life in Cornwall is generally just as prosaic as anywhere else!

It is true that many people living in Cornwall do work independently, or at least in very small companies, and many people who move to live in Cornwall from other parts of the country do so for the outdoor lifestyle. As for the surfing, well that is the preserve mostly of the relatively young, although the number of older surfers is steadily increasing as the early pioneers of the sport in Cornwall start to age.

Cornwall does somehow cast a spell over anyone who lives there for any length of time, the roar of its surf, the ruggedness of its cliffs, the loneliness of the moors, the cry of gulls and even the smell of seaweed and fish working their way into the psyche

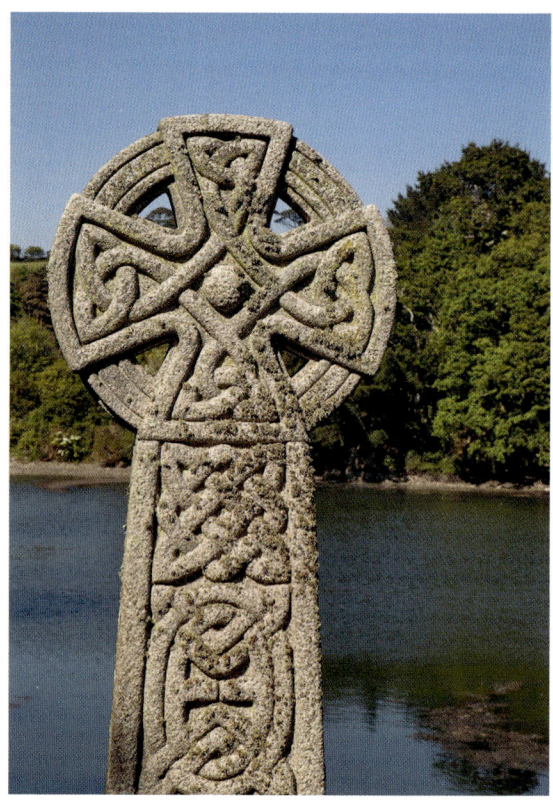

Above: A classic Celtic cross in a graveyard at St Just-in-Roseland, near St Mawes.

to drive home a very strong sense of belonging and even loyalty.

Pride in a Cornish identity has for many years been expressed in calls for Cornwall's independence, or at least autonomy, led by Mebyon Kernow, the Cornish Nationalist Party. While independence does seem rather unlikely, the growing sense of a Cornish 'separateness' has led to a steady revival in many old Cornish traditions. One of these is the widespread flying of the flag of St Piran, a white cross on a black background, for many years now Cornwall's 'national' flag, regularly seen just about everywhere, even on government buildings.

Such uniquely Cornish festivals as Padstow's Obby Oss, Mousehole's Tom Bawcock's Eve

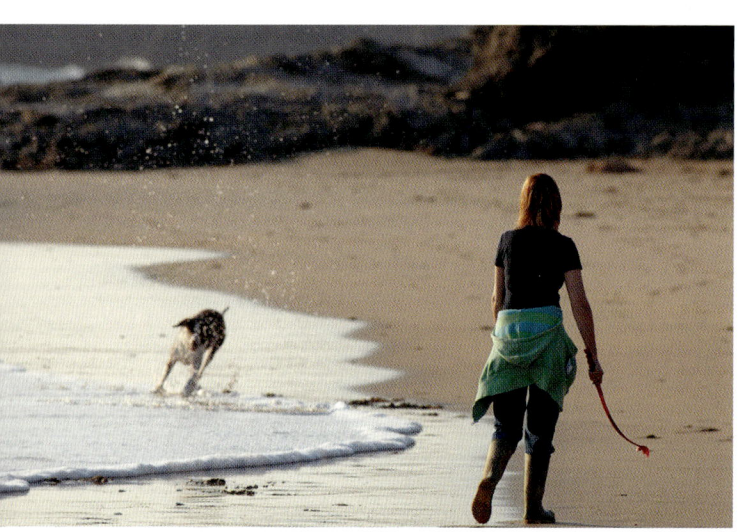

Above: Walking the dog on the beach at Constantine Bay. Living in Cornwall gives plenty of opportunity for an outdoor lifestyle.

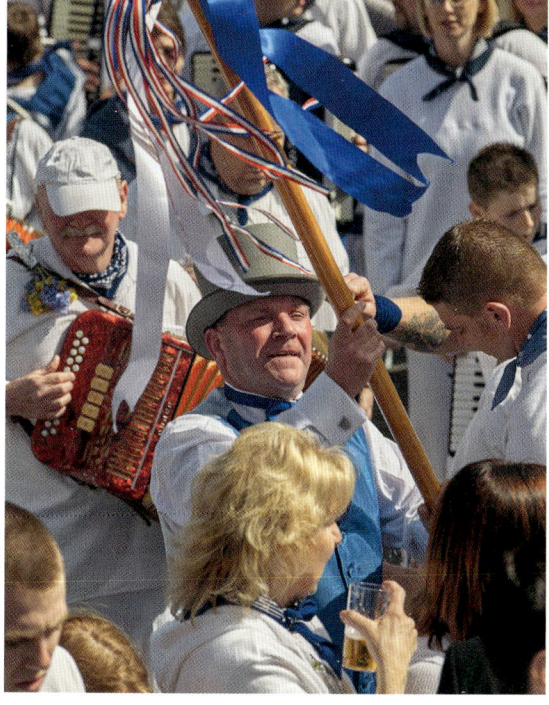

Above: Crowds gather around the master of ceremonies at Padstow's Obby Oss Festival, held every 1st May.

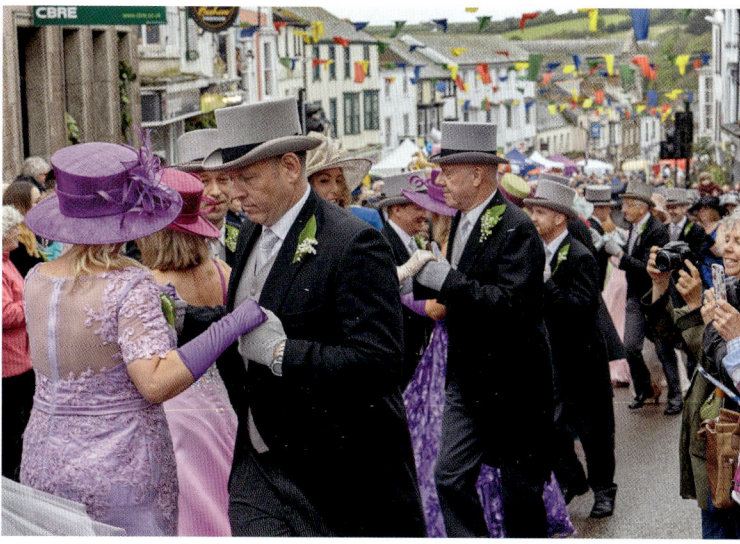

Above: Helston's Flora Day, held every 8th May, consists of a series of very stylish dances through the town's streets.

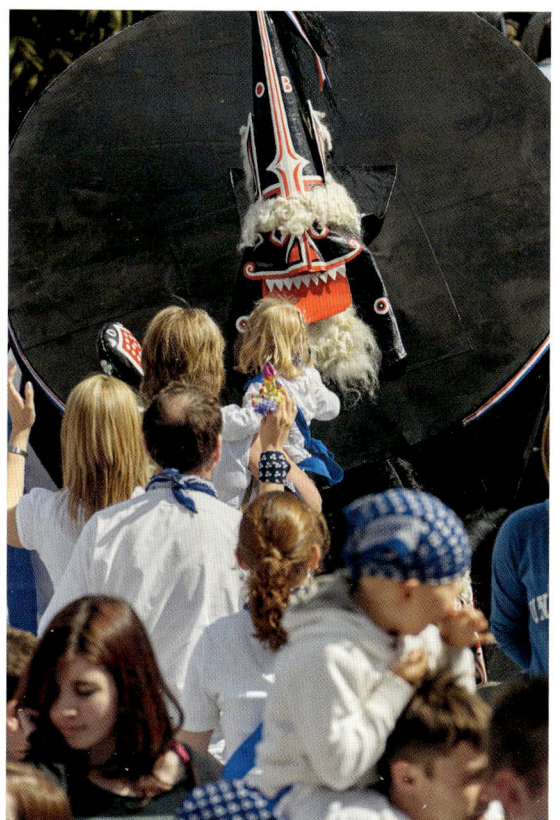

Above: The Obby Oss, the centre of attention during Padstow's Obby Oss Festival.

and Helston's Floral Dance are celebrations of Cornishness as much as anything else. Penzance's Golowan is a mid-summer festival that died out in the 19th century, but which was very successfully revived in the 1990s, culminating in the Mazey Day parades through the town.

Perhaps paramount among the traditions is the restoration of the Cornish language, a form of Gaelic closely related to both Welsh and Breton. The language fell out of use as a daily language in the 18th century – its last native speaker is said to have been one Dolly Pentreath, who lived in Mousehole and who died in 1777 – and for many years it lived on only in place names. Over the past 20 years, however, scholars have started to revive its use, and it is now estimated that about 300 people are fluent in speaking the language, with perhaps 5000 having a moderate ability. Out of a total population of over 500,000 this is still rather small, but it is an interesting beginning. Cornish Gaelic is being taught in a few schools across the county, and it is now not uncommon to see bilingual place names. Everyone living in Cornwall will be fully aware of at least one word: *Kernow*, the Cornish Gaelic word for Cornwall.

Beautiful Cornwall: A Portrait of a County

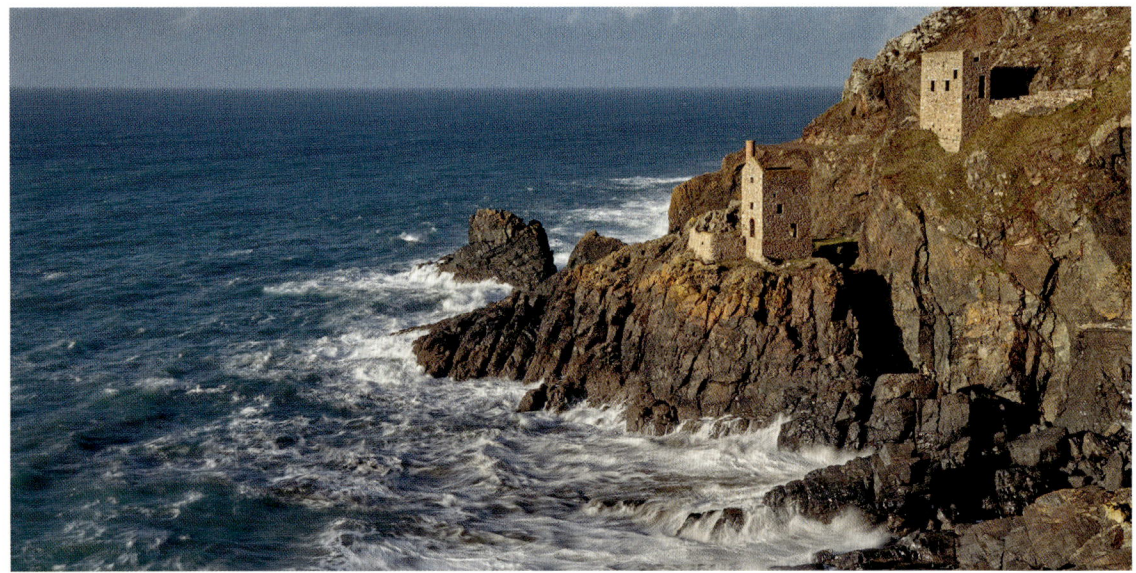

Above: One of Cornwall's most famous tin mine views: that of Botallack, standing right on the cliff edge, in the county's far west.

Below: The ruins of Carn Galver mine, a short-lived 19th century tin mine, that sits beside the Land's End to St Ives road in Cornwall's far west.

An ancient heritage

Cornwall has been lived in for a very long time, as clearly illustrated by the huge number of prehistoric remains that litter the landscape. They consist of a plethora of stone circles, burial mounds and dolmen, village remnants and hill forts, all standing as silent monuments to peoples long gone.

They are largely concentrated into particular areas, with Bodmin Moor quite well endowed, and the Penwith peninsula – that last promontory of land between St Ives and Land's End - positively strewn with all kinds of remains. As usual, tales have built up around many, giving them great mystical status, ranging from offering a cure for rickets to being the petrified remains of men who dared to play sport on a Sunday!

Ruins from historical times are also common, including a number of castles, the most well known of which is undoubtedly the spectacular clifftop Tintagel. Its fame stems from claims that this was the birthplace of King Arthur, whose legends are closely tied with much of Cornwall.

But it is the ruined mines that are Cornwall's quintessential manmade landscape feature, most especially the engine houses, their chimneys and vaulted roofs an essential inclusion in many Cornish views. Mining for tin and copper is believed to have begun as early as the Bronze Age, and there are some unsubstantiated claims that even the Phoenicians traded the metals with the Cornish.

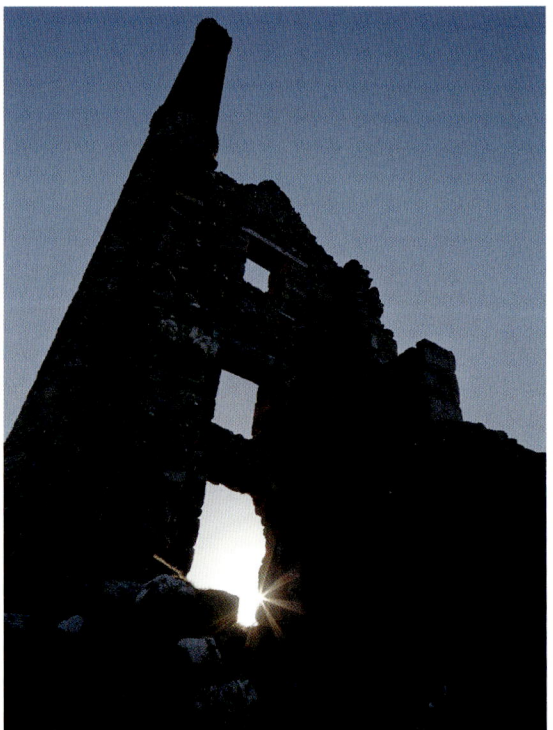

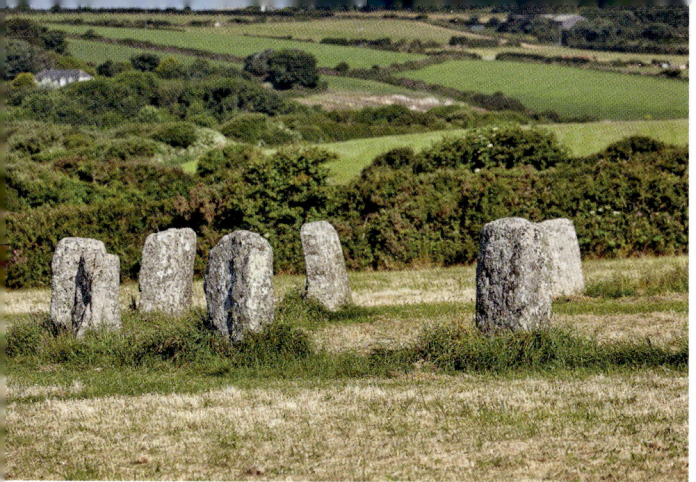

Above: The Merry Maidens, a stone circle near Mousehole, said to be all that's left of children that dared to play on the Sabbath!

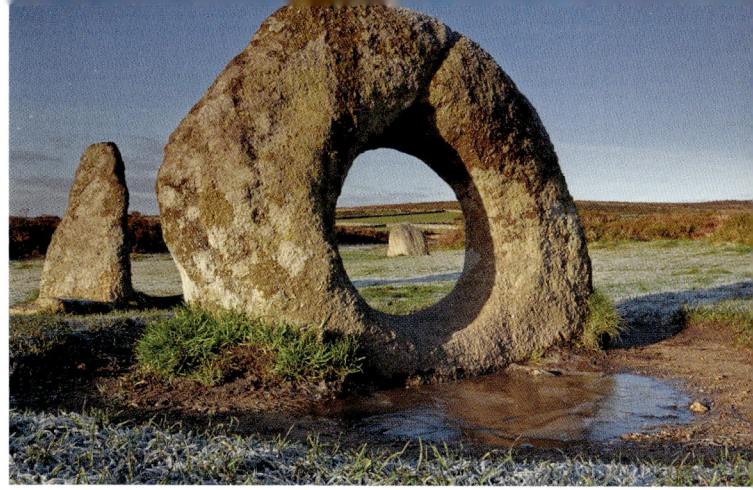

Above: The standing stones and ring of Men-an-Tol, near Penzance, are one of Cornwall's most enigmatic prehistoric remains.

It was from the 17th century onwards that copper mining in particular really gathered momentum, making it Cornwall's largest employer, and a little later putting the county in the vanguard of the Industrial Revolution. Cornishman Richard Trevithick developed the high pressure steam engine, initially to work the mines but subsequently forming the prototypes for the world's first railway locomotives.

By the middle of the 19th century copper mining was in decline, but tin took over, Cornish tin dominating the world for the rest of the century. By the early part of the 20th century, however, competition from mines around the world drove down prices, steadily putting the Cornish mines out of business. The last tin mines survived until the 1990s, Geevor (at Pendeen, close to Land's End) and South Crofty (near Camborne) closing in 1990 and 1998 respectively, the very last two mines to go. The loss of South Crofty brought to an end a 2000-year mining heritage in the county, though that may not actually be the end of the story. In 2016 Canadian mining company Strongbow Exploration bought the site, with a view to trying to reopen the mine. Since then the company has been renamed Cornish Metals, has been given permission to pump out the flooded mine, has started some test drilling, and has greatly increased its estimates of the amount of tin still present in the mine. It is just possible that the mine will eventually reopen.

Today, it is not uncommon for Cornish historians and independence activists to bask in the perceived glory of Cornwall's past industrial heritage, conveniently overlooking the fact that mining caused both huge pollution to the county's land and coast, and often made life short and brutal for the miners. Life expectancy was frequently as low as 35, particularly for those unlucky enough to be in those mines that also produced lead and/or arsenic.

Such criticisms notwithstanding, Cornwall's mining heritage is a formidable feature of the county's history, as well as that of the world's Industrial Revolution. It is not surprising, then, that all the southwest's old mining areas, from the far west of Devon and throughout Cornwall have been proclaimed by UNESCO as a World Heritage Site.

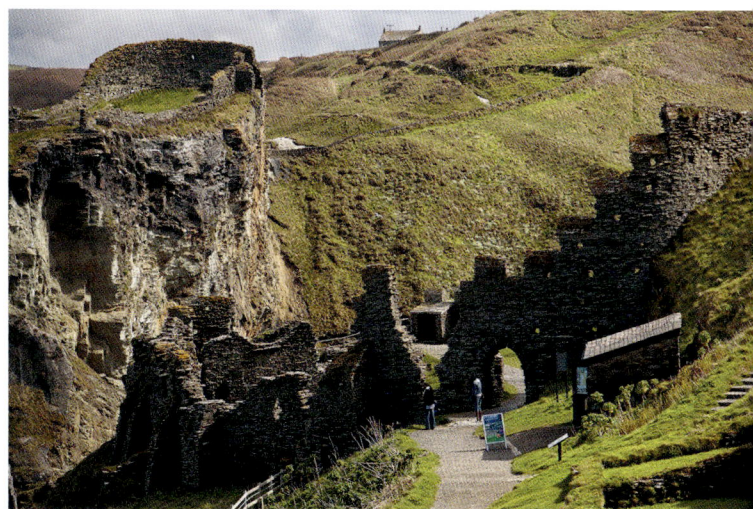

Above: Loaded with folklore, the ruins of Tintagel Castle are said to have been the birthplace of King Arthur.

Beautiful Cornwall: A Portrait of a County

Town and country

Although the legacy of mining still looms large in Cornwall, and some areas are still badly scarred by the aftermath, much is now slowly crumbling picturesquely into the landscape. Perhaps the biggest physical reminder today is the continued existence of Camborne and Redruth, two conjoined towns that were the epicentre of Cornish mining, and which continue to be Cornwall's industrial centre and its largest urban area.

Of course, even in its heyday, mining was not the only industry, for there were also quarrying (particularly of china clay), farming and fishing. Concentrated mainly around the town of St Austell, the china clay is noteworthy for the huge white waste heaps that used to be generated, nicknamed rather tongue-in-cheek as the 'White Alps', and which once dominated the skyline. Today, the quarryng continues, but the White Alps have mostly disappeared, cleverly contoured into the natural hillsides and covered with vegetation.

Fishing has always been hugely important to Cornwall. From the 18th century onwards it was largely fuelled by enormous shoals of pilchards that migrated annually into Cornish waters. They provided catches that numbered tens of millions of fish annually until the 20th century. It remained the dominant fish landed at Newlyn right up until the 1960s, but then the prolonged over-fishing saw the shoals decline, bringing pilchard fishing almost to an end.

Today, large fishing fleets have all but disappeared from the majority of the small harbours and coves, and there are less than 1000 fishermen left in the county. Places like Looe, Mevigissey, Padstow and St Ives do continue with quite a healthy fishing industry, but dominating them all is Newlyn, by far the largest fishing port in Cornwall.

Over 600 boats are registered at Newlyn, mostly relatively small inshore craft. It is said that in any given day up to 40 species may be landed at its wharfs, crabs the most common of them all. In terms of

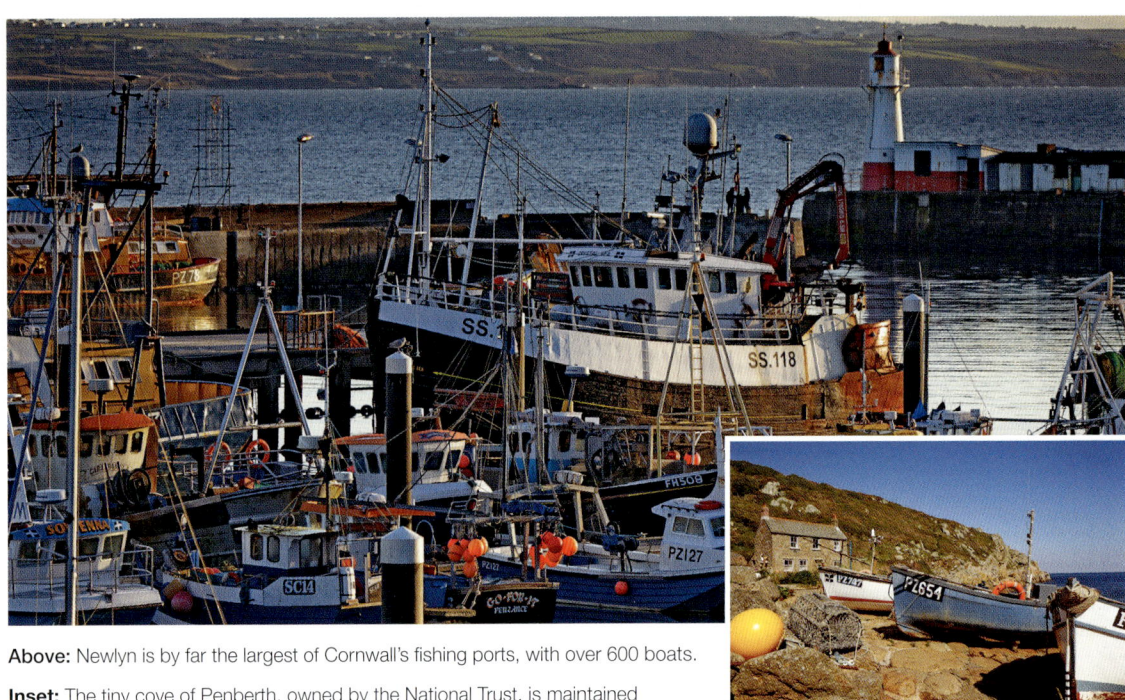

Above: Newlyn is by far the largest of Cornwall's fishing ports, with over 600 boats.

Inset: The tiny cove of Penberth, owned by the National Trust, is maintained as a very traditional fishing village.

All About Cornwall

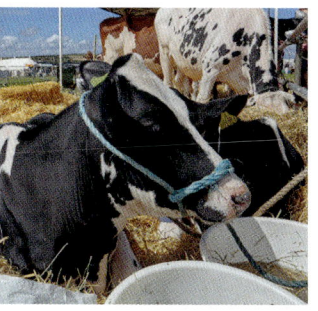 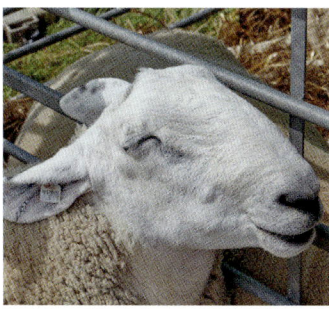

Above: Livestock at the Camelford Agricultural Show, a local event held every August, showcases the farming that is still so important to north Cornwall.

value, crab and monkfish compete for the number one slot, but other highly valued fish include lemon sole, hake, haddock, plaice, turbot, pollack, sardines and scallops.

In such a largely rural county farming remains important, with an estimated 74% of the land in some form of farming. Much of this is pasture, used for grazing animals, mainly sheep and cattle, concentrated especially in areas of poorer soil, such as on Bodmin Moor and along exposed coasts. Only 20% of the farmland is given over to crops, mostly cereals.

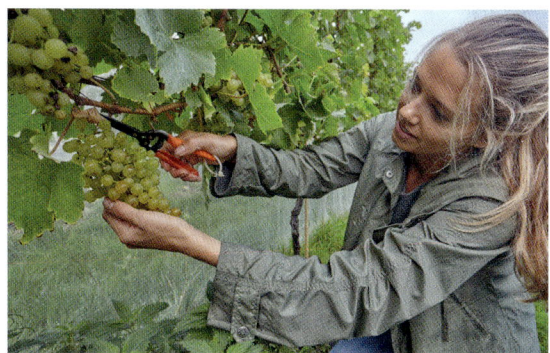

Above: The autumn grape harvest at Trevibban Mill vineyard, near Padstow, illustrates the diversification of farming.

The opening of the Eden Project (see pages 50-51) in 2001 kick-started a process of moving Cornwall away from looking at its past, and instead towards a future where it could be at the leading edge of new industries that promote environmental technology and sustainability. There had already been some progress towards this in the 1990s, with the opening of the UK's first commercial windfarm at

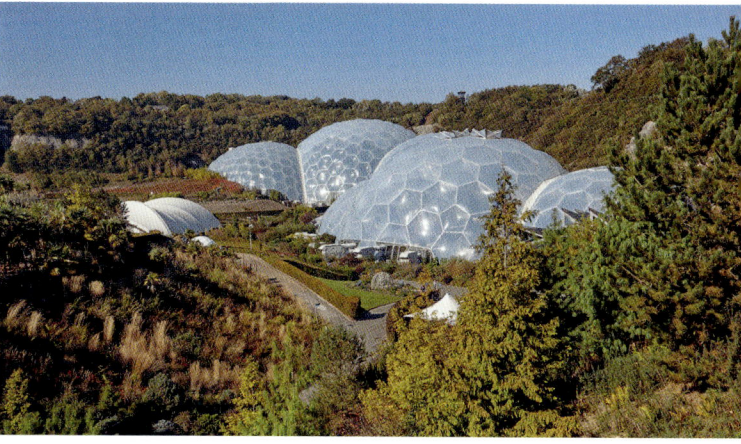

Above: The spectacular habitat domes of the Eden Project have become symbolic of a 'new' Cornwall, one looking towards a future that promotes environmental sustainability.

Delabole (near Wadebridge), but the huge momentum generated by the Eden Project has carried this forward to the extent that wind turbines and banks of solar photovoltaic cells are now a very common feature of rural Cornwall's landscape.

This has been coupled with the development of the University of Cornwall, with a campus near Falmouth (funded largely by EU money), and the growth of some space technology industries around Newquay, the latter growing from a belief that Newquay Airport may become the UK's first commercial spaceport.

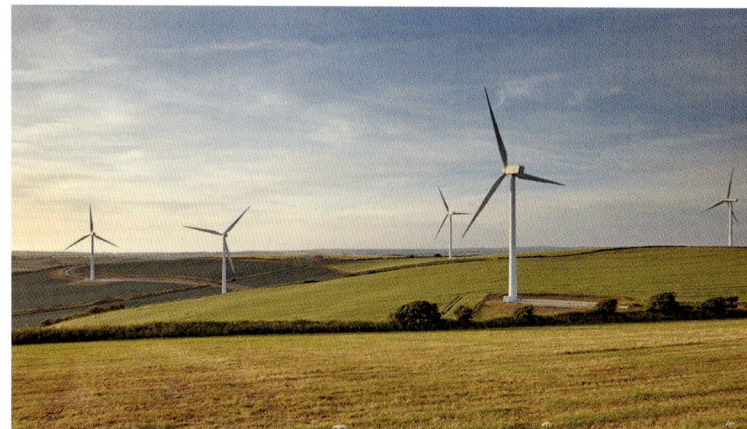

Above: One of the rapidly growing number of windfarms spreading across the Cornish landscape, here seen near Truro.

13

Beautiful Cornwall: A Portrait of a County

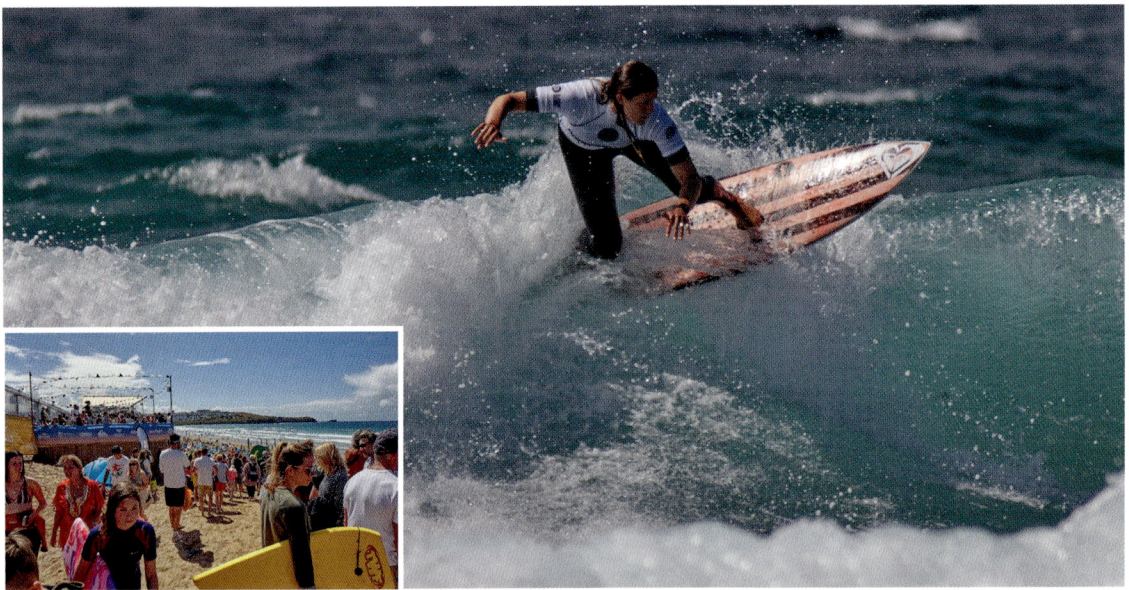

Above: A pro surfer shows how it is done, during the Boardmasters festival on Fistral Beach, Newquay.

Inset: Fistral Beach crowded with visitors equipped with all kinds of hired surf boards.

Cornwall's Tourism

The problem with all the industries described in the last section is that they still employ relatively small numbers of people. Today Cornwall's biggest boom industry, and on which the county largely depends, is tourism.

Cornwall has been a popular holiday destination since the 1960s, but today it is really riding high on a wave of prestige as a truly cool or chic place to spend the summer, visitors from all over the UK and Europe swept in on a tide of enthusiasm for its beaches, surfing and super-fresh seafood.

The beaches have, of course, always been a feature of the Cornish coast, spectacularly long stretches of golden sand, particularly on the north coast, backed by either rugged cliffs or grassy dunes, fronted by a foaming surf-lined azure sea. The surfing is something of a relatively modern phenomenon, arriving in the late 1960s but at that time largely the preserve of bronzed devotees. The advent of surfboards and wetsuits to hire, along with surfing schools at many of the most popular beaches revolutionised the sport in Cornwall. Suddenly

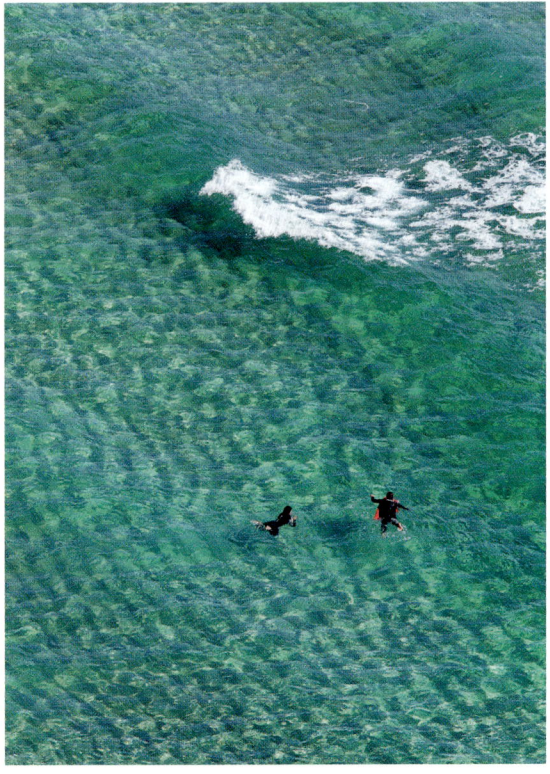

Above: Swimming with wetsuits, in the crystal clear waters off Pedn Vounder beach, near Porthcurno.

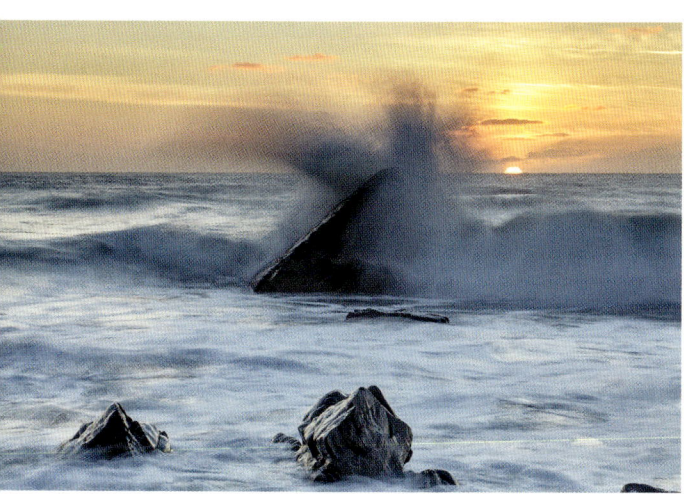

Above: Atlantic surf crashes over rocks just as the sun is setting, at Sandy Mouth, near Bude.

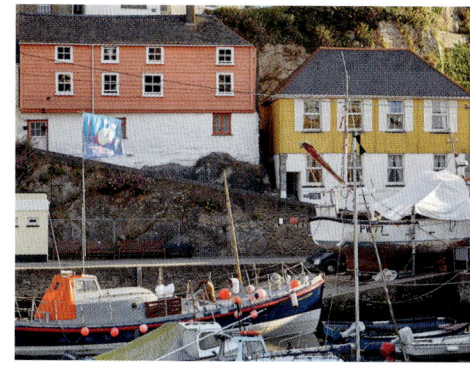

Above: Mevigissey is a classic Cornish fishing village, though one that still has a very active and successful fishing fleet.

everyone could give it a go and today the waves are frequently packed with novices, hardly a soul in the water without a wetsuit and board.

The growing popularity of Cornish seafood is closely linked to the development of the celebrity chef phenomenon, a number of whom have opened now-famous restaurants in Cornwall, sparking the enthusiasm of food afficionados to come to the county. Of course, this is good news for Cornwall's fishing industry, which has benefitted from the good prices they can demand as a result.

Fishing packs a punch well beyond its relatively small size, indirectly creating a major tourism attraction, and not just the seafood they produce. It is those oh-so-quaint little fishing harbours, filled with colourful boats and ringed by a crowd of cottages, usually grey stone walls, but often white-washed and almost luminous in the sunlight. Newlyn may be very much a working port that few visitors explore, but places like Mousehole, Polperro, St Ives and Mevigissey absolutely define the very essence of the traditional Cornish fishing harbour.

A more subtle but nevertheless hugely important attraction is the arts. Since the 19th century Cornwall has increasingly attracted artists, who have been drawn in both by the region's clear light and its rural lifestyle. They initially came mostly to Newlyn and St Ives, where first the Newlyn School was established, followed after the First World War by the St Ives School. Over time, the latter has rather eclipsed the Newlyn School, largely due to some of its world-famous members, which include the sculptor Barbara Hepworth and potter Bernard Leach. The importance of the St Ives artists became sealed in the 1990s with the opening in the town of a branch of the Tate, now a major showcase for the greatest of Cornwall's artists.

Finally, but by no means least, for those who tire of art galleries, seafood restaurants, fishing harbours, surfing and just lazing on a beach, there is Cornwall's superb walking, most especially its coast path. The trail follows the county's entire coast, making it possible to explore some of the region's most spectacular views. To get a taste of this, as well as many of Cornwall's other amazing sights, already described, start by exploring the photo essays that follow through the rest of this book.

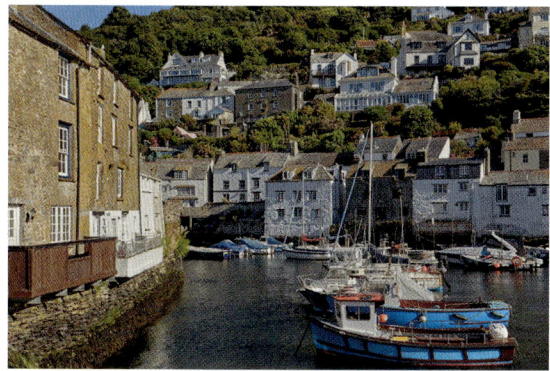

Above: Polperro is the number one quintessential quaint Cornish fishing harbour, set in a deep valley and surrounded by historic cottages that crowd in all around.

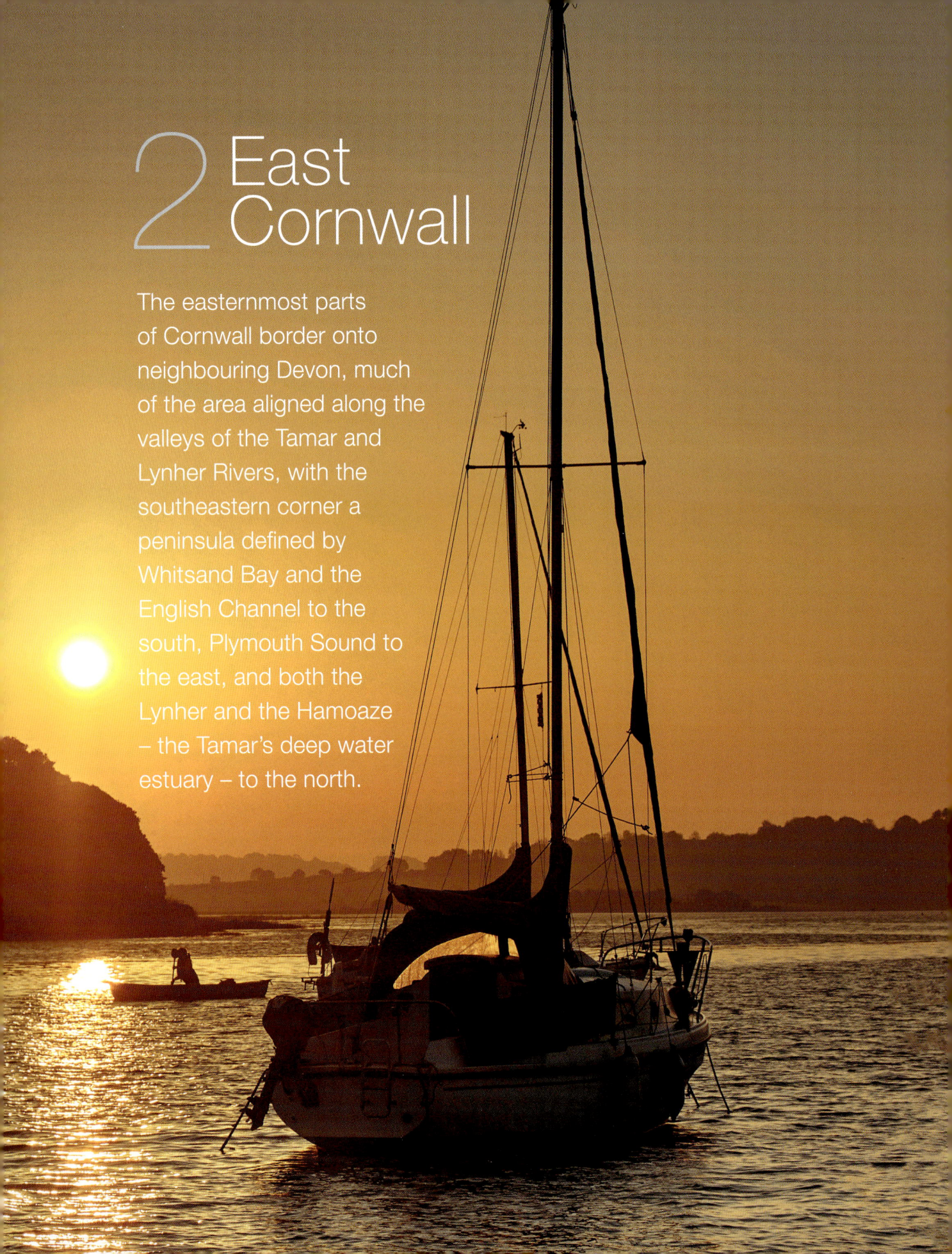

2 East Cornwall

The easternmost parts of Cornwall border onto neighbouring Devon, much of the area aligned along the valleys of the Tamar and Lynher Rivers, with the southeastern corner a peninsula defined by Whitsand Bay and the English Channel to the south, Plymouth Sound to the east, and both the Lynher and the Hamoaze – the Tamar's deep water estuary – to the north.

East Cornwall

Many would argue that this is the least Cornish part of Cornwall: with its rolling hills, deep, wooded valleys and extensive agriculture, much of the area still feels rather like Devon. However, in its place names and grey stone towns, the sense of 'Cornwall' does start to make itself felt almost as soon as the Tamar is crossed, and by the time the westernmost areas at Looe and Polperro are reached we are well and truly into quintessential Cornish fishing village territory.

Towards the north, the hilltop town of Launceston sits almost on the Devon border, dominated by the ruins of its historic castle, and with magnificent views out across the surrounding countryside to Dartmoor in the east and Bodmin Moor in the west.

To the south, lies rolling open farmland, all the way to Callington, overshadowed on its northeast side by the enormous Kit Hill. The highest peak in this part of Cornwall, Kit Hill is a swathe of rocky, open moorland, with wonderful 360° views deep into Cornwall and across the Tamar valley into Devon.

Further east, right on the border, the small towns of Calstock and Gunnislake nestle on the banks of the Tamar, set in deep valleys and the latter especially enveloped in dense woodland. Southwest of Callington the Lynher River meanders through verdant countryside, Cadsonbury one of its most scenic spots, site of a riverside prehistoric hill fort, with more wonderful views and dense riverside woodland.

At the southernmost end of this Tamar/Lynher border region sits the Rame peninsula, almost cut off from all the main roads by the Lynher and Tamar estuaries, and as a result a rather forgotten corner of Cornwall. It is well worth the effort to reach, for it is stunningly beautiful. Its southern coast is marked by Whitsand Bay's magnificent stretch of golden sand, and its outermost points consist of the rugged Penlee Point and Rame Heads. Inland are the very quiet and lovely Millbrook and St John's Lakes, sheltered inlets

Left: Sunrise over the lovely Lynher River at St Germans.

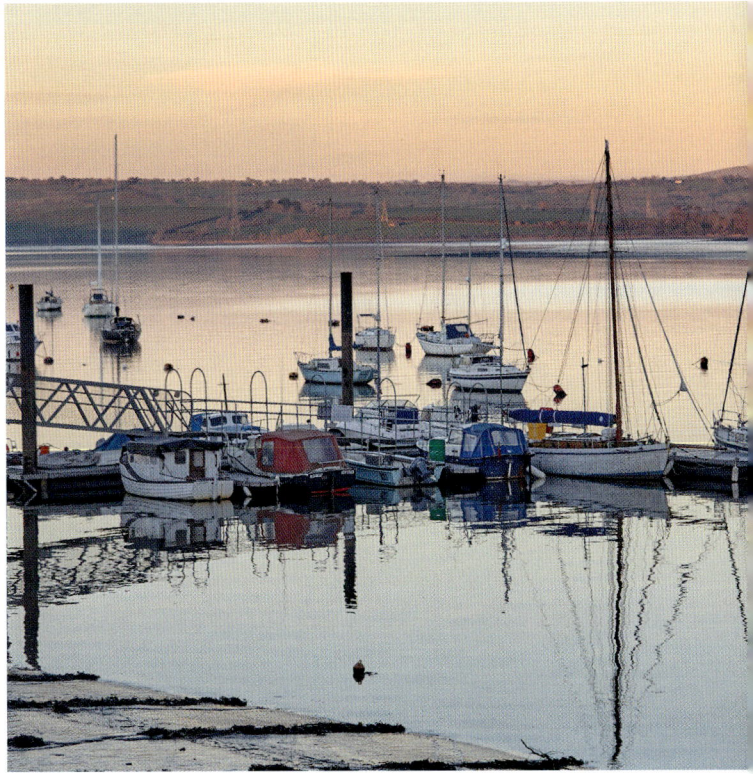

Above: The Hamoaze, the wide waters of the Tamar estuary, lit by the last rays of the setting sun, seen from Saltash on the Cornish shore.

of the Hamoaze that provide valuable mud banks to thousands of over-wintering wading birds. At the peninsula's easternmost end sits Mt Edgcumbe Country Park, site of a deer park, a stately home and a wonderful shoreside formal garden.

The western part of this region is very much on the tourist trail, consisting of the twin fishing towns of Looe and Polperro, the former a lively town with an active fishing port built along the banks of the Looe River. Polperro, by contrast, looks as though it were created specifically to encapsulate the perception of the archetypal Cornish fishing village; a cramped harbour surrounded by high hills, hundreds of cottages crowding around the harbour walls and climbing the hills above, roads consisting solely of narrow cobbled footpaths. With Looe and Polperro, you have quite definitely reached the 'real' Cornwall!

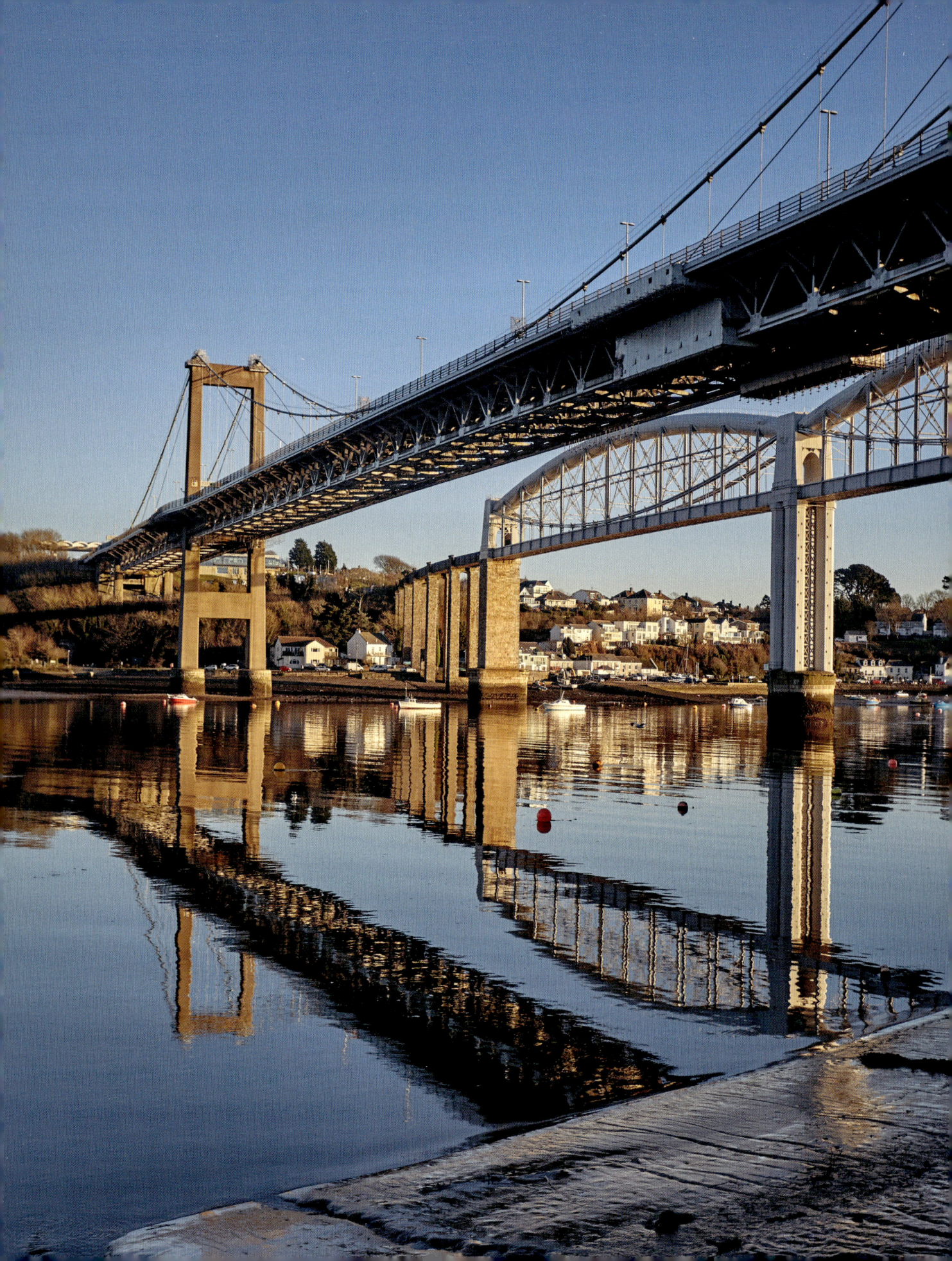

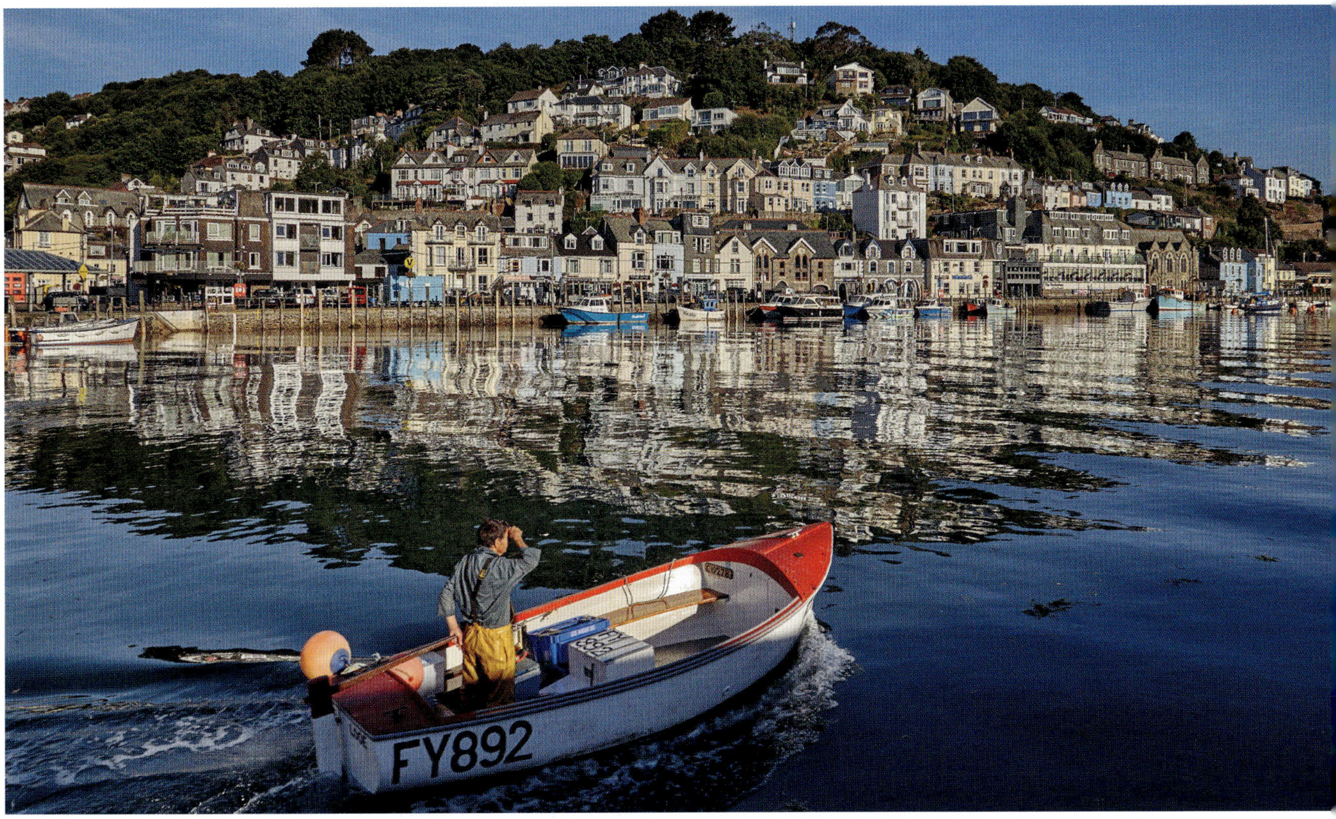

East Cornwall

Above: The fishing harbour and town at Looe, bathed in early morning sunlight.

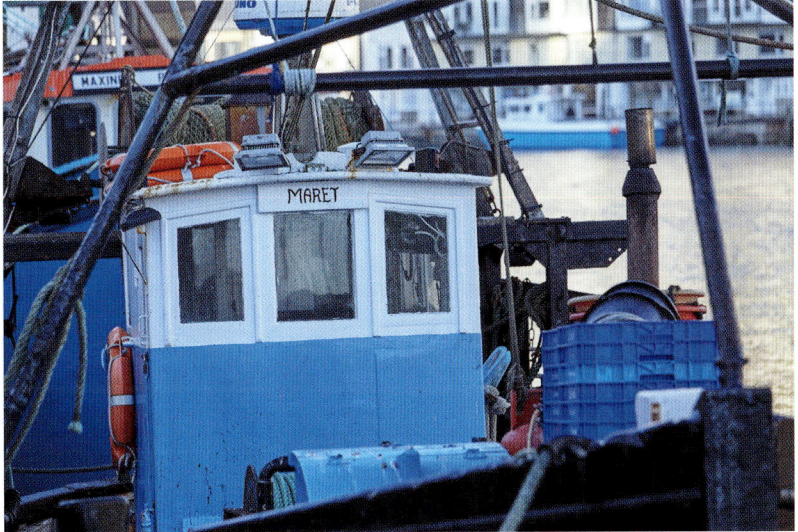

Left: The twin road and rail bridges that span the Tamar estuary at Saltash, linking Cornwall with Plymouth.

Above: Fishing boats tied up along the wharf beside Looe's fish market, waiting for the next fishing expedition.

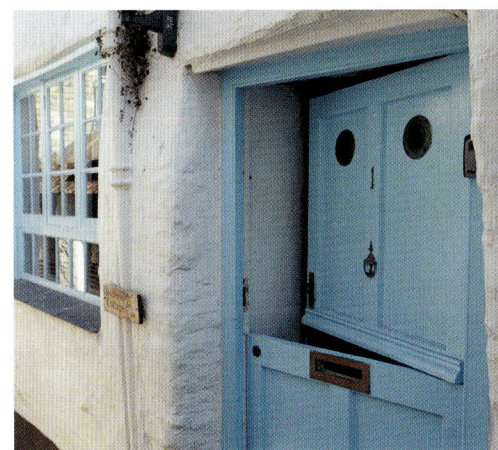

Above: Most of Polperro's harbourside cottages are hundreds of years old, with whitewashed walls and traditional doors.

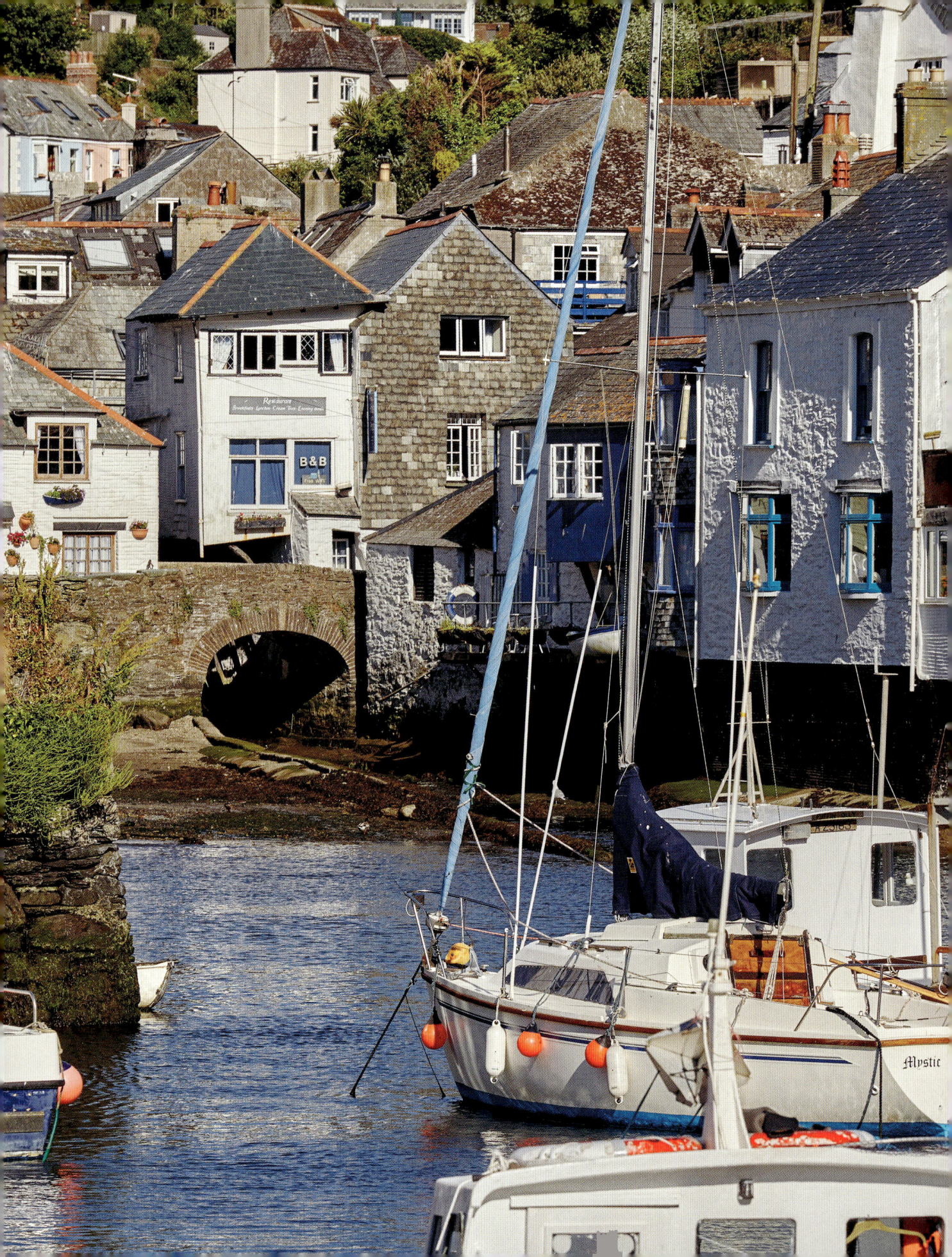

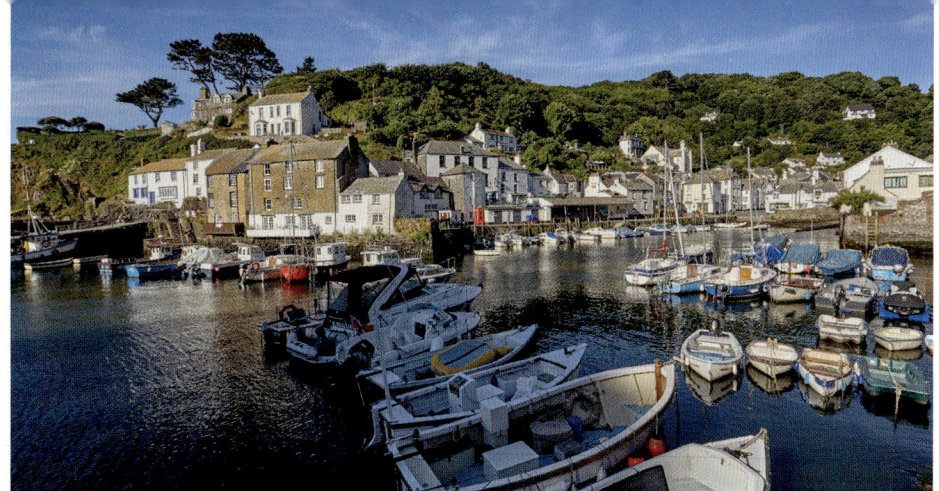

East Cornwall

Opposite and Left: Polperro is absolutely the quintessential old Cornish fishing harbour, hemmed in by hills, the waterways filled with boats, historic stone cottages crowding in all around and climbing the hills above.

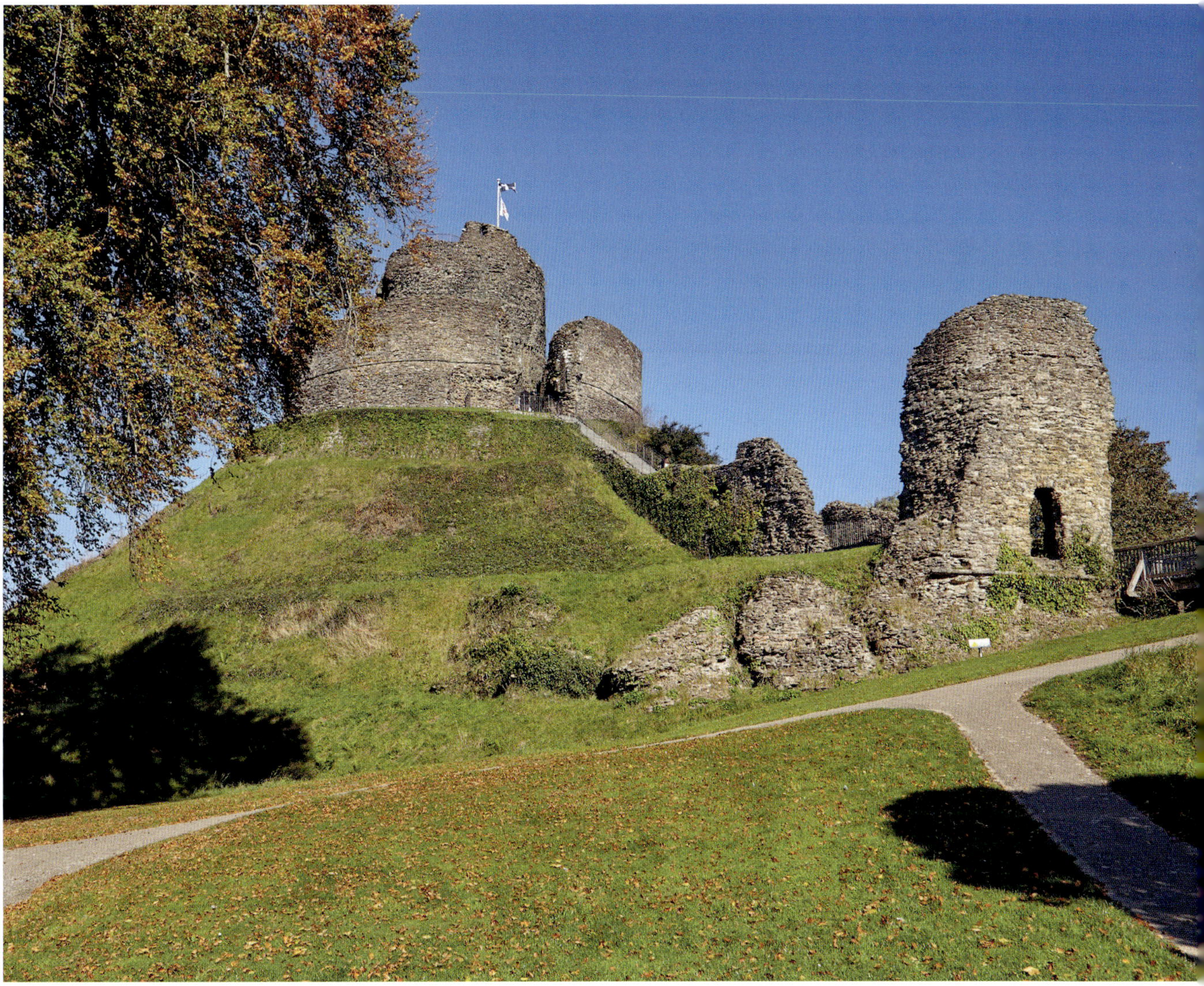

Above: Right at the hilltop heart of Launceston is the town's ruined castle. Originally established in the 11th century, just a few years after the Norman invasion, the stone walls date from 13th century improvements. The highest part of the castle's keep has superb views of the surrounding countryside.

Beautiful Cornwall: A Portrait of a County

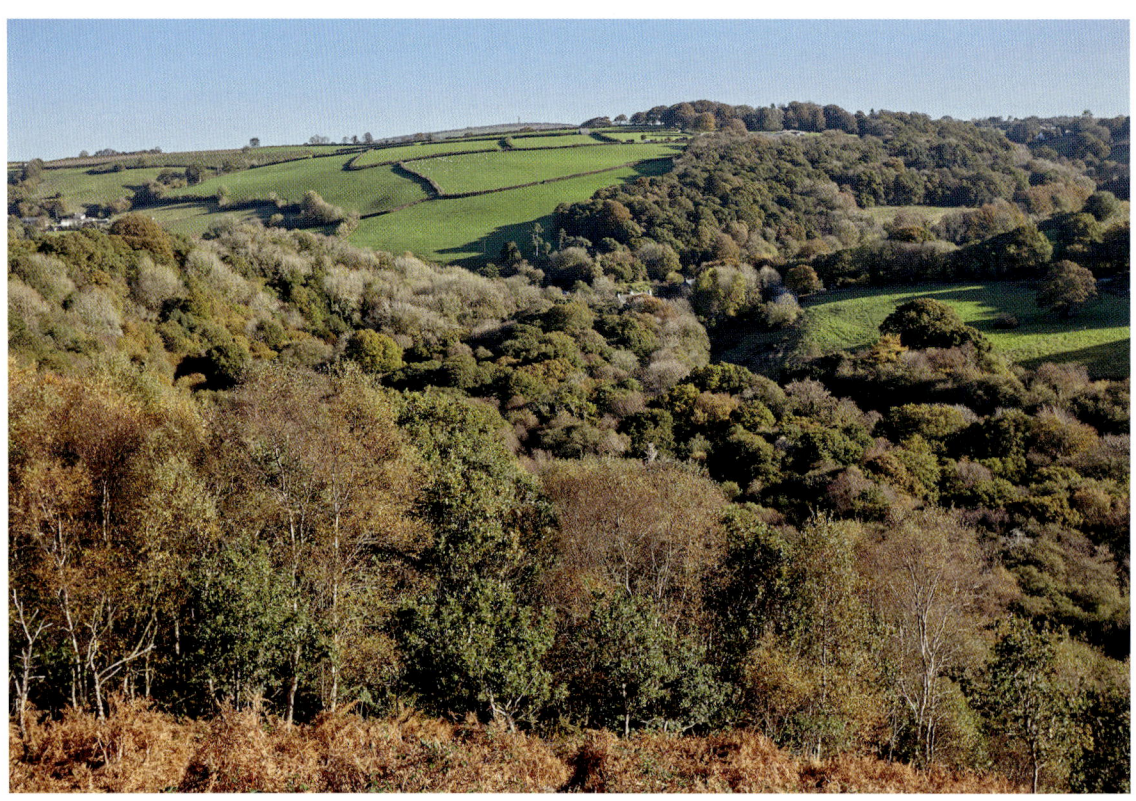

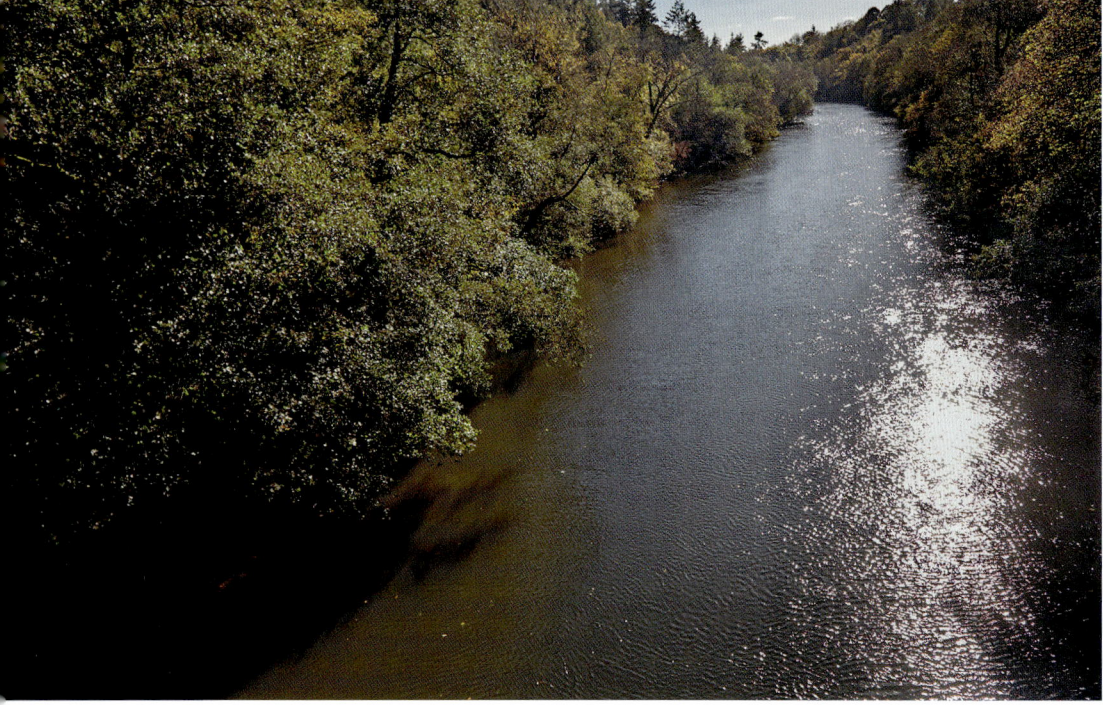

Above: An autumnal view of Cadsonbury Woods around the prehistoric Cadsonbury hill fort, and in the valley of the River Lynher, near Callington.

Left: At Gunnislake, the Tamar is enveloped in dense ancient woodland on both the Devon and Cornish *(to the right)* shores, making the river quite remote and rather inaccessible for long stretches.

Right: At Calstock, the Tamar is spanned by a huge railway viaduct, a tribute to Victorian engineering skills, bringing a railway line up the valley from Plymouth to nearby Gunnislake.

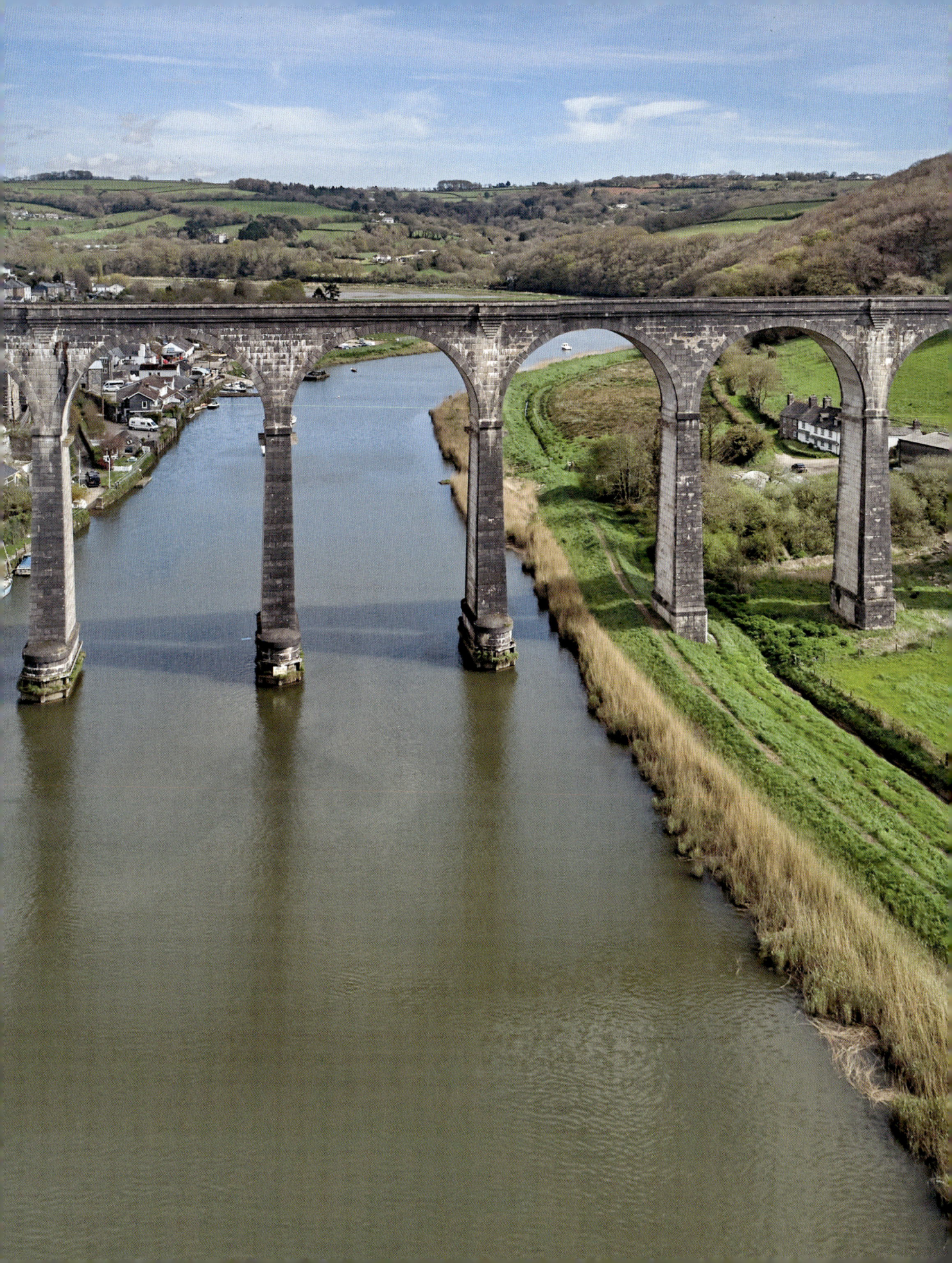

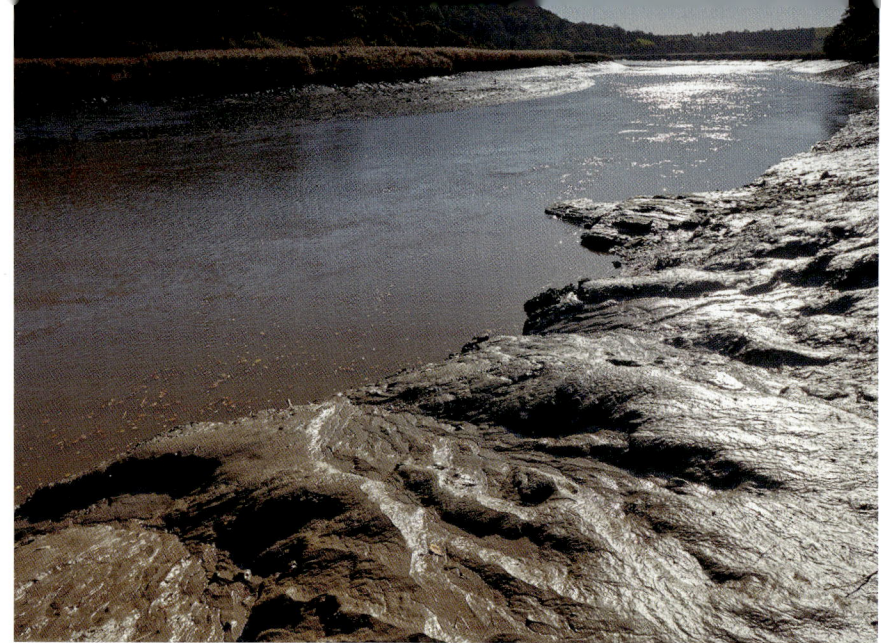

Left: The tidal range along the Tamar's lower reaches is such that at low tide large mud banks are left exposed, as seen here at Cotehele. Particularly in the estuary, the mud banks are hugely important as feeding grounds for wading birds, especially in winter.

Below: The riverside Cotehele Mill, now a museum, is in an immensely beautiful rural part of the Tamar Valley. It is part of a large estate that is now owned by the National Trust.

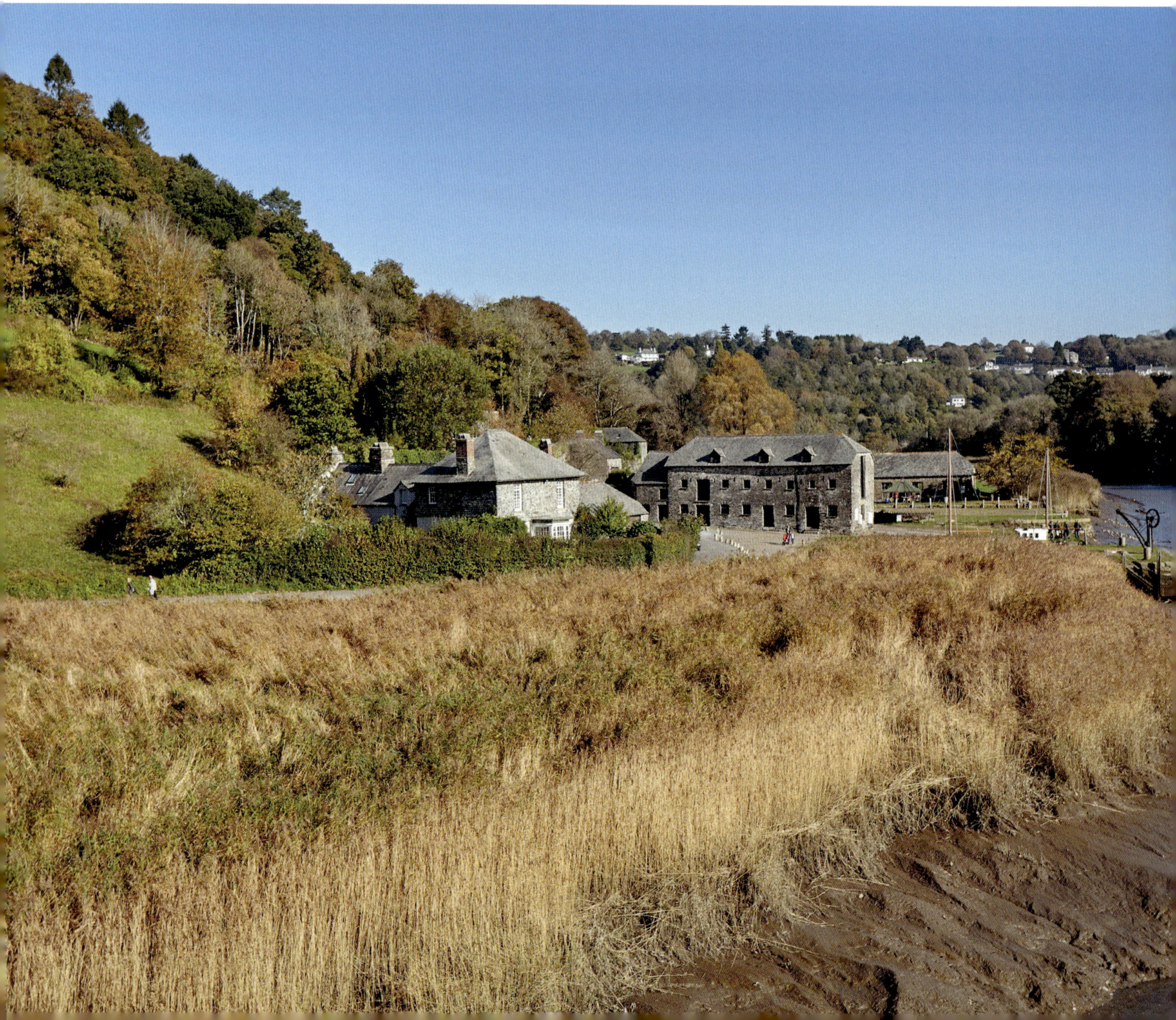

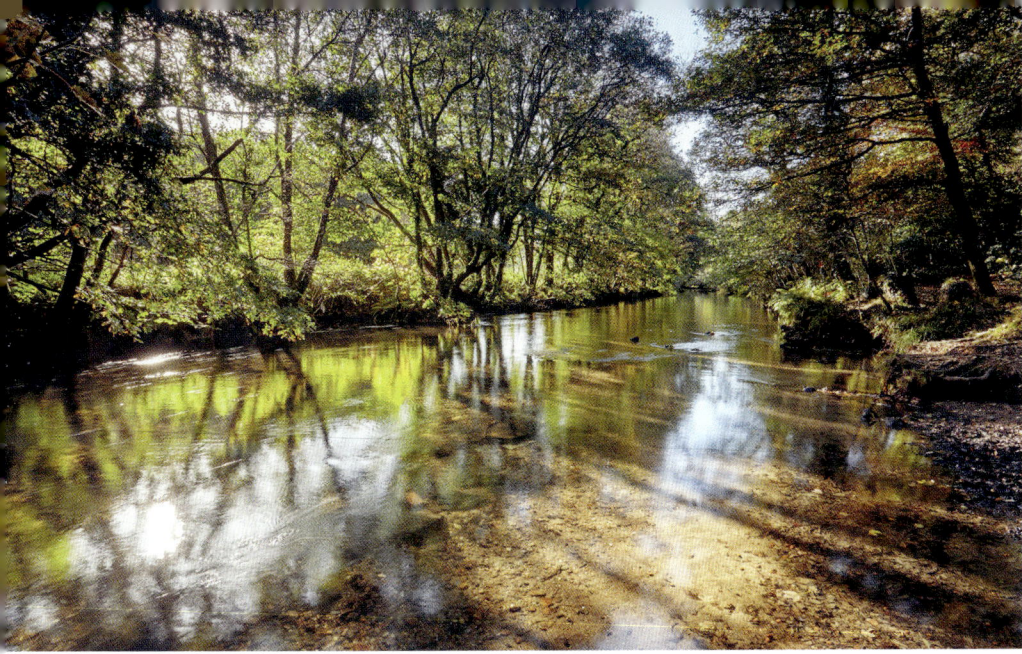

Left: A very calm, quiet and woodland-lined stretch of the Lynher River at Cadsonbury, at the foot of the Cadsonbury hill fort, a few miles southwest of Callington. The Lynher flows down from the eastern slopes of Bodmin Moor, draining much of east Cornwall.

Below: Sunrise over the harbour at St Germans, at the head of the estuary of the Lynher River, an extremely rural location surrounded by farmland in Cornwall's southeast corner.

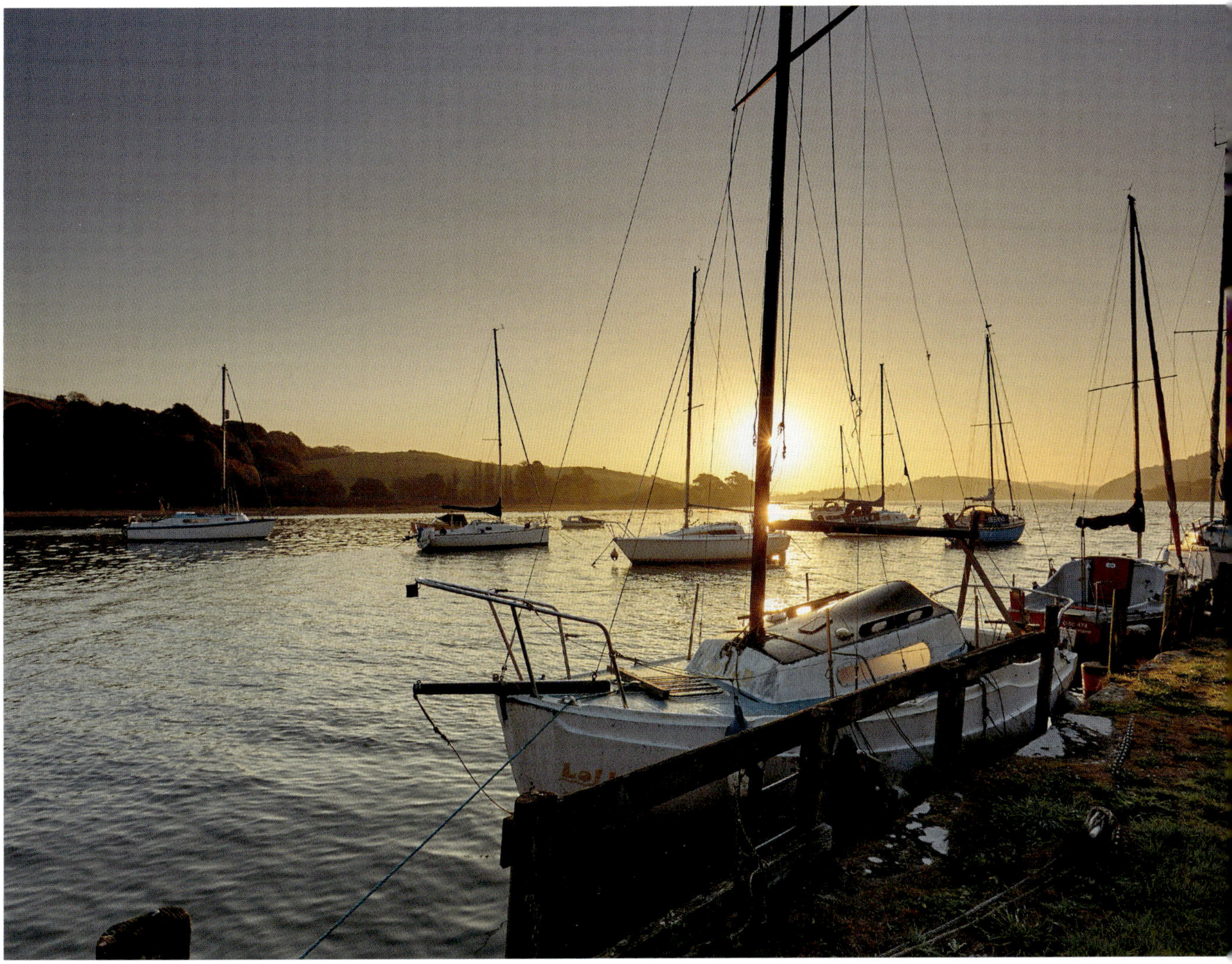

Beautiful Cornwall: A Portrait of a County

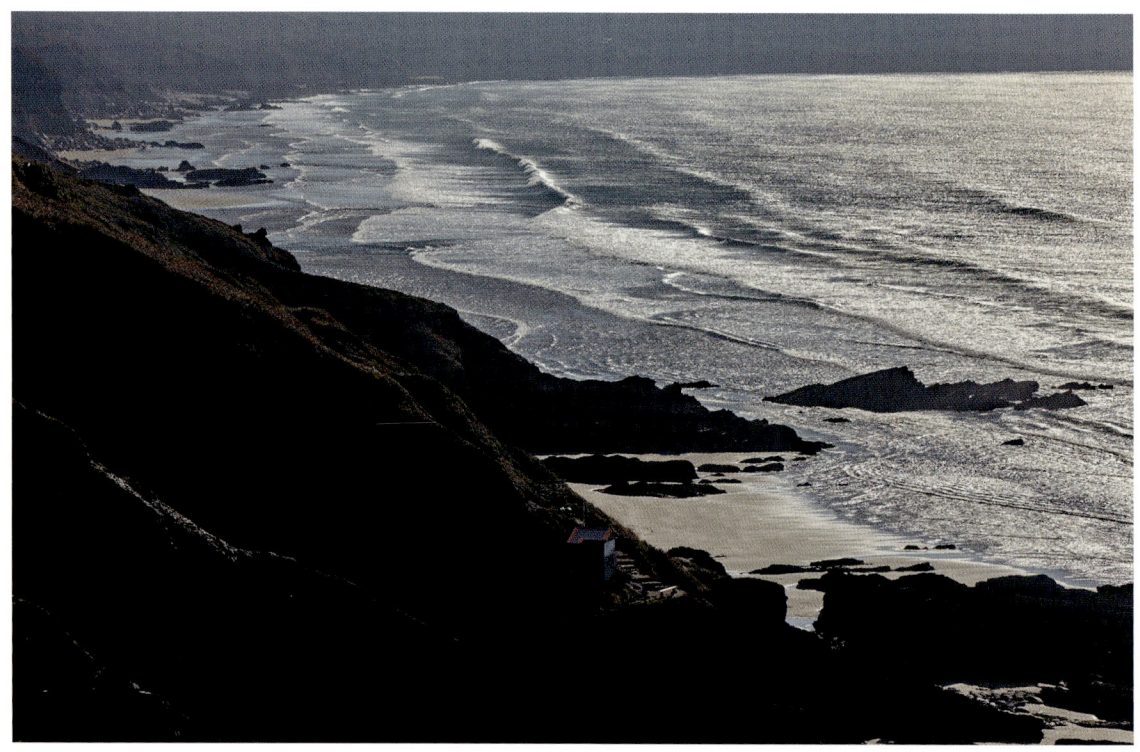

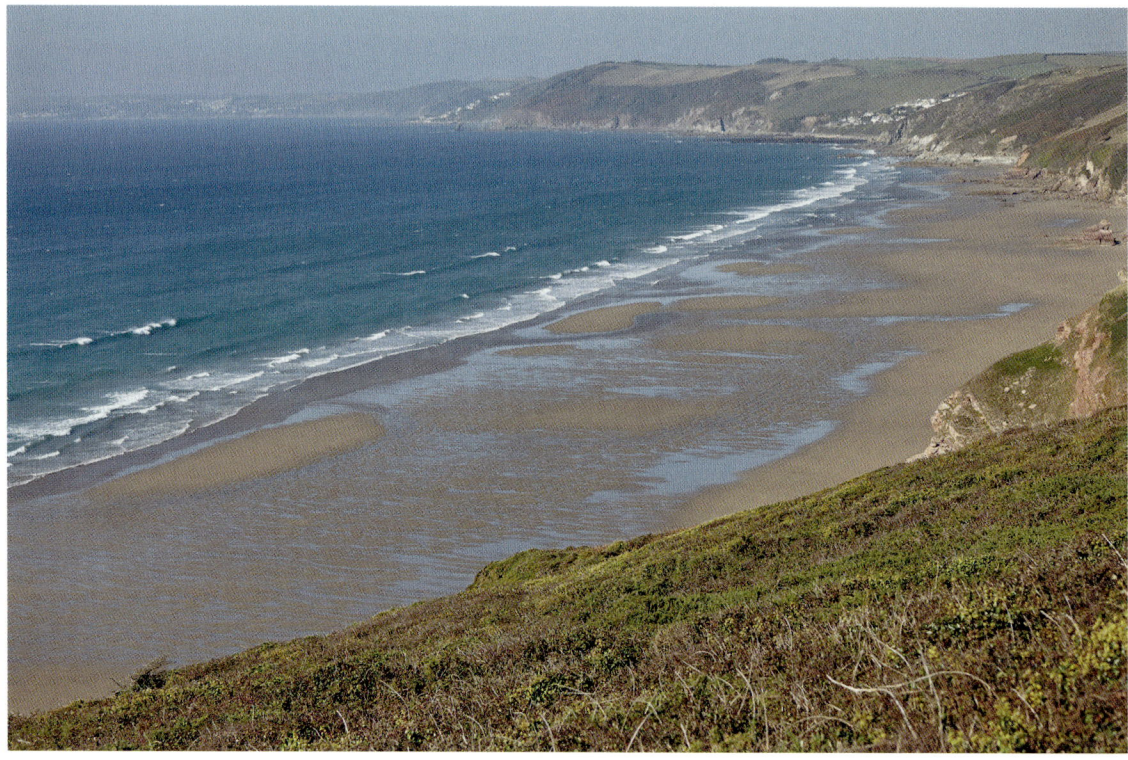

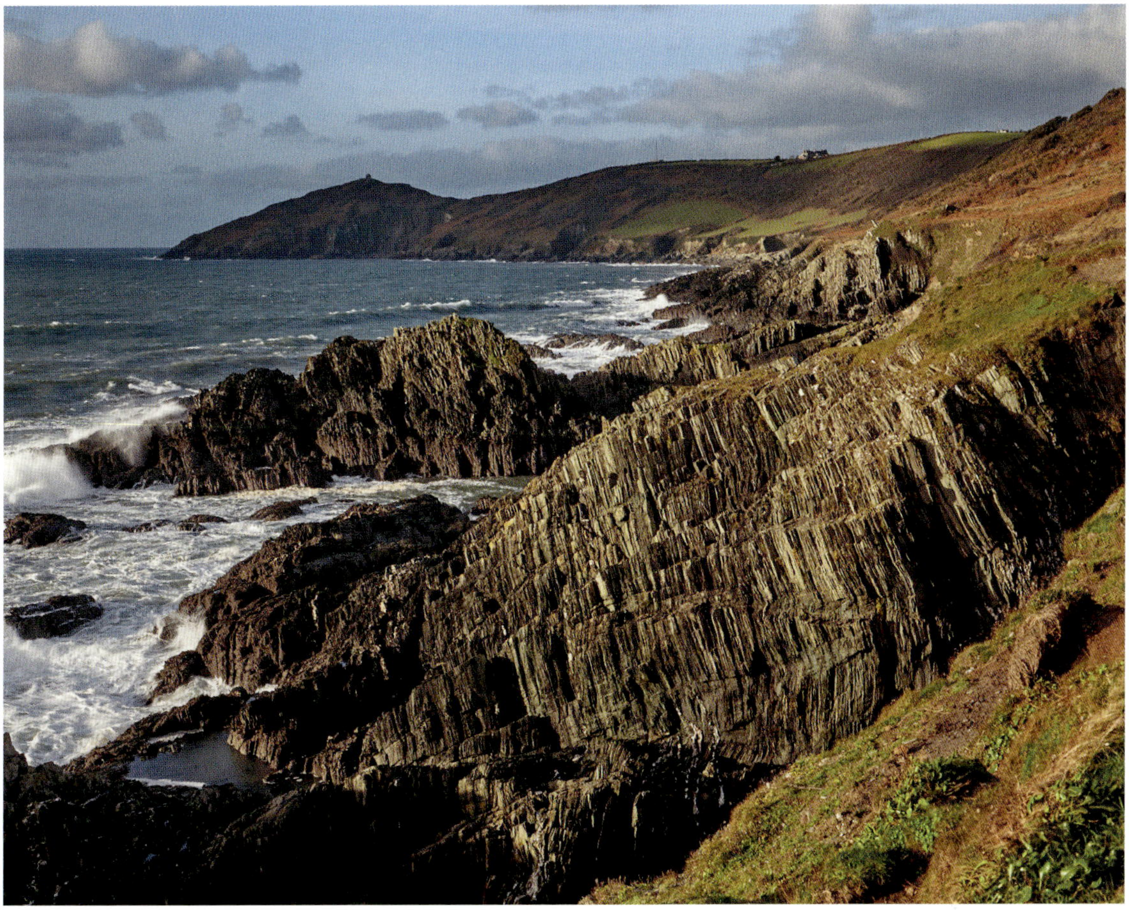

East Cornwall

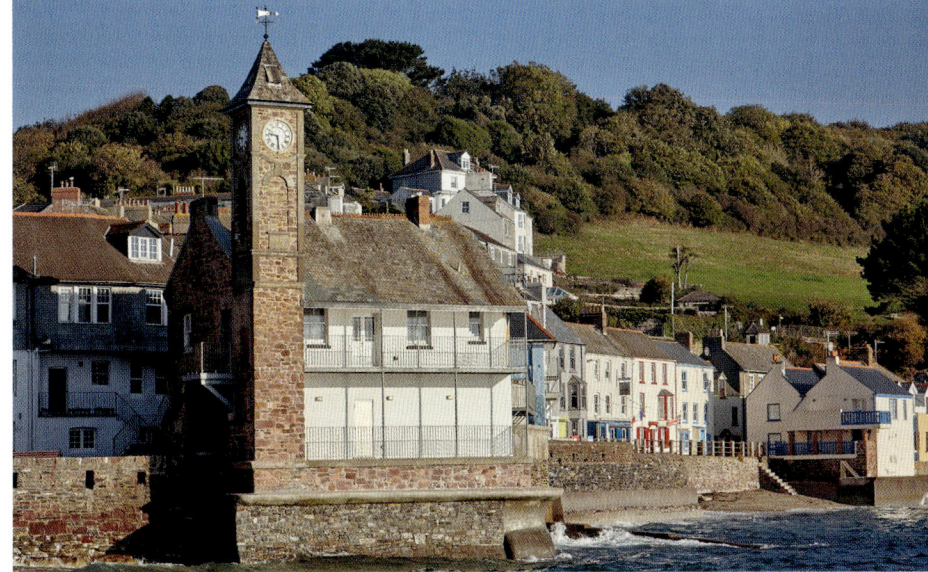

Top and Bottom Left: The spectacular stretch of sand that is Whitsand Bay, seen from Freathy cliff, on the Rame peninsula. Despite being one of Cornwall's most spectacular beaches, it is also one of the most under-used, partly due to the area's relative isolation, but also due to many of the cliff areas once upon a time being closed as military sites, though this is no longer so.

Above: An early morning view from Penlee Point towards Rame Head, the twin headlands that mark the outermost entrance towards Plymouth Sound and from there the River Tamar.

Right: The lovely little seaside village of Kingsand, tucked away on the southeast shore of the Rame peninsula. Contiguous with the adjacent village of Cawsand, the two villages sit at the outer edge of Plymouth Sound, sheltered from westerly storms by nearby Penlee Point.

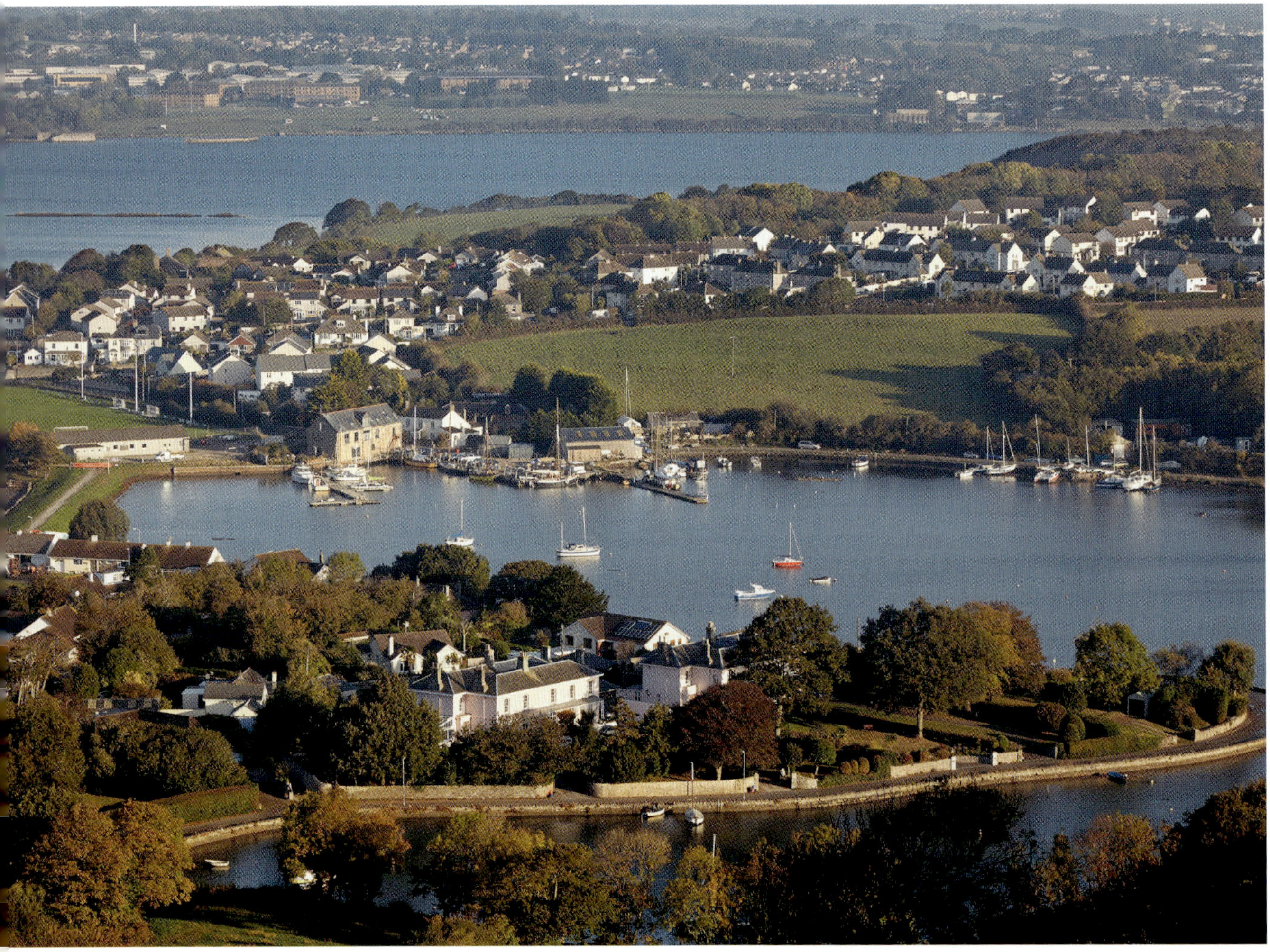

Beautiful Cornwall: A Portrait of a County

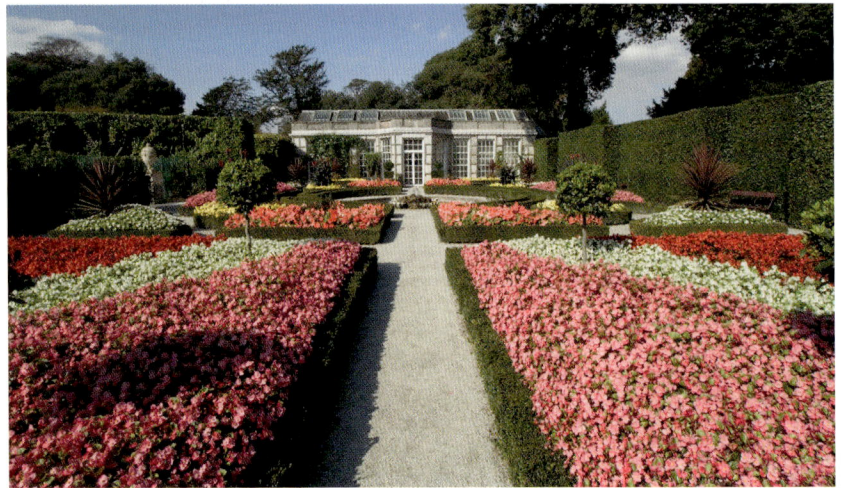

Above: A view across the inlet and village of Millbrook to the much larger St John's Lake, another inlet of the Hamoaze, or Tamar estuary, a truly beautiful part of the Rame peninsula.

Left: The French Garden, part of the ornamental gardens at Mt Edgcumbe Country Park. Lying on the easternmost tip of the Rame peninsula, near Torpoint, Mt Edgcumbe consists of a mansion, ornamental gardens and a deer park, covering over 350 ha (865 acres), established in the 16th century.

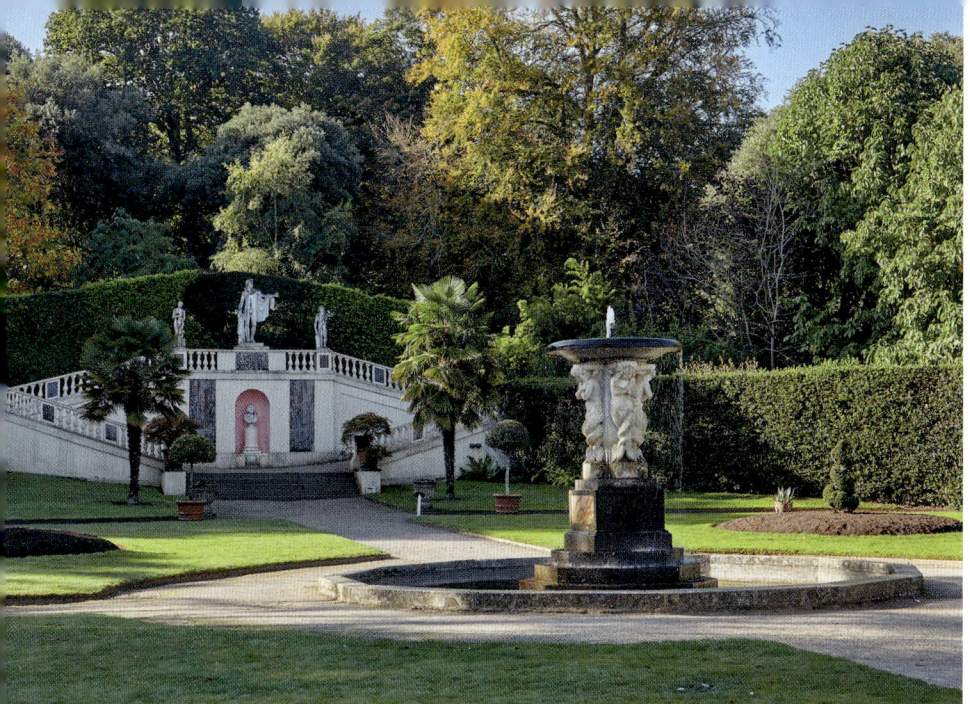

East Cornwall

Left: One of the loveliest parts of Mt Edgcumbe's ornamental gardens is the Italian Garden, complete with ornate fountains and Romanesque statues. One of the first parts of the ornamental gardens reached by visitors after they arrive, the Italian Garden fronts onto the Orangery, an historic airy building that is the gardens' attractive cafe.

Below: Sunrise seen from Rame Head, the final promontory of the Rame peninsula, looking eastwards across the area where Plymouth Sound and the open seas of the English Channel meet.

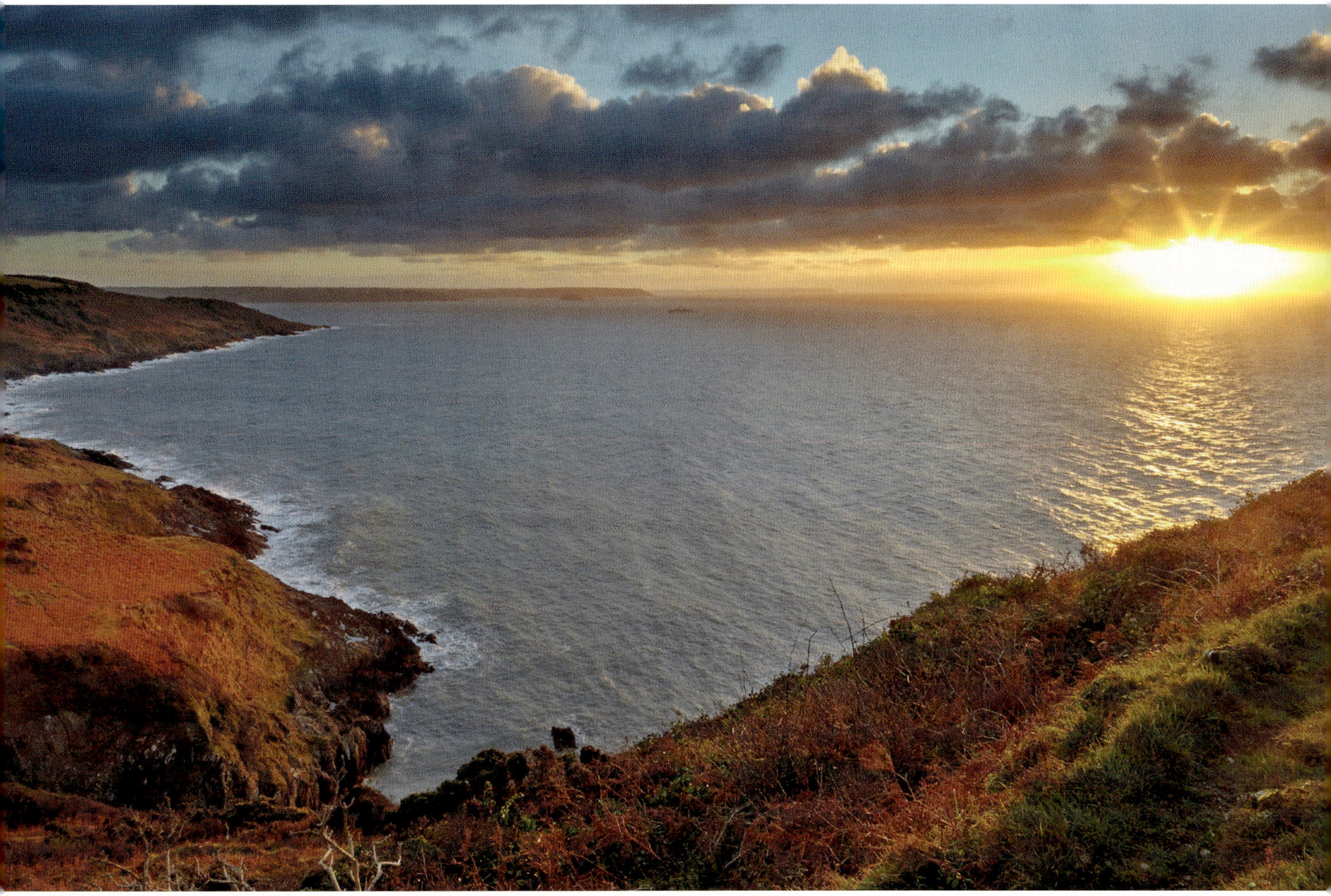

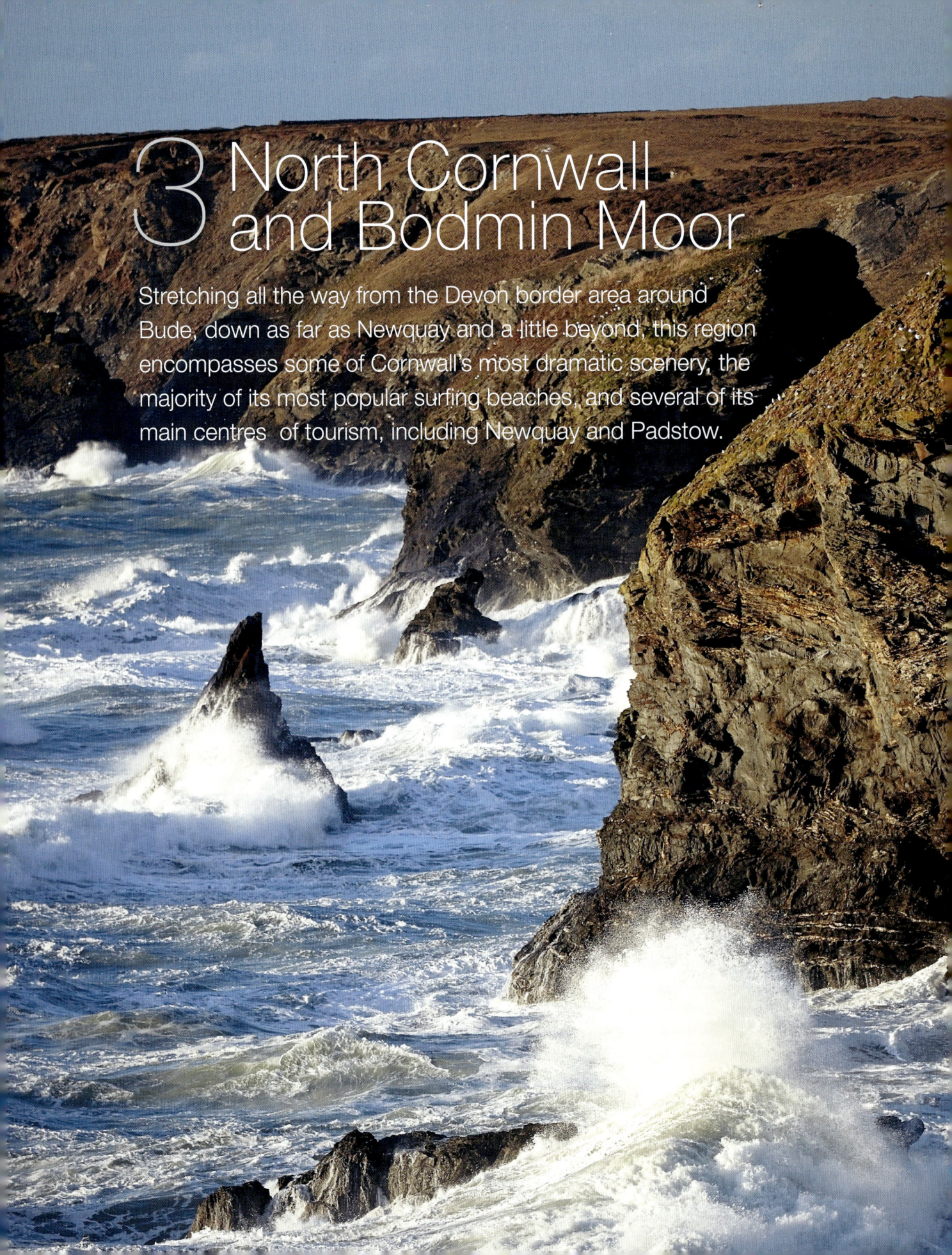

3 North Cornwall and Bodmin Moor

Stretching all the way from the Devon border area around Bude, down as far as Newquay and a little beyond, this region encompasses some of Cornwall's most dramatic scenery, the majority of its most popular surfing beaches, and several of its main centres of tourism, including Newquay and Padstow.

North Cornwall and Bodmin Moor

The magnificent show starts with the sandy beaches, and the hugely folded cliffs around Bude itself and Sandy Mouth (a dream for geologists), and continues a little further south at the great surfing beach of Widemouth Bay. From here, high cliffs continue almost unbroken several miles to the tiny, cliff-encircled harbour at Boscastle. Just a few miles beyond lies world-famous Tintagel, renowned for its castle ruins, situated on a spectacular peninsula. Visitors are drawn in from all over the world, not so much for its location, but due to its inseparable links with King Arthur, Tintagel supposedly his birthplace.

The next major attraction is the little fishing village of Port Isaac, not so long ago quite off the tourism trail, until its discovery and setting for television drama *Doc Martin*. Beyond here are the popular surfing beach of Polzeath, and then the stunning Camel estuary, by far the largest river mouth on the north coast. The little town of Padstow sits on the estuary's west shore, one of Cornwall's most popular visitor attractions, thanks at least in part to the annual Obby Oss Festival, and to celebrity chef Rick Stein, who has several restaurants here.

Inland from Padstow, to the east of Wadebridge, rise the rugged hills of Bodmin Moor, a huge uprising of granite similar to Devon's Dartmoor, many of its highest points, such as Brown Willy and Rough Tor, topped with bare boulder outcrops known as tors. Much of this high, windswept massif consists of open grasslands and bogs, the sources of several of Cornwall's rivers, including the Lynher, Fowey and Looe. The south and eastern slopes are a lot more sheltered than the exposed north and west, and have been gouged by the rivers into a number of valleys that contain rushing streams and dense woodlands. An example of the latter is the lovely Cardinham Woods, east of Bodmin town, while the former includes stunning Golitha Falls, a steep boulder-strewn section of the River Fowey, enveloped in verdant ancient woodland.

Back on the coast and continuing west from Padstow, spectacular vistas follow quickly one after another, including rugged Trevose Head, Constantine Bay and Bedruthan Steps. The last of these is a series of rocky islets standing close to equally rocky and rugged cliffs, one of Cornwall's iconic views. Further west is Watergate Bay, shortly before the town of Newquay, probably Cornwall's biggest centre of tourism and epicentre for the region's surfing, most especially at its Fistral Beach. Newquay is very much at the focus of the 'Cornish Riviera', making it a very popular place in summer. As if it did not already attract enough people, in August it becomes even more crowded when it hosts Boardmasters, Cornwall's biggest annual event, a surfing-cum-rock music festival that draws in tens of thousands of people.

To the southwest, after a string of headlands, is Perranporth, a vast beach backed by a huge area of dunes, a major surfing centre and something of a Newquay 'overspill'. Finally, we then reach the high cliffs of St Agnes, with some fabulous sea views and heather-covered cliff-top moors. From here we enter into the lands of Cornwall's far west.

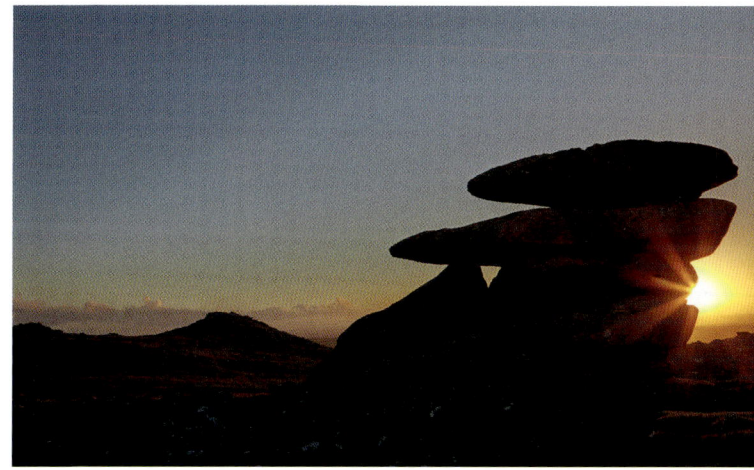

Above: Massive granite boulders on Bodmin Moor's Rough Tor, silhouetted against the setting sun.

Left: Dramatic Atlantic surf crashes against the rocks and cliffs at Bedruthan Steps, near Newquay, on Cornwall's north coast.

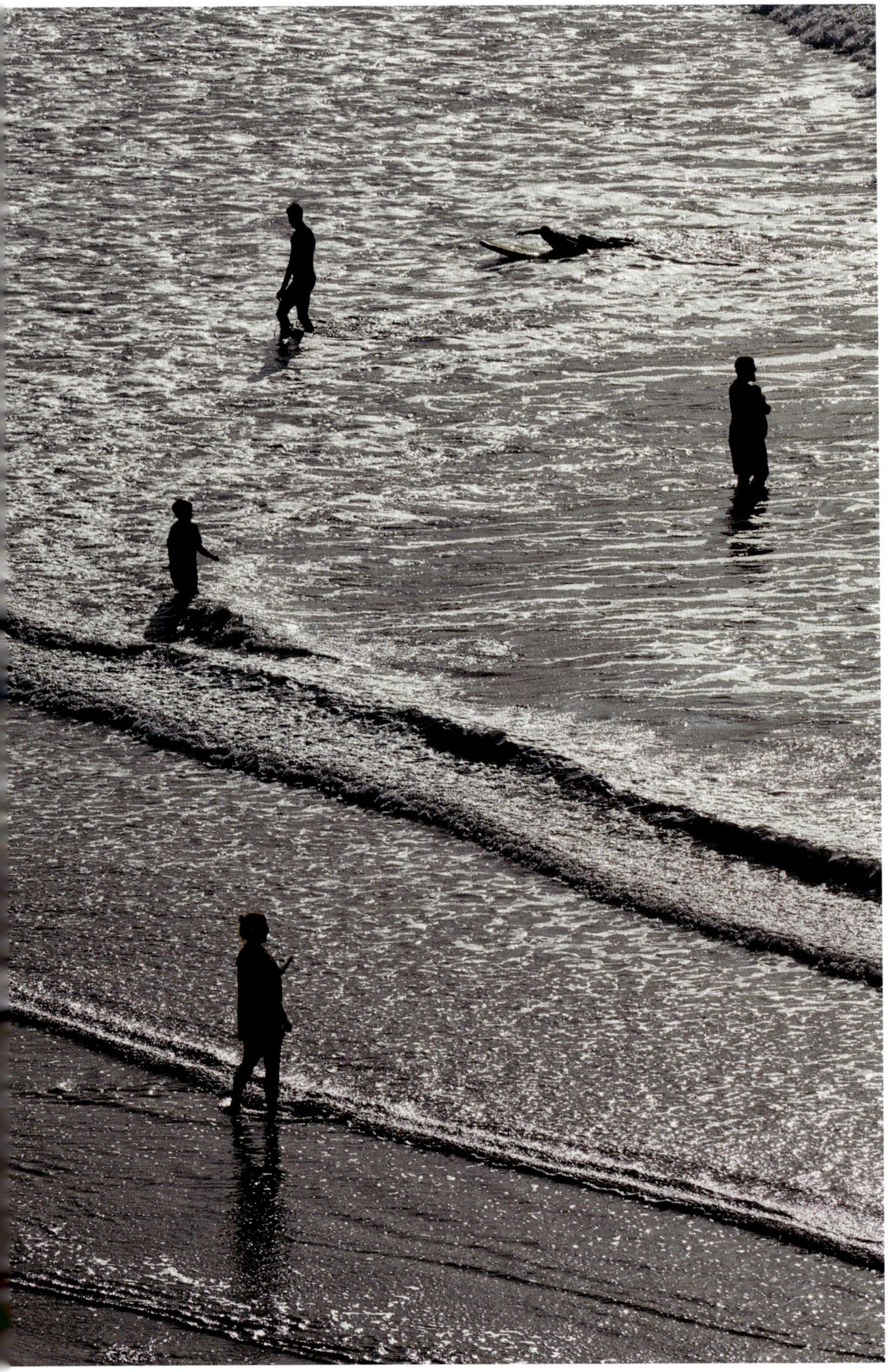

Beautiful Cornwall: A Portrait of a County

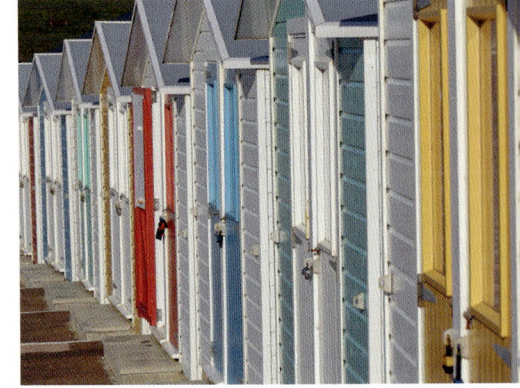

Above: Colourful beach huts line the shore at Bude's Summerleaze Beach.

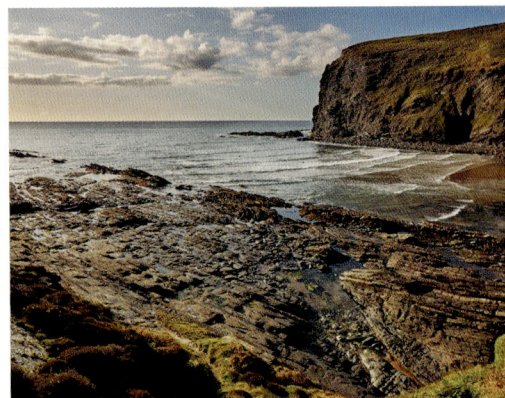

Above: Diminutive Crackington Haven, a small cove on the north coast, enclosed by high, sheer cliffs.

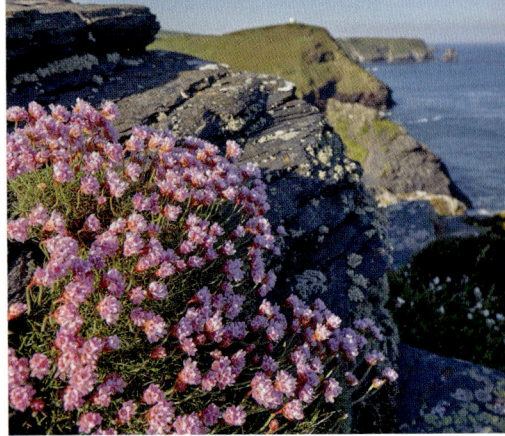

Above: In late May, sea pink, or thrift, puts a blaze of colour across the clifftops at Boscastle.

Above: Beachgoers splashing in the shallows at Summerleaze Beach, in Bude, one of Cornwall's most popular north coast locations.

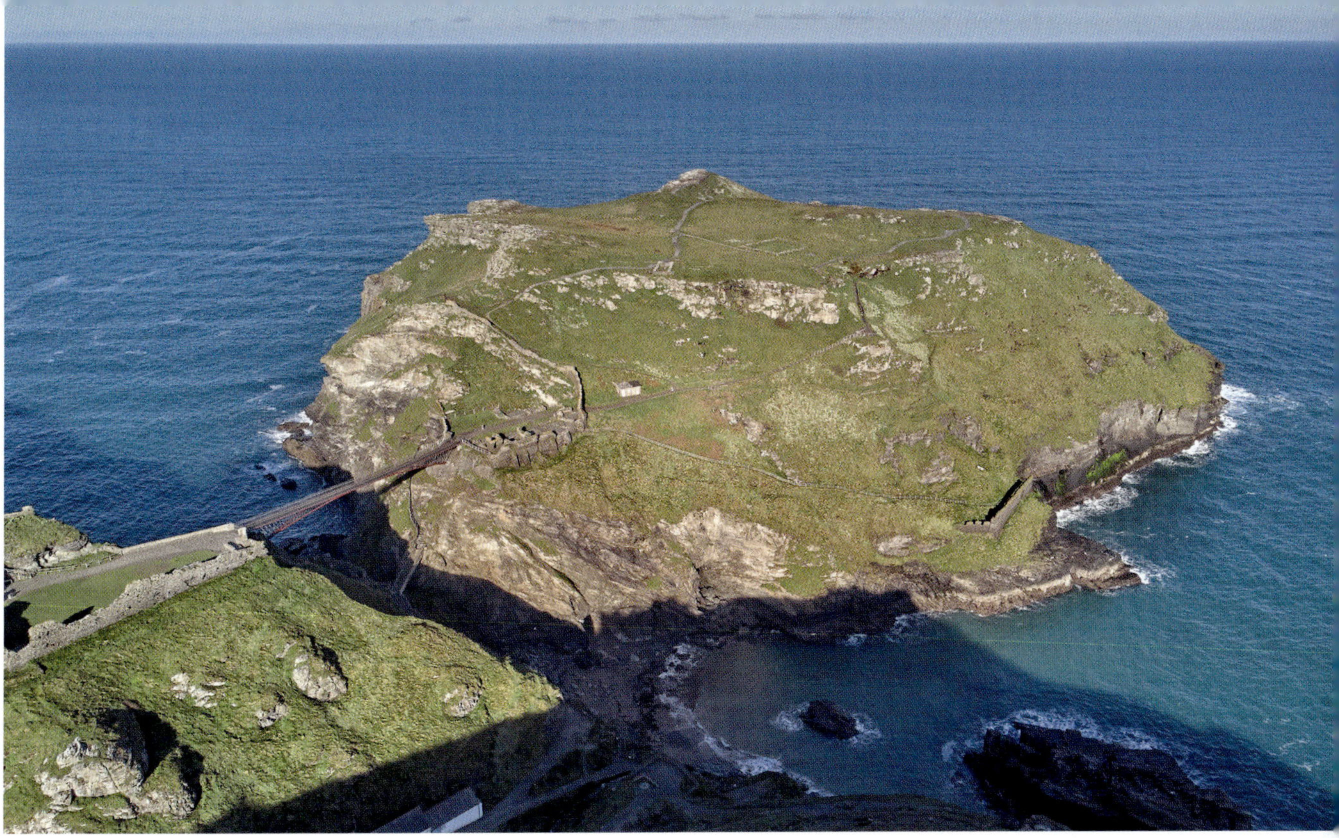

Above and Below Left: The rocky peninsula – almost an island – that is site of the ruins of Tintagel Castle, if legend is to be believed, the birthplace of King Arthur. Here, ruined walls hang precariously over sheer drops into the sea far below.

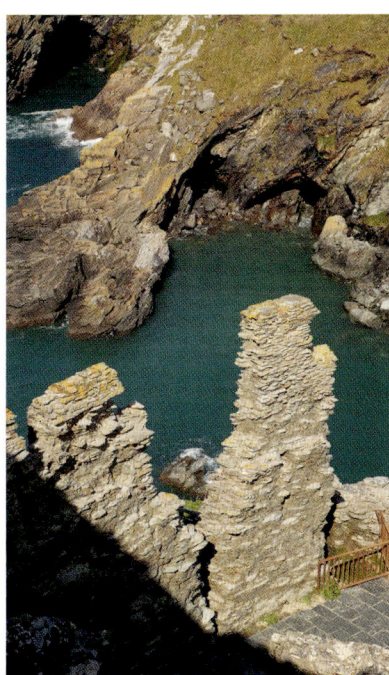

Right: The quaint village and harbour of Port Isaac was right off the tourism trail, but has been made well known by TV series *Doc Martin*.

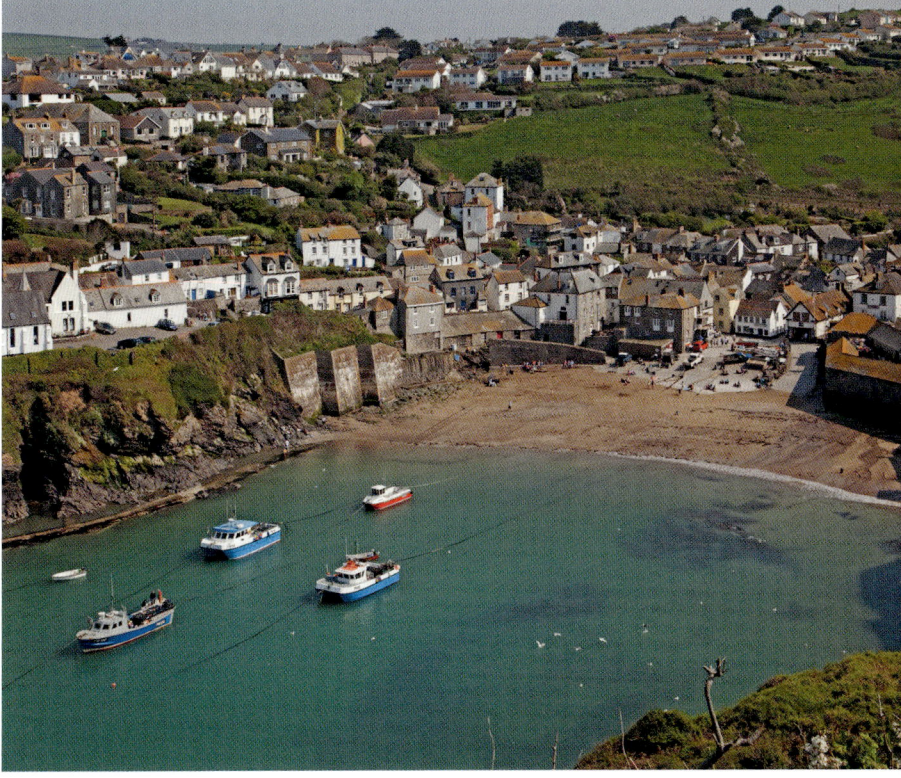

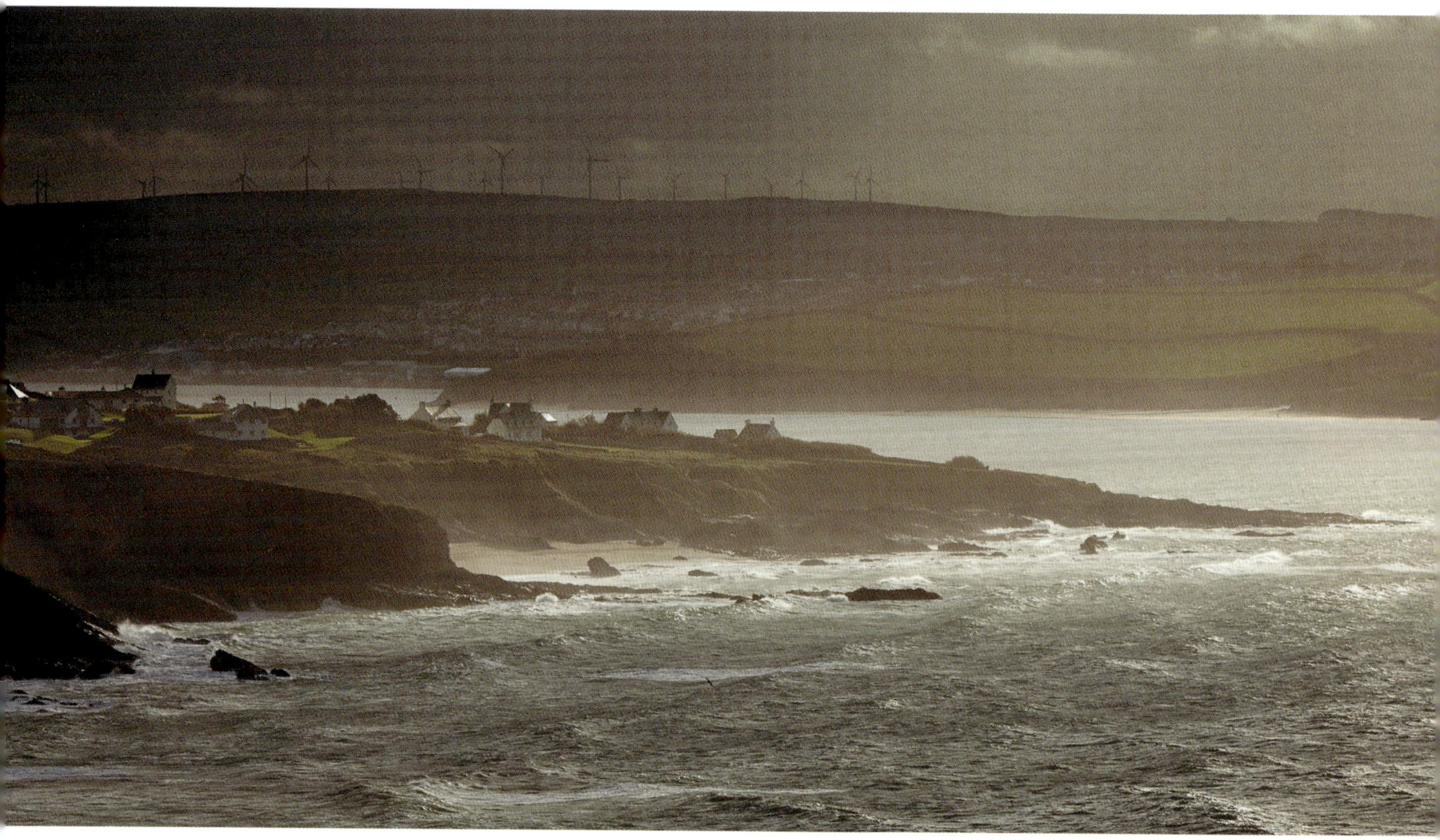

Beautiful Cornwall: A Portrait of a County

Above: A view on a breezy autumn day from Pentire Point across the mouth of the Camel River, to the distant town of Padstow.

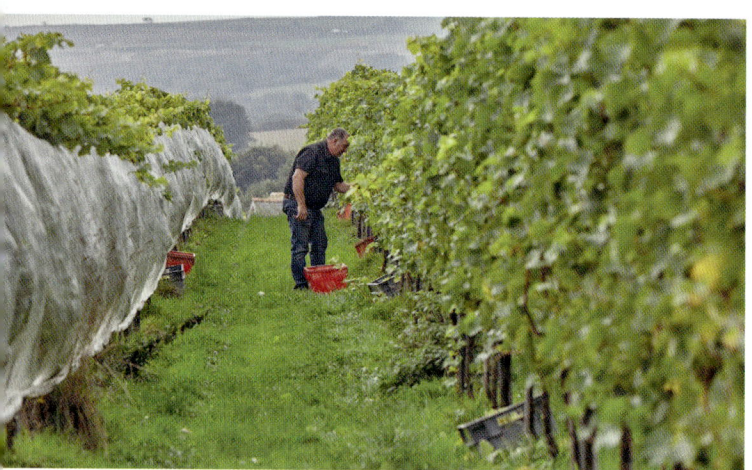
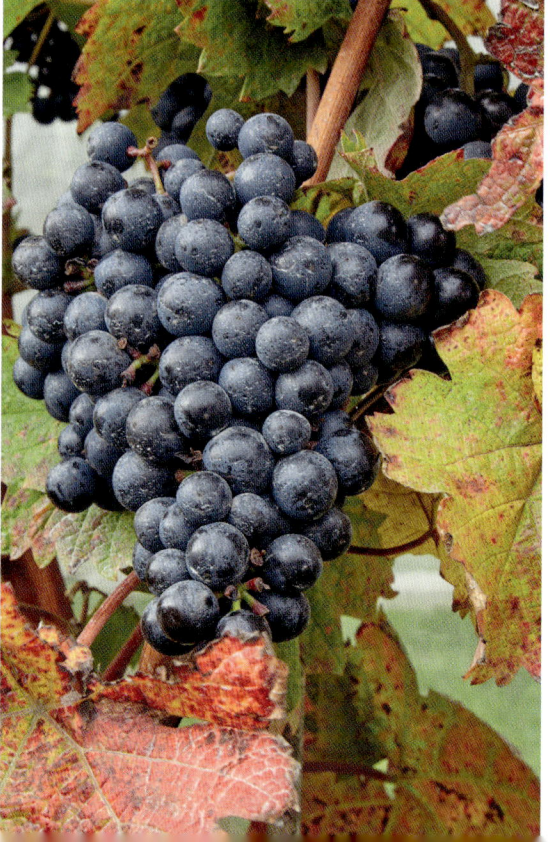

Above and Right: Autumn brings the grape harvest at Cornwall's slowly growing number of vineyards, as seen here at Trevibban Mill, near Padstow. Although most of Trevibban's grapes are white, they do also have the richly red Dornfelder variety, whose leaves also go a striking red at this time of year.

North Cornwall and Bodmin Moor

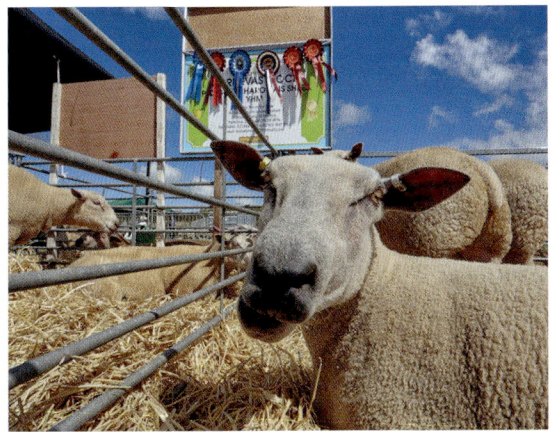 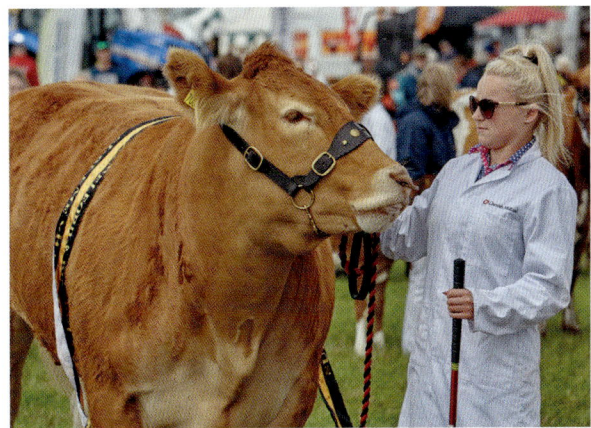

Above and Above Right: Prize livestock at the Camelford Agricultural Show, held every August. The show gives north Cornwall's farming community a good chance to show off the best of their animals – a very important part of quality breeding – as well as providing a rare opportunity for a social gathering.

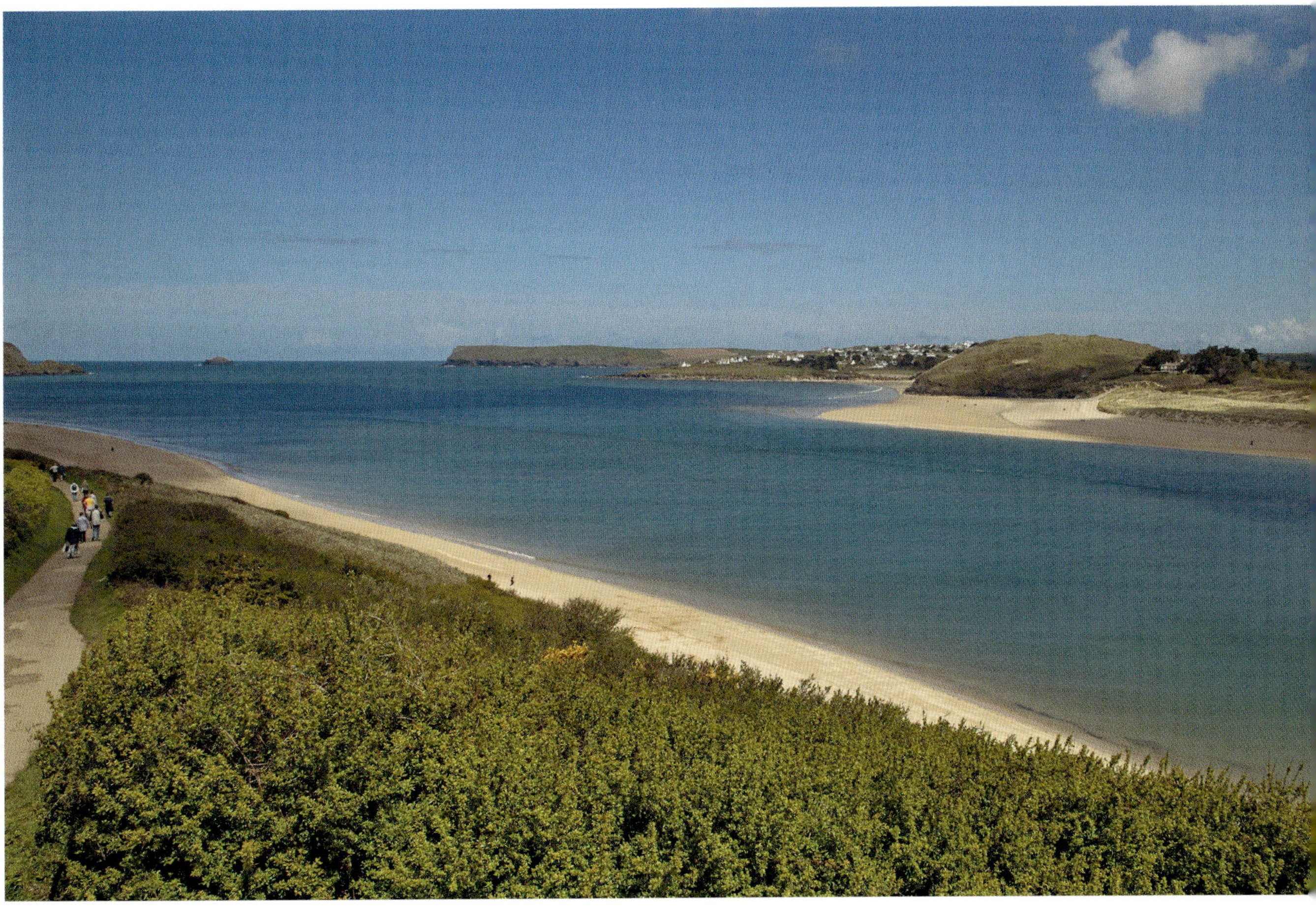

Above: A magnificent summer view of the Camel estuary, seen from the northern edge of Padstow, along the coastpath leading from the town to Stepper Point, at the river's mouth.

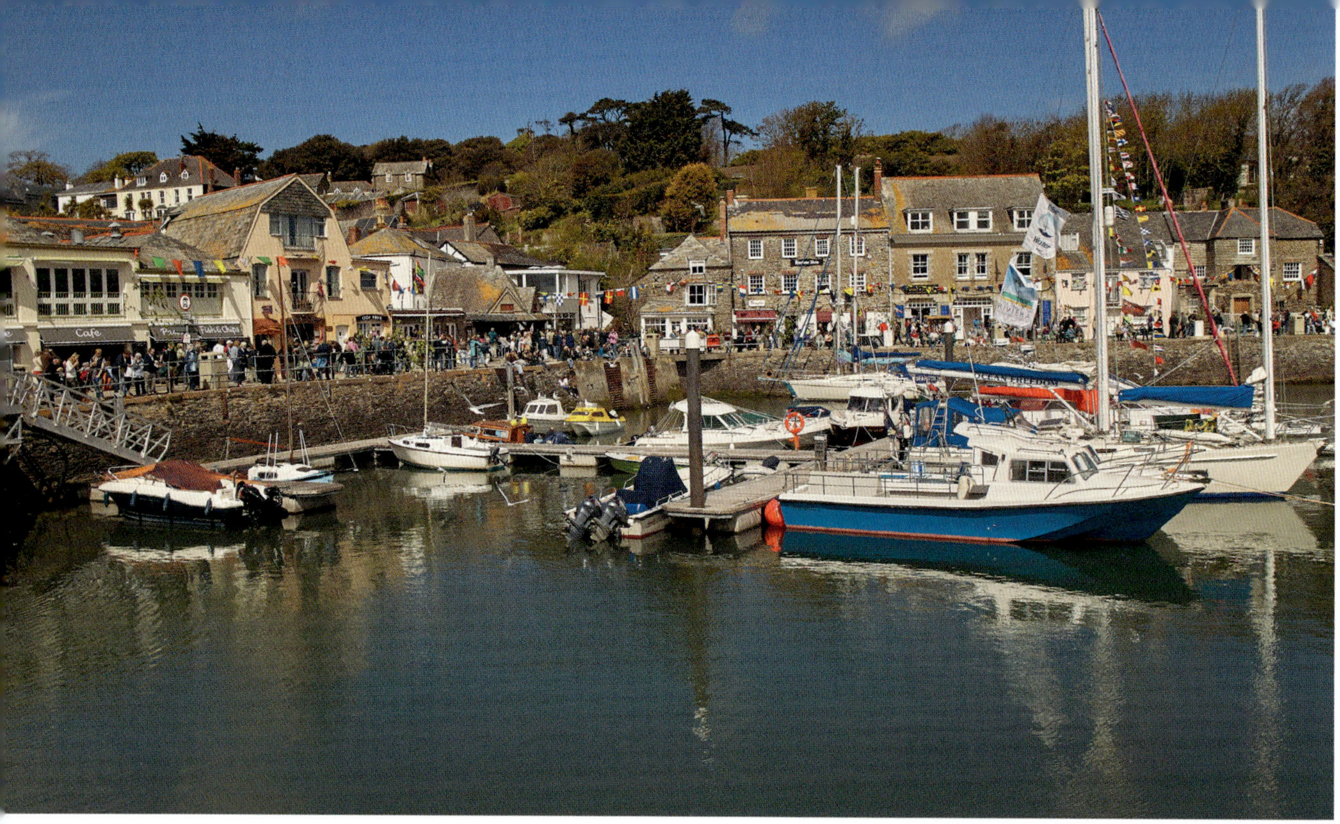

Padstow is one of Cornwall's major attractions, the old town crowding around the harbour gaining most attention. On 1st May each year the crowd is rather different from the usual, on this day consisting of locals and visitors alike, drawn in by the raucous Obby Oss Festival, a day when two Obby Osses dance through the streets accompanied by musicians to welcome in the spring and summer.

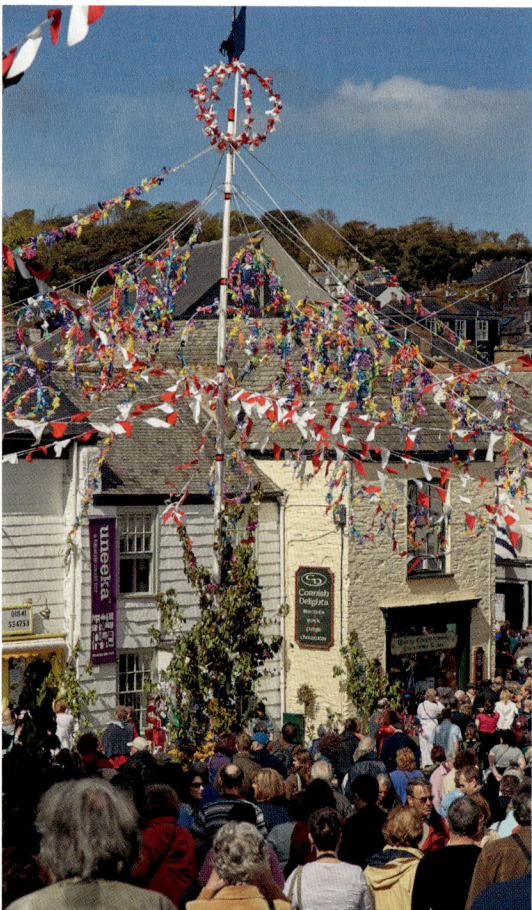

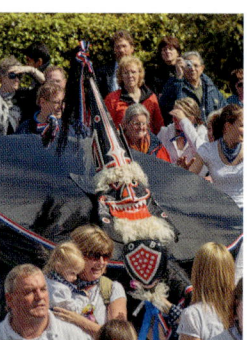

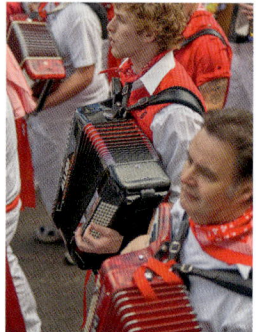

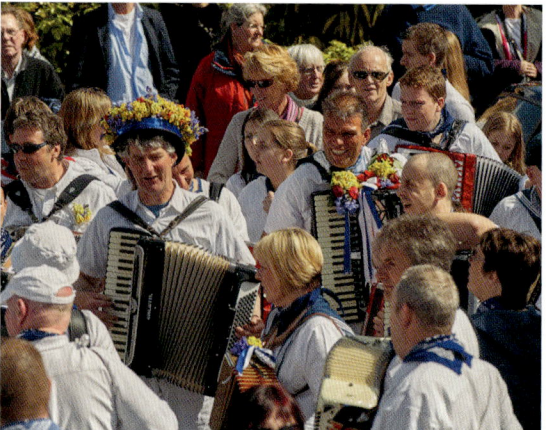

Right: The surf along north Cornwall's Atlantic coast is among the best in the UK, attracting many leading surfers.

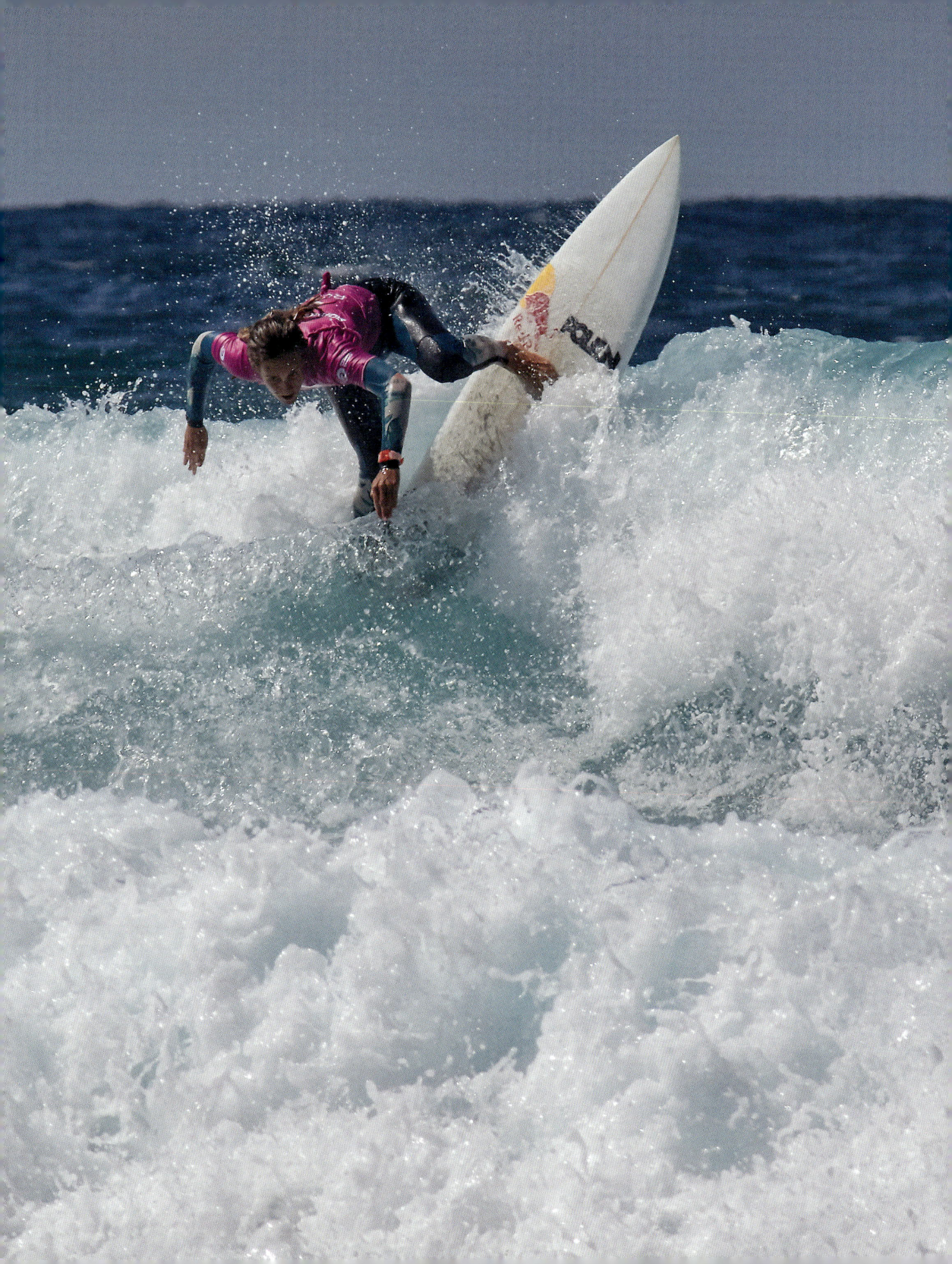

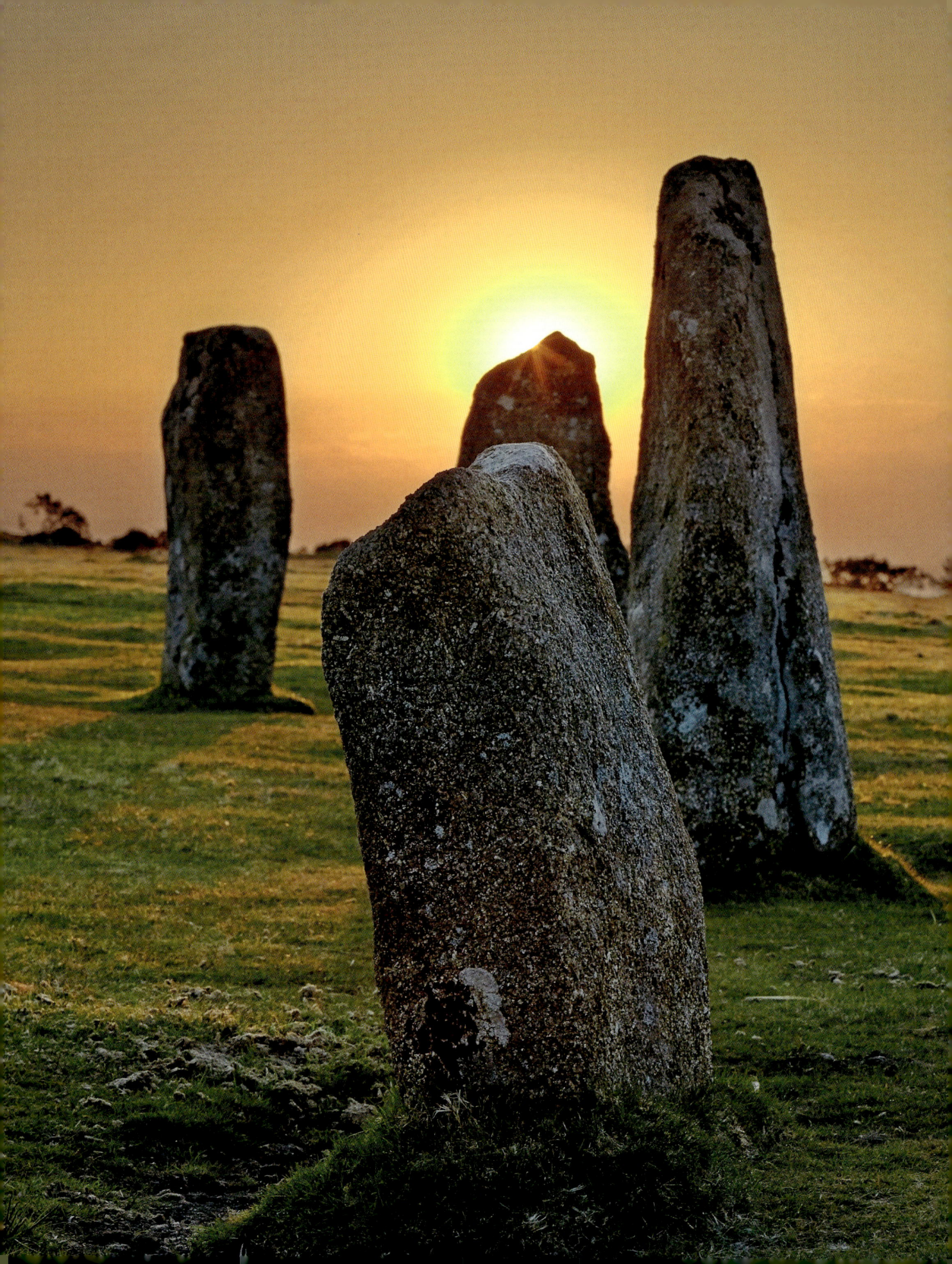

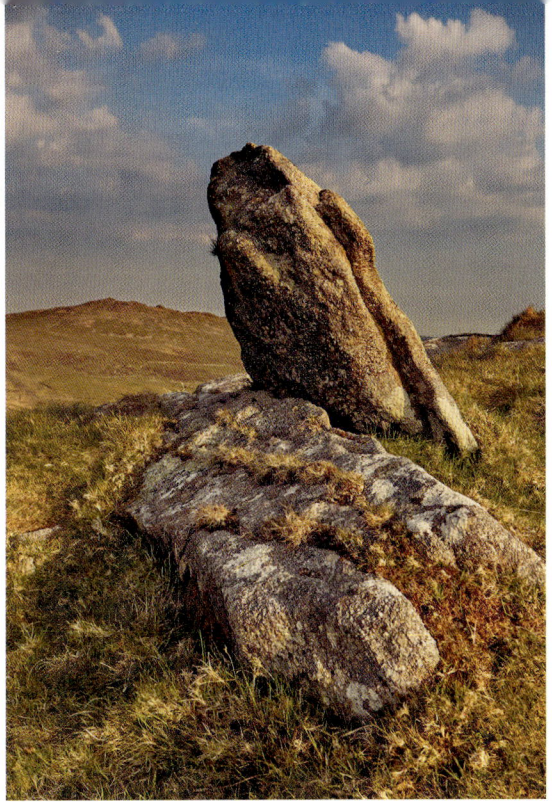

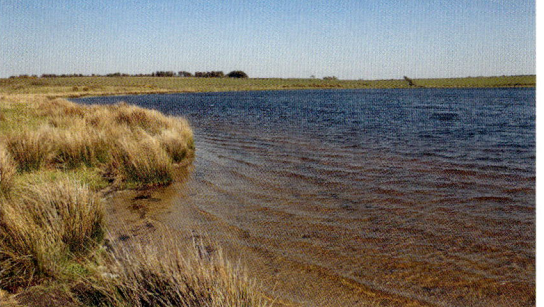

Above: Dozmary Pool, on Bodmin Moor, is said to have been the place where King Arthur was given his sword Excalibur by *'the Lady of the Lake'*.

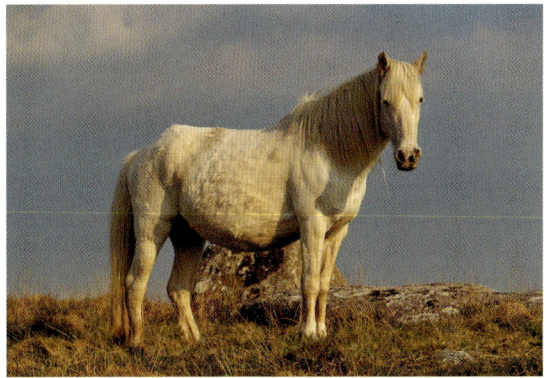

Above: Granite rocks lit by the light of sunset are a typical scene on the summit of Rough Tor, one of Cornwall's highest and wildest points, in the heart of Bodmin Moor.

Above: As with Devon's Dartmoor, so on Bodmin Moor ponies are able to wander freely, usually seen moving around in small herds across some of the remoter moorlands.

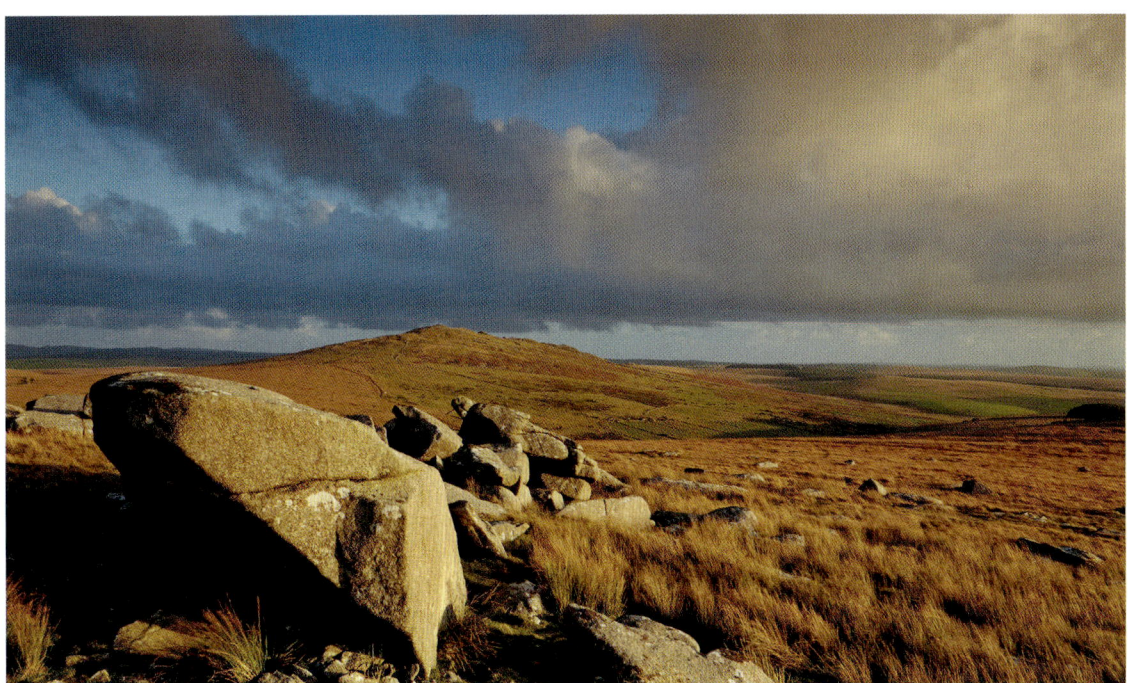

Left: A sunrise view of some of the standing stones at the Hurlers, an extensive series of prehistoric stone circles on the southern side of Bodmin Moor, and one of Cornwall's most well known ancient sites.

Above: An autumnal evening's view from the summit of Rough Tor towards Brown Willy, at 420 metres (1378 ft) Cornwall's highest point, set in the wild heart of Bodmin Moor.

Beautiful Cornwall: A Portrait of a County

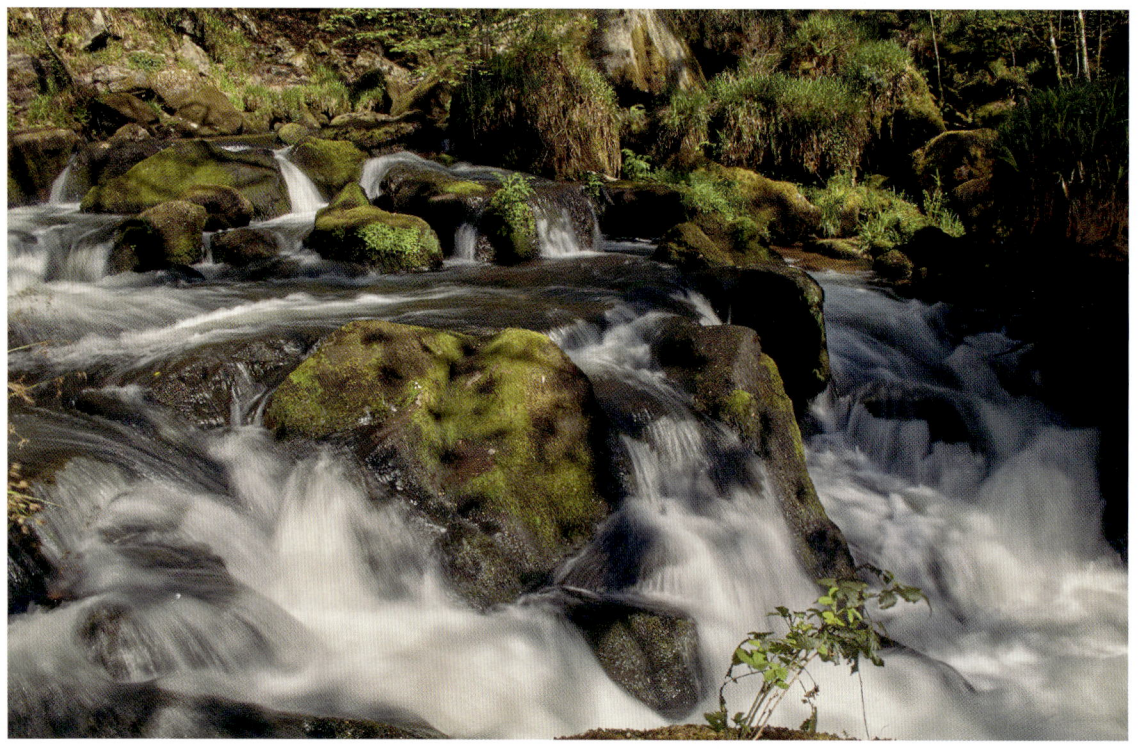

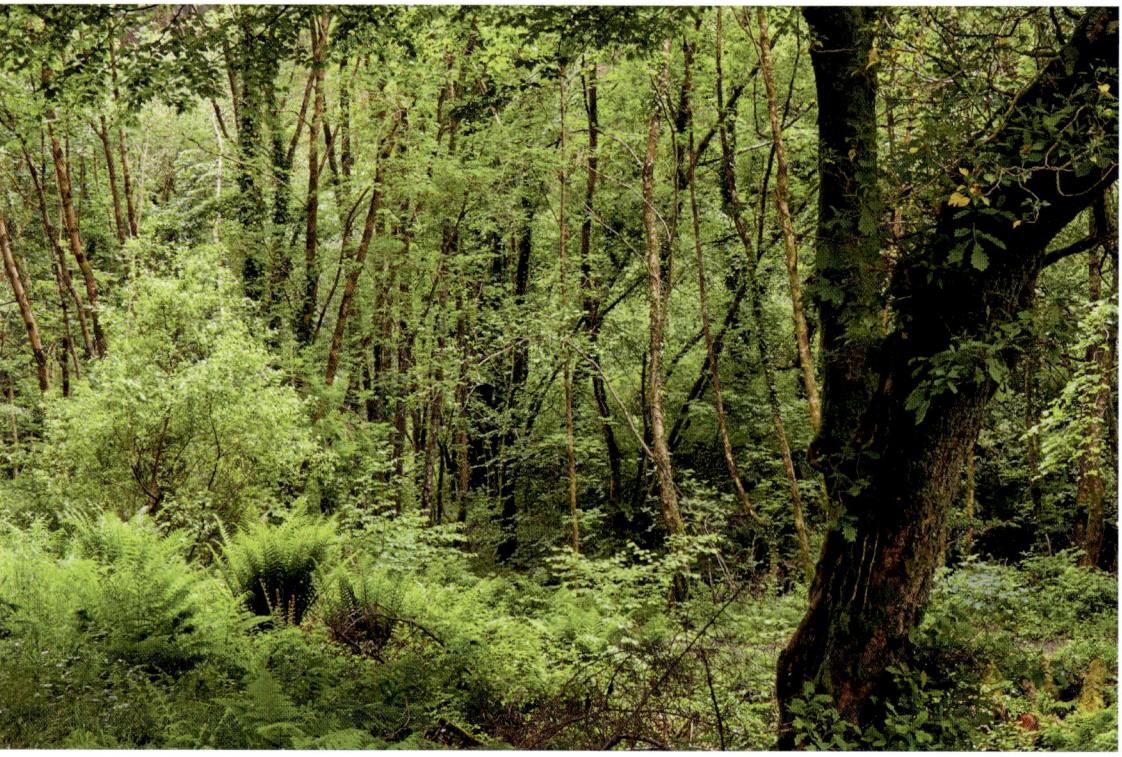

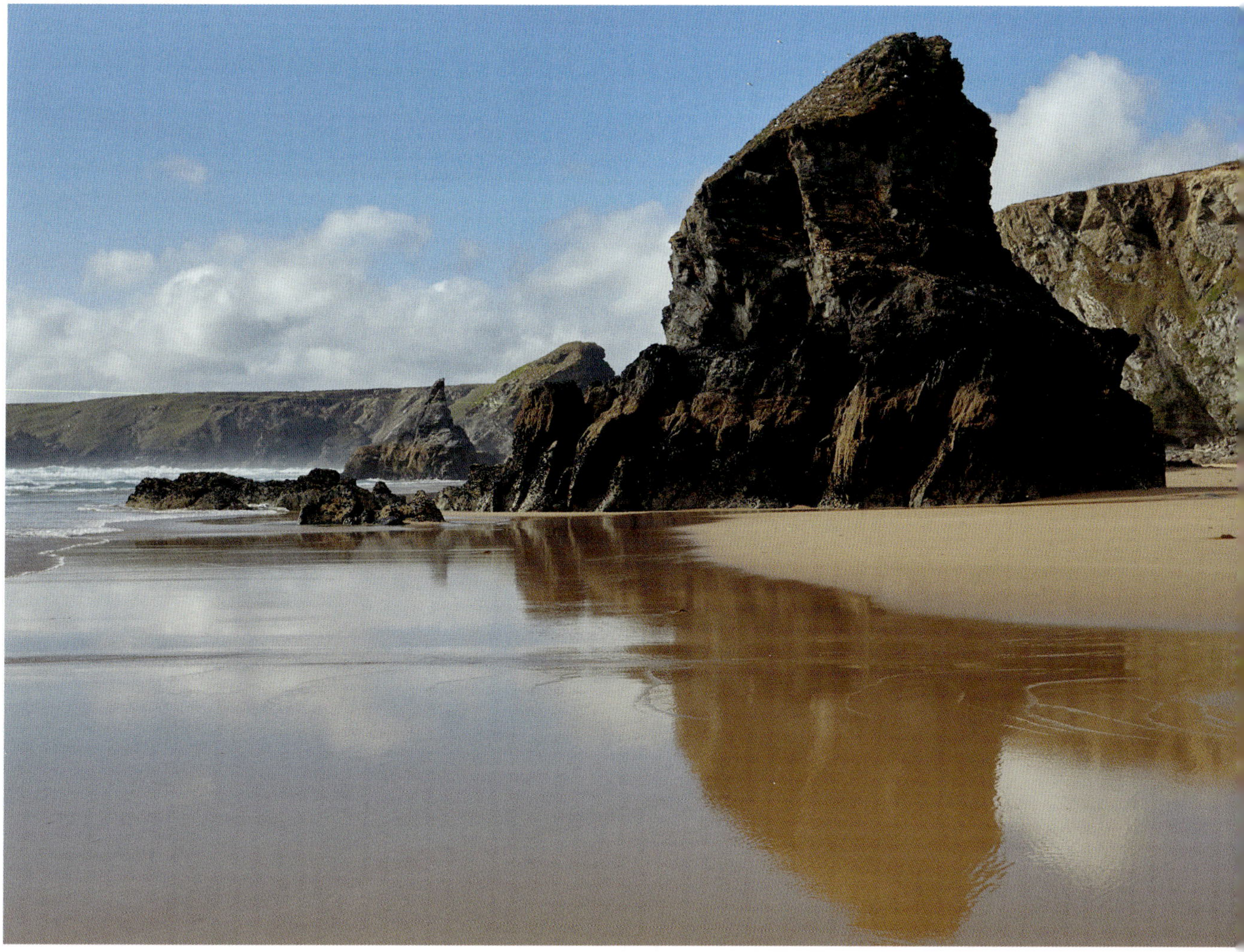

North Cornwall and Bodmin Moor

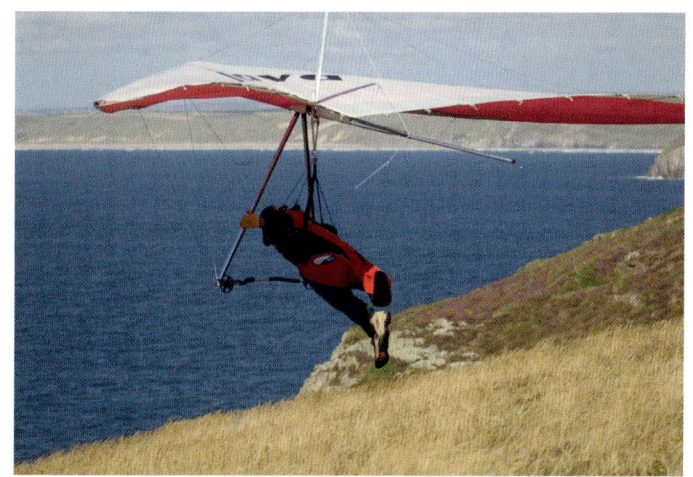

Above Left: A section of the lovely Golitha Falls, a steep, fast-flowing stretch of the River Fowey, as it tumbles down off the southern slopes of Bodmin Moor.

Bottom Left: A dense stand of trees in Cardinham Woods, one of Cornwall's rather rare larger woodlands, sheltered in a valley on the southern edge of Bodmin Moor.

Above: One of the mighty rocks that constitute Bedruthan Steps, seen from an unusual angle; the surrounding beach, which is accessible only at low tide.

Right: A hang-glider launching off the cliffs at St Agnes Head. In the right weather, these high cliffs can generate strong upward thermals that allow hang-gliders to both launch from and land again on these cliffs.

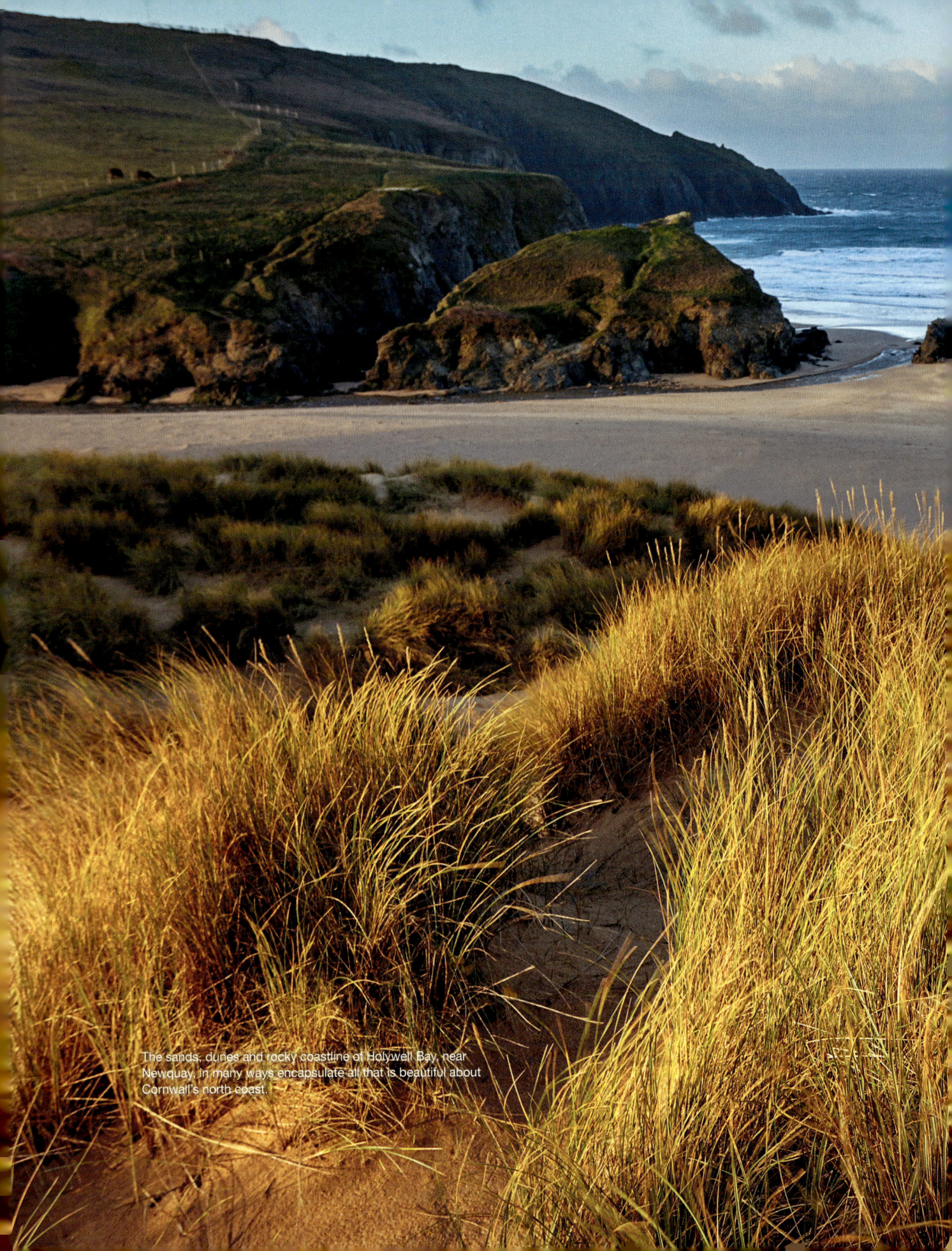

The sands, dunes and rocky coastline of Holywell Bay, near Newquay, in many ways encapsulate all that is beautiful about Cornwall's north coast.

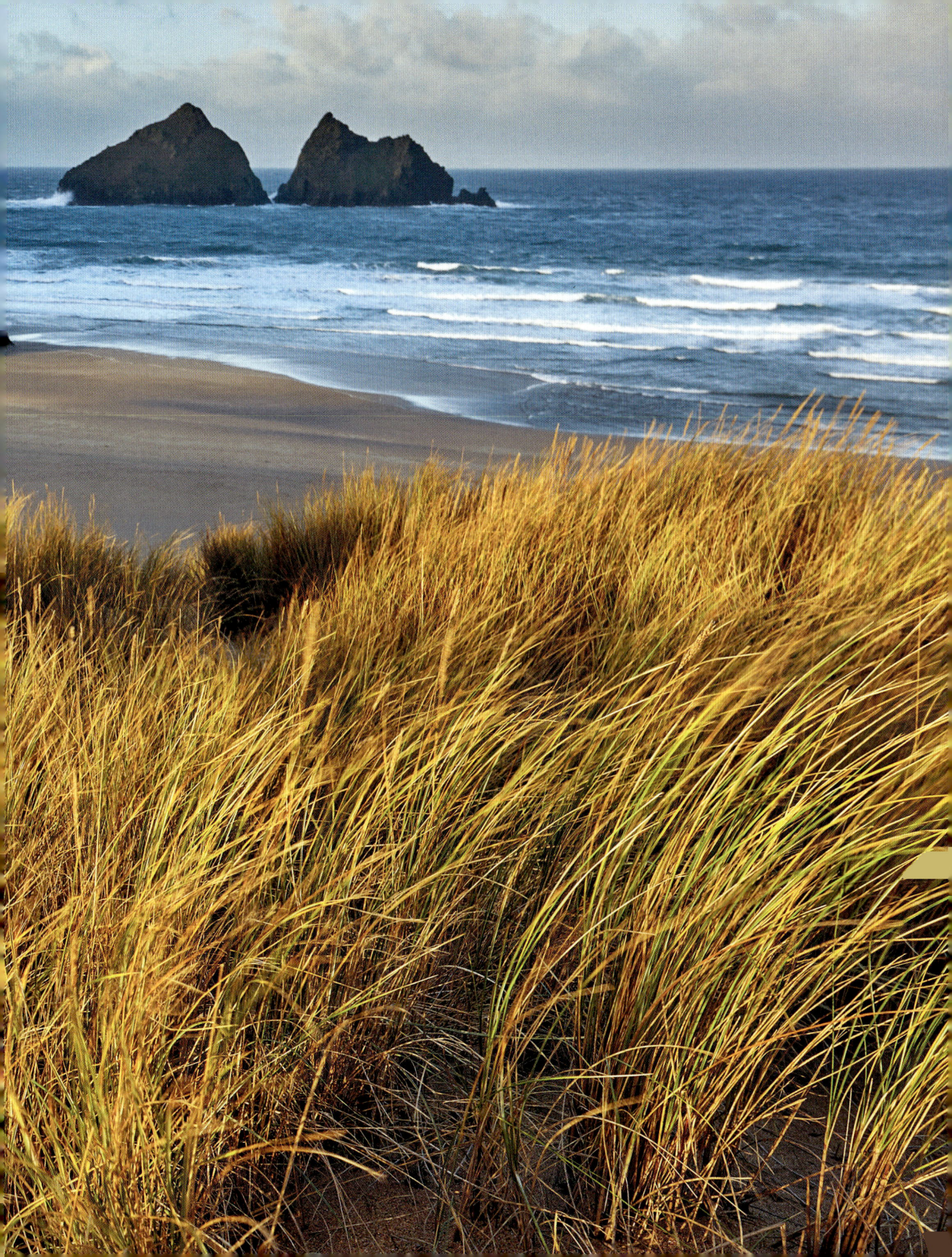

Beautiful Cornwall: A Portrait of a County

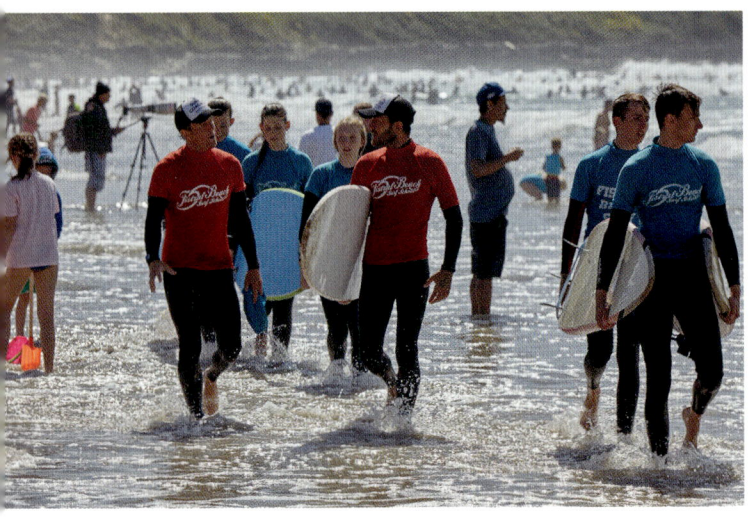

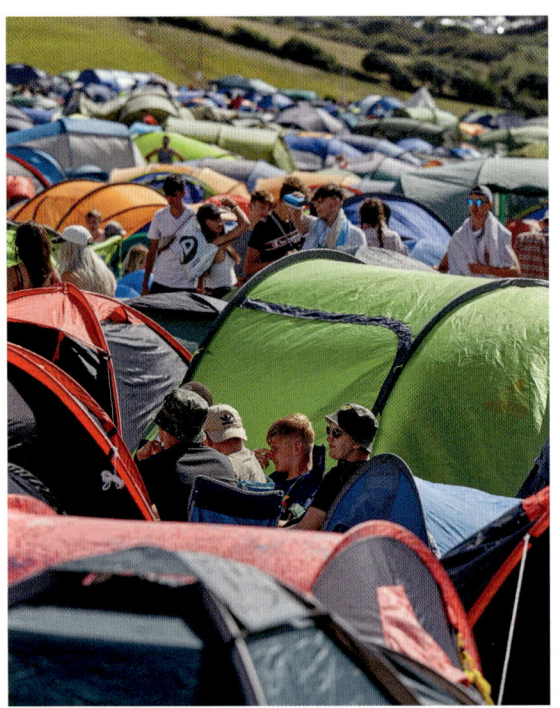

Newquay's Boardmasters, held every August, draws tens of thousands of people to the area, making Fistral Beach packed, and establishing a tent city near Watergate Bay, to the northeast of the town, site of the event's rock music festival.

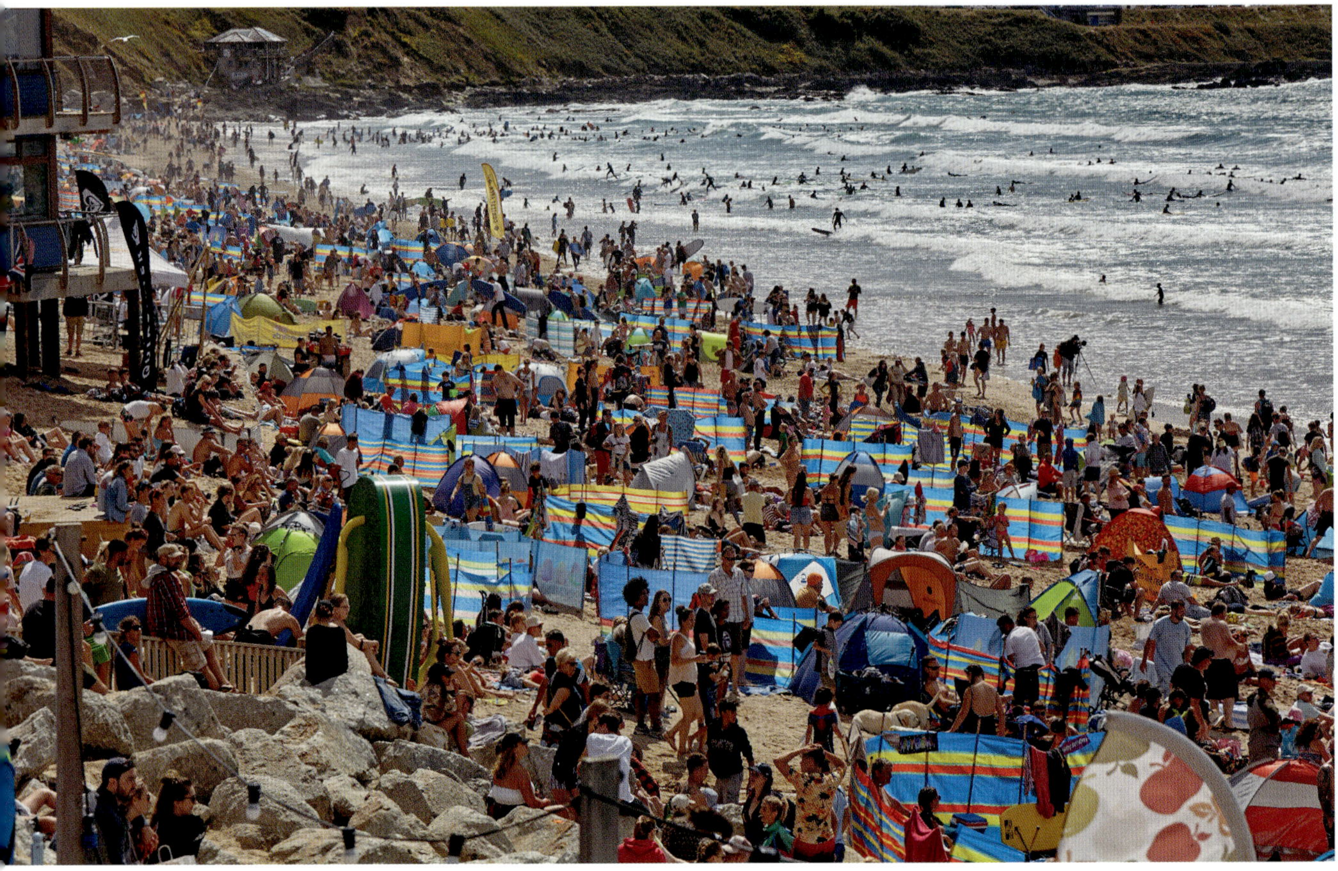

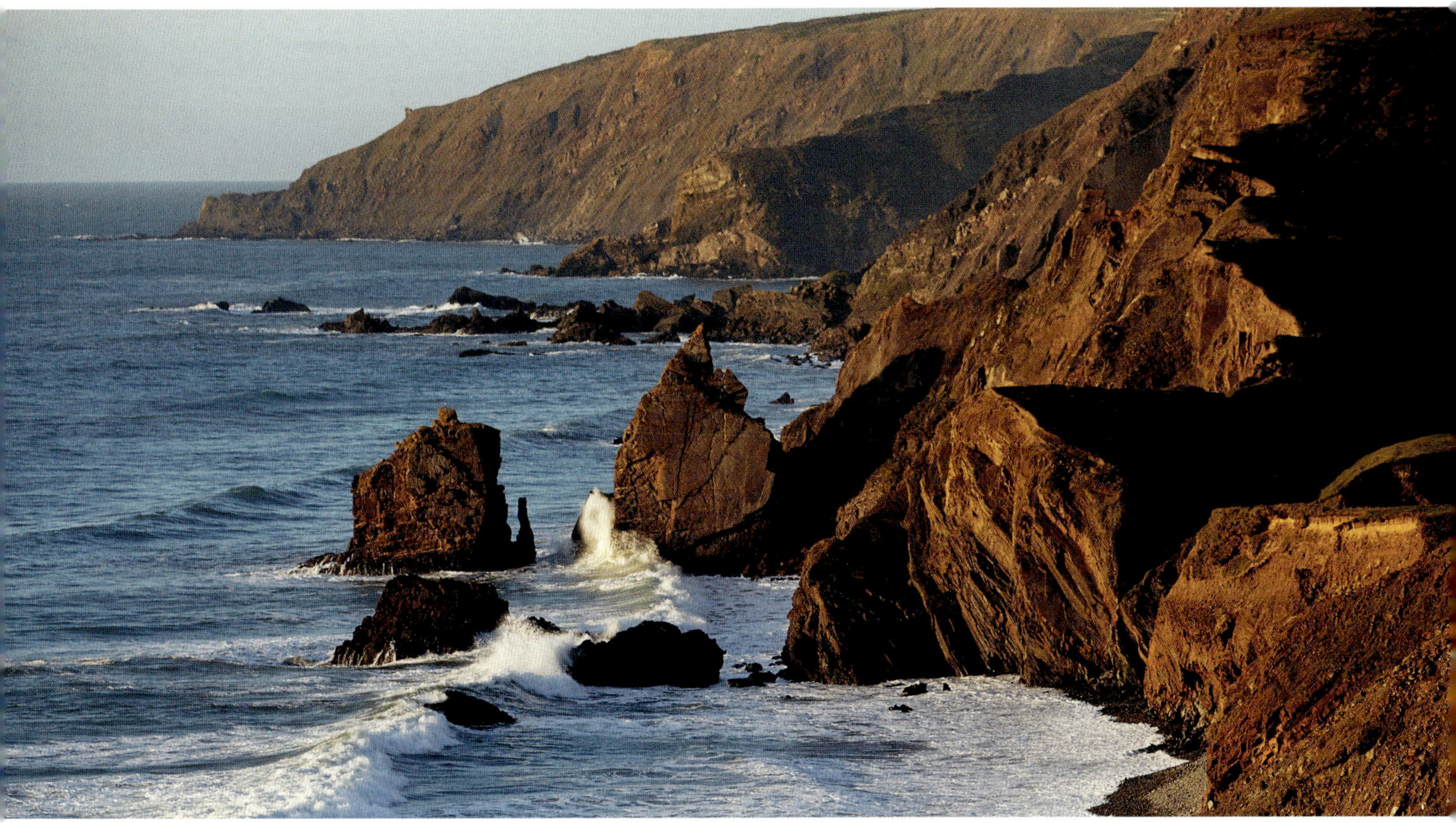

North Cornwall and Bodmin Moor

Above: North of Bude, as you approach the border with Devon, the soft cliffs are heavily eroded into jagged shapes and large numbers of offshore rocks. One of the most spectacular is Sandy Mouth, seen here bathed in evening sunlight.

Right: In close-up, the cliffs in and around Sandy Mouth reveal tortuous patterns of uplifting and twisting, generating superb patterns that only add to the already bright orange hues of much of the rock.

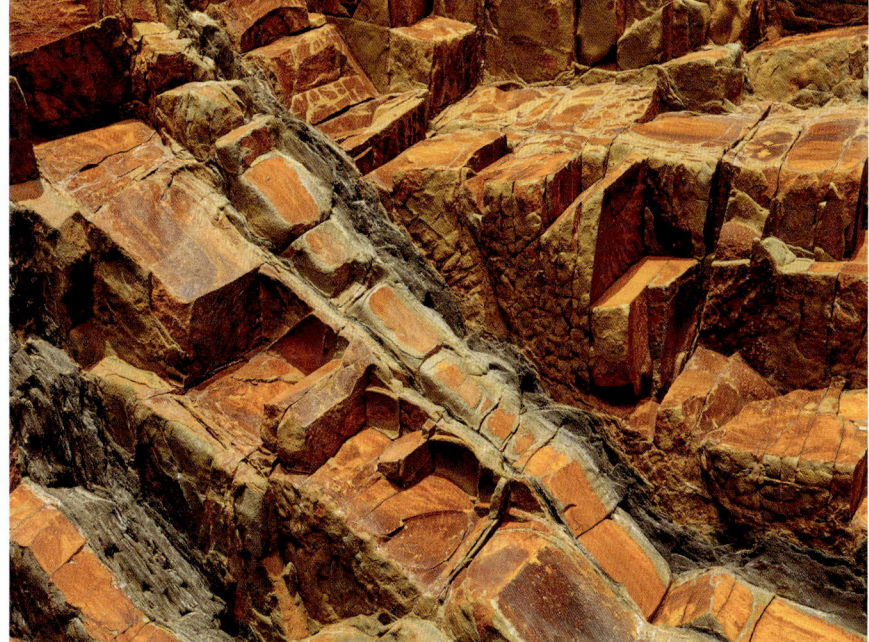

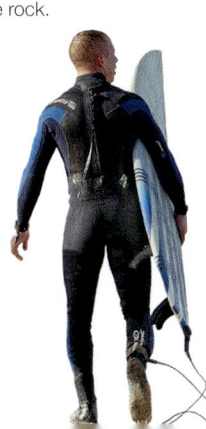

4 The South Coast

Stretching from Fowey in the east all the way down to the Helford River area, this region encompasses Cornwall's English Channel coastline, a much gentler environment than the rugged north coast. Here, rolling agricultural hills drop down towards the coast, marked mostly by much smaller, less rugged cliffs.

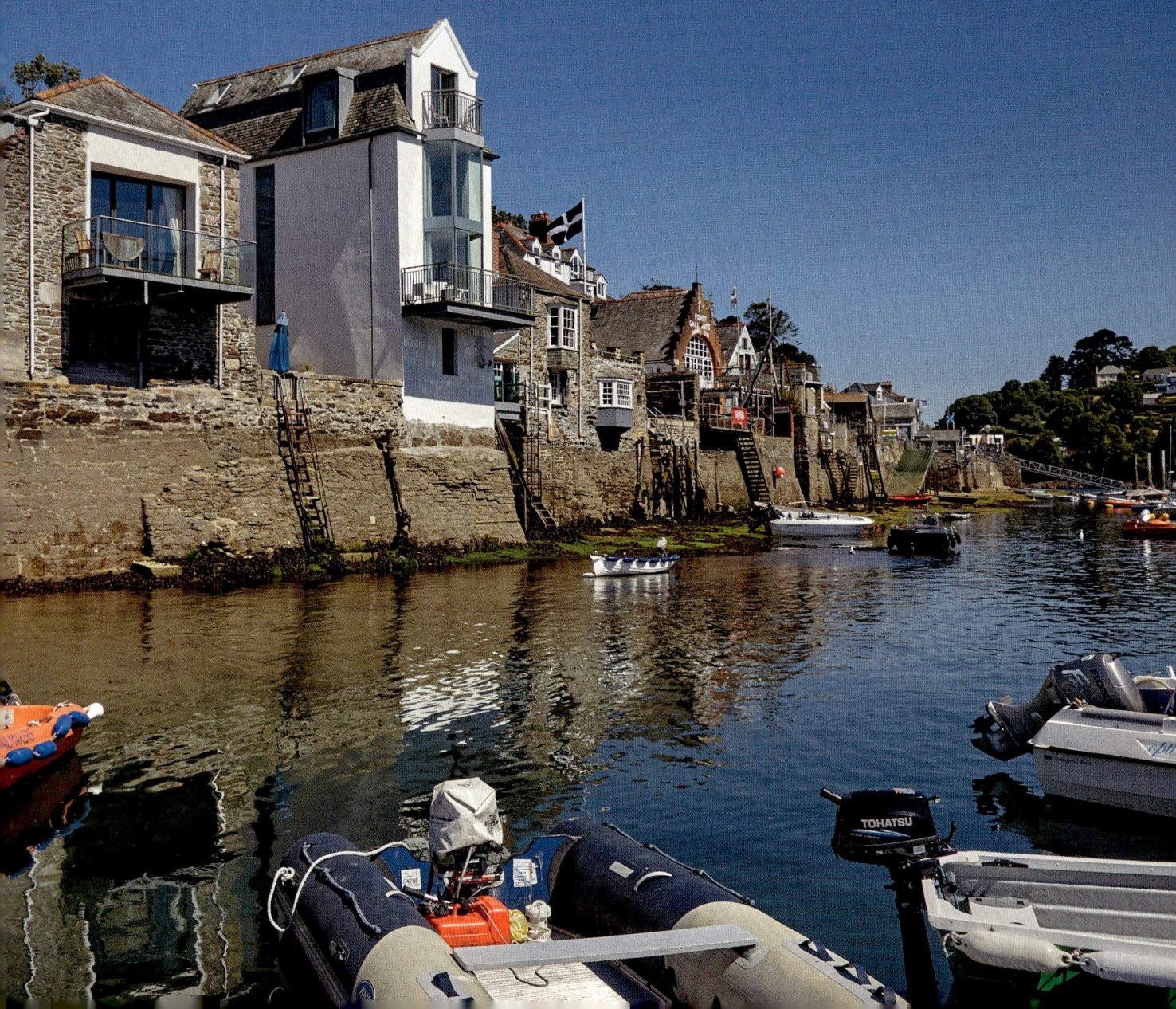

Several rivers have gouged deep valleys, the Fowey, Fal and Helford, creating some magnificent natural harbours. Towns and harbours are quite frequent, interspersed with mostly relatively small surf-free beaches. The easternmost town in this region is Fowey, nestling in a river valley and on the shores of the River Fowey estuary, a deepwater natural harbour. An historic town, today it still bustles with activity, mostly yachts, plus a modest fishing fleet and a small port.

Heading west leads to St Austell, a busy working town, and although the town itself is not much of an attraction, it is surrounded by places that are. Firstly, on its southern fringe lies the historic port of Charlestown, no longer working as such, but with its permanently moored tallships it is rather a museum to the past. In total contrast, to the north sits one of Cornwall's most modern and forward-looking visitor attractions, the Eden Project. An awe-inspiring concept, it sits at the bottom of a disused quarry and consists of two huge domes that almost unbelievably contain a tropical rainforest and a Mediterranean environment.

A rather more traditional garden on the edge of St Austell is the Pinetum, while to the south is the now-famous Lost Gardens of Heligan. Also south of St Austell is Mevigissey, one of those quaint quintessential Cornish fishing villages, this one still busy with a very active and successful fishing fleet. Beyond Mevigissey lies the little harbour village of Gorran Haven, and then Dodman Point, whose rugged cliffs are more reminiscent of the north coast than the gentler south.

To the west we come to the area of the River Fal and its magnificent estuary. Sitting on one of its northern arms is Truro, Cornwall's only city, the county capital, dominated by the spires of its 19th century

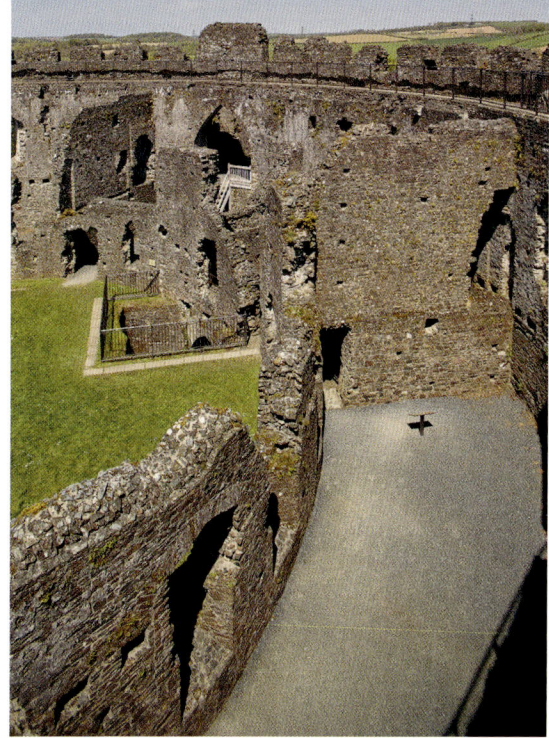

Above: The ruins of the perfectly circular Restormel Castle, dating from the Norman era, that stands above the River Fowey, near Lostwithiel.

cathedral. To the south, on the western shore of the estuary is Falmouth, arguably one of the most enviably well-placed towns in southern England. It has a fabulous prospect overlooking the vast Carrick Roads, the sheltered waters of the Fal's estuary and one of the world's largest natural harbours. The land around the Fal estuary is one of Cornwall's jewels, rolling hills, deep valleys and tiny roads hiding a string of lovely riverside villages and harbours, paramount among which are Mylor Harbour and St Mawes.

South of Falmouth lies the Helford River, a smaller version of the Fal though perhaps even more sublimely bucolic. Lost in deep valleys and served by very few roads, much of it is barely accessible to anything other than a boat. Gweek is one of the few easily reachable places, its tidal creeks home to several boat repair yards and the Cornish Seal Sanctuary, a place to which injured or sick seals are brought for rehabilitation. On the river's very sheltered northern shores are two more of Cornwall's most famous gardens, the neighbouring Glendurgan and Trebah, both almost buried in lush, verdant valleys, a great finale to this region.

Left: The harbour at Fowey, in the mouth of the Fowey River, is characterized by historic buildings crowding down to the water's edge, leaving little room for any kind of quay that might provide a series of viewpoints.

Beautiful Cornwall: A Portrait of a County

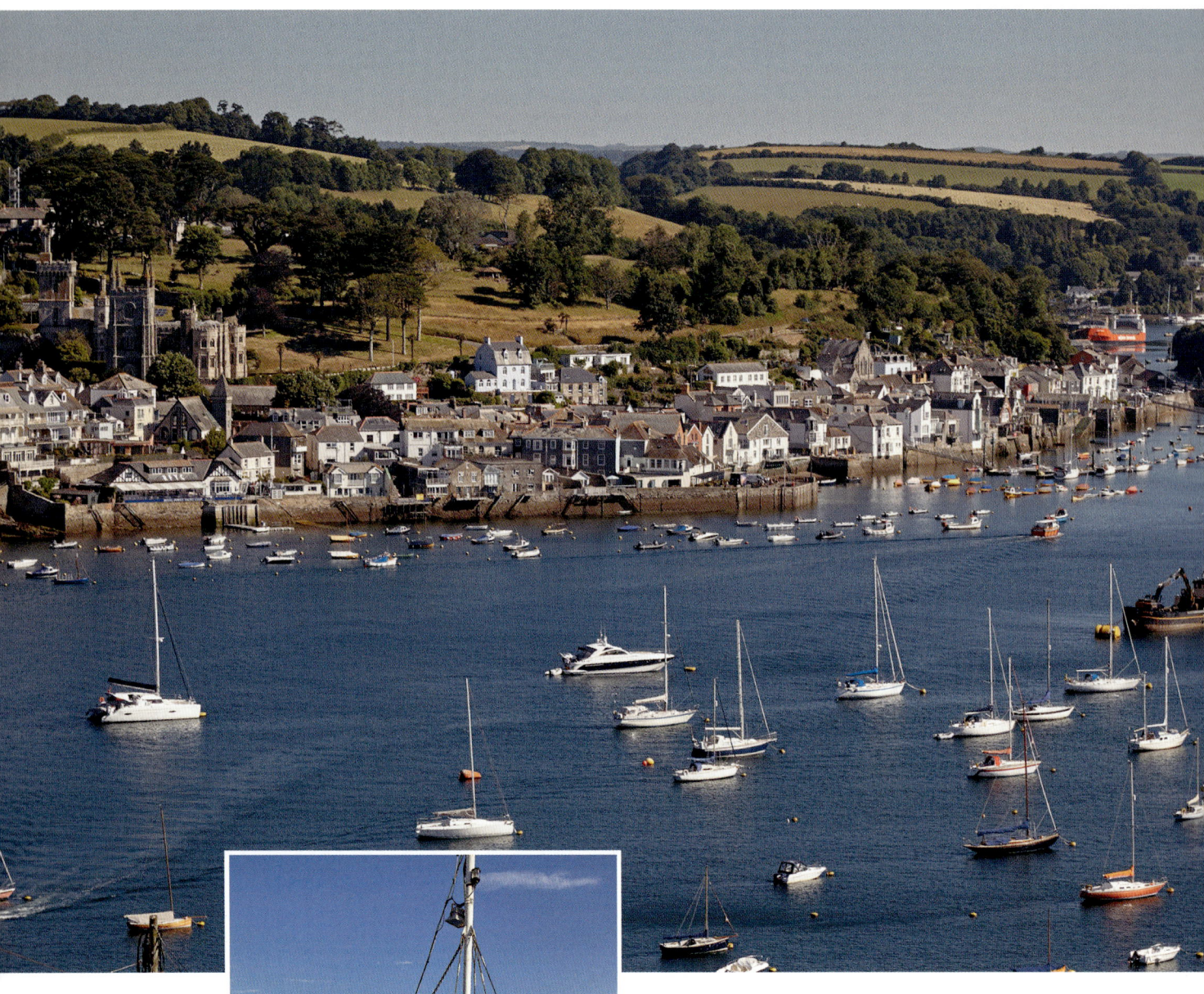

Above: Fowey is an attractive, old harbour town sitting in a very well protected position on the shore of the Fowey estuary. It bustles with life, mainly yachts, though it does still have a small commercial port.

Left: A very traditional kind of fishing boat rests, tied up to one of the quays with the town of Mevigissey behind, seen in early morning sunlight.

Right: The historic harbour of Charlestown, on the southern edge of St Austell, was once busy with ships carrying away china clay. Today, it serves as something of a tallships museum, as well as a very handy and convincing film set.

The South Coast

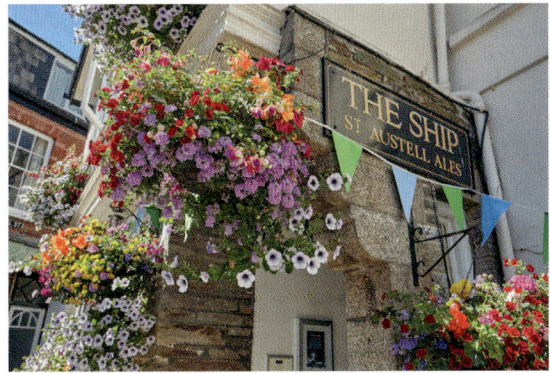

Above: In a town like Fowey, the pubs inevitably have very maritime names, in summer bedecked with enormous flower displays to add appeal for the many visitors.

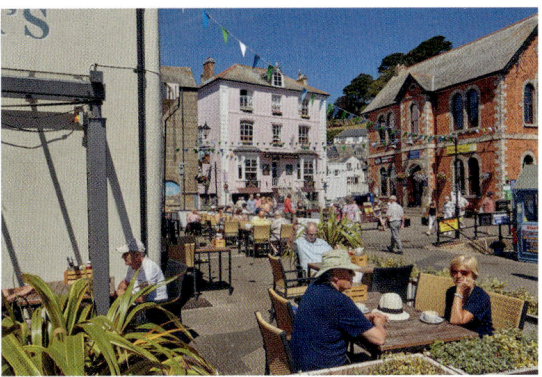

Above: The area around the Town Quay is very much at the heart of Fowey's visitor attractions, with several cafes and pubs, as well as some of the only views of the harbour and estuary.

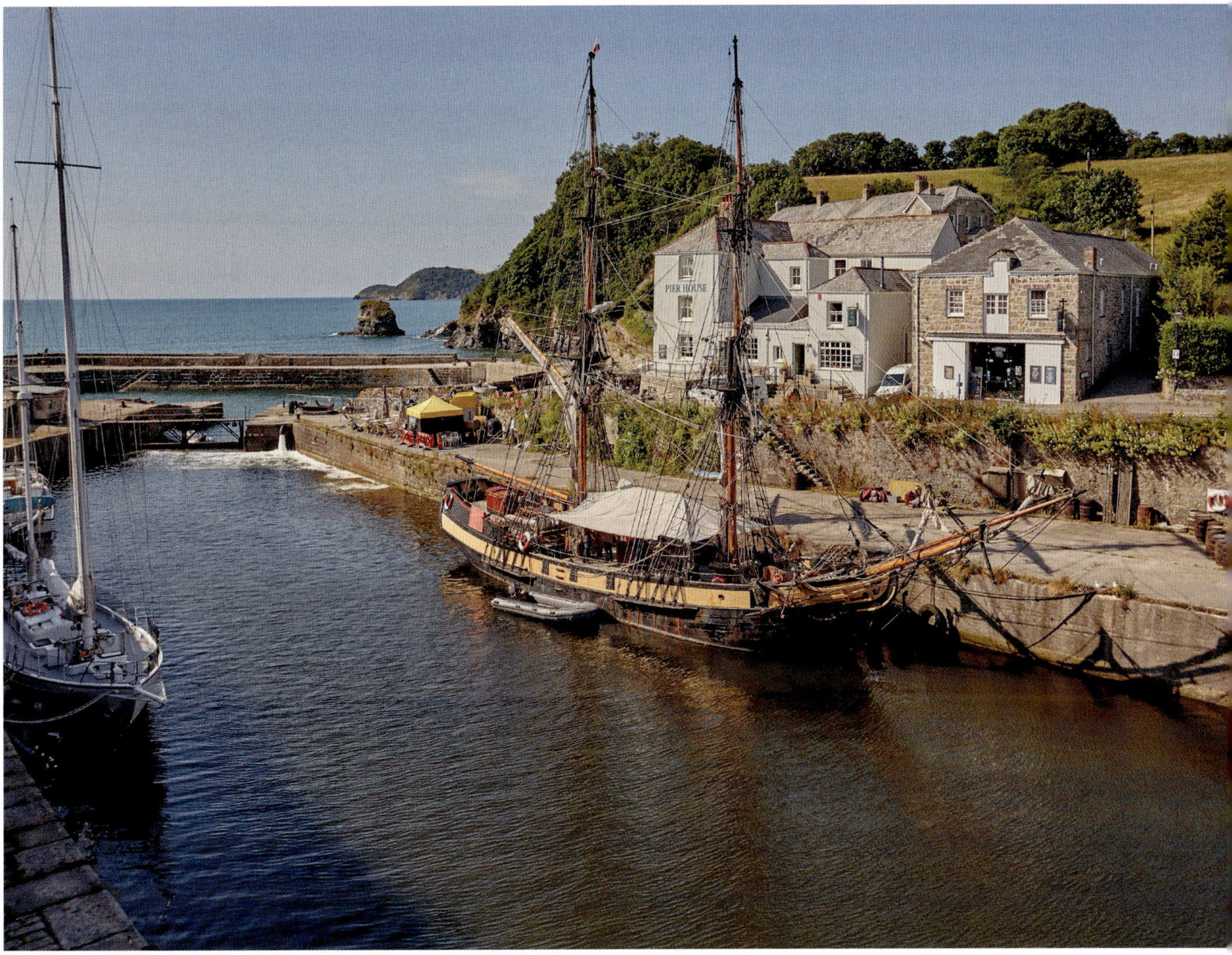

Beautiful Cornwall: A Portrait of a County

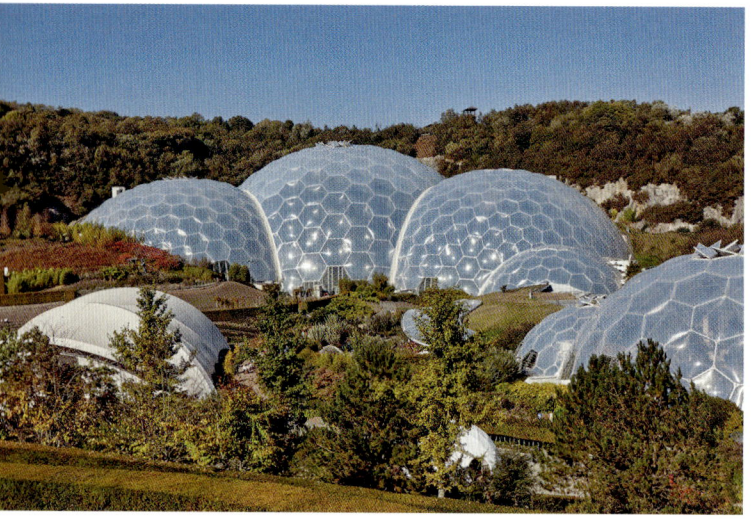

Above: One of modern Cornwall's most iconic views, that of the domes of the Eden Project's Rainforest Biome, housing full-sized tropical rainforest trees, showcasing some of the world's most useful plants.

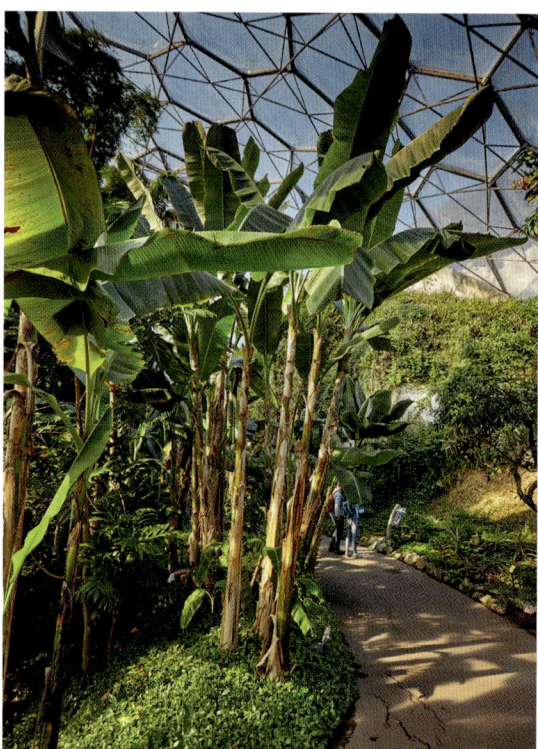

Above: In the Rainforest Biome a display of banana plants recalls the importance of this single crop in many tropical countries, thriving in the hot, humid atmosphere under the protective dome.

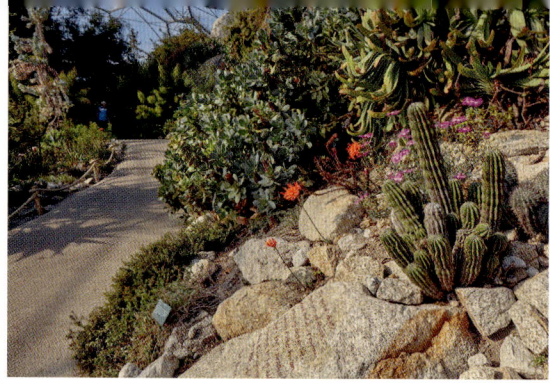

Above: Plants of a dry climate – cacti and other succulents – from South Africa, displayed in the Eden Project's Mediterranean Biome, where plants from several of the world's warm temperate regions are displayed, thriving in a protected warm, dry climate under the huge dome.

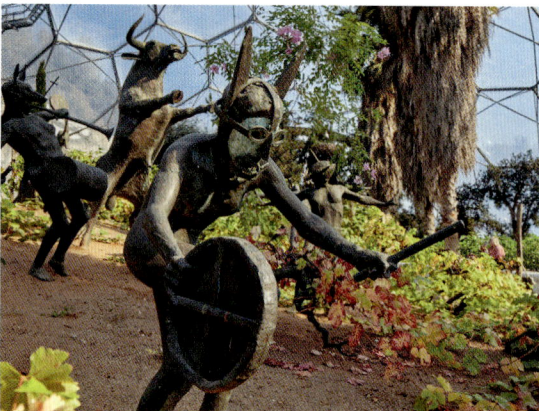

Above: Bacchanalian sculptures depicting the story of Dionysus, the Greek god of the vine, his followers 'dancing' within the mini-vineyard inside the Mediterranean biome.

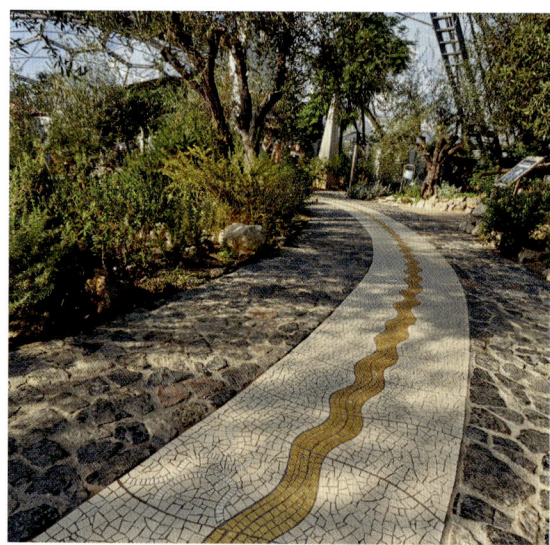

Above: A river of gold on one of the Mediterranean Biome's paths is symbolic of the wealth that olive oil has delivered to the Mediterranean world. The path is lined by trees of an olive grove.

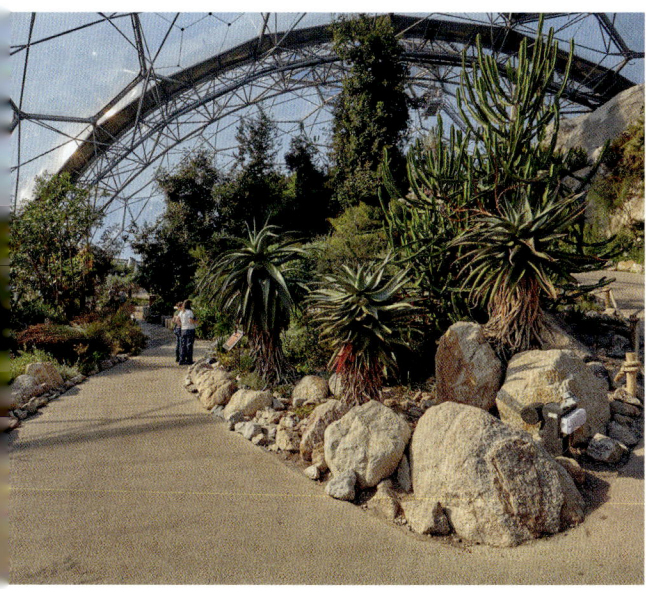

Above: The Mediterranean Biome, protected under its huge dome, houses thousands of plants from around the world, plants originating in a variety of dry, warm temperate, Mediterranean-type climates.

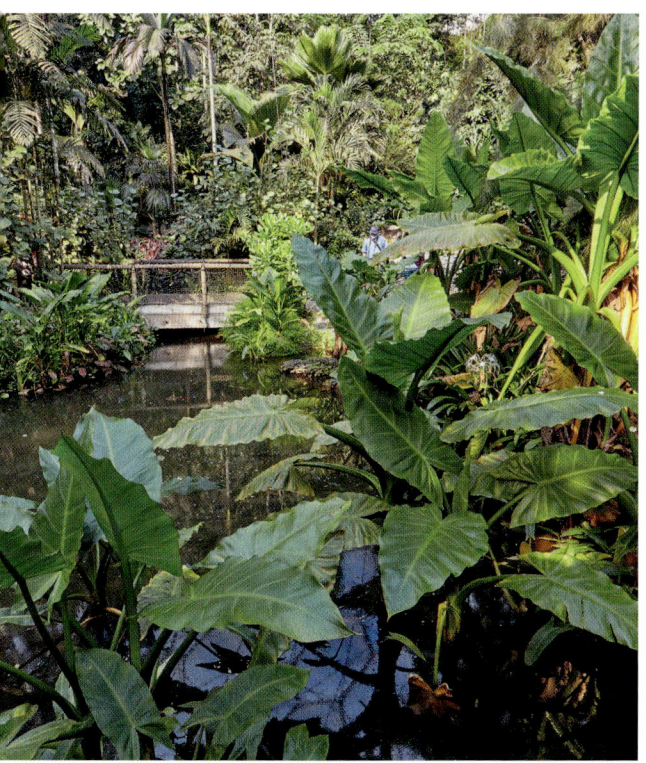

Above: The tropical climate within the Rainforest Biome allows wild yams to grow in the shallow waters around the edge of a pool, with rainforest crowding in the background.

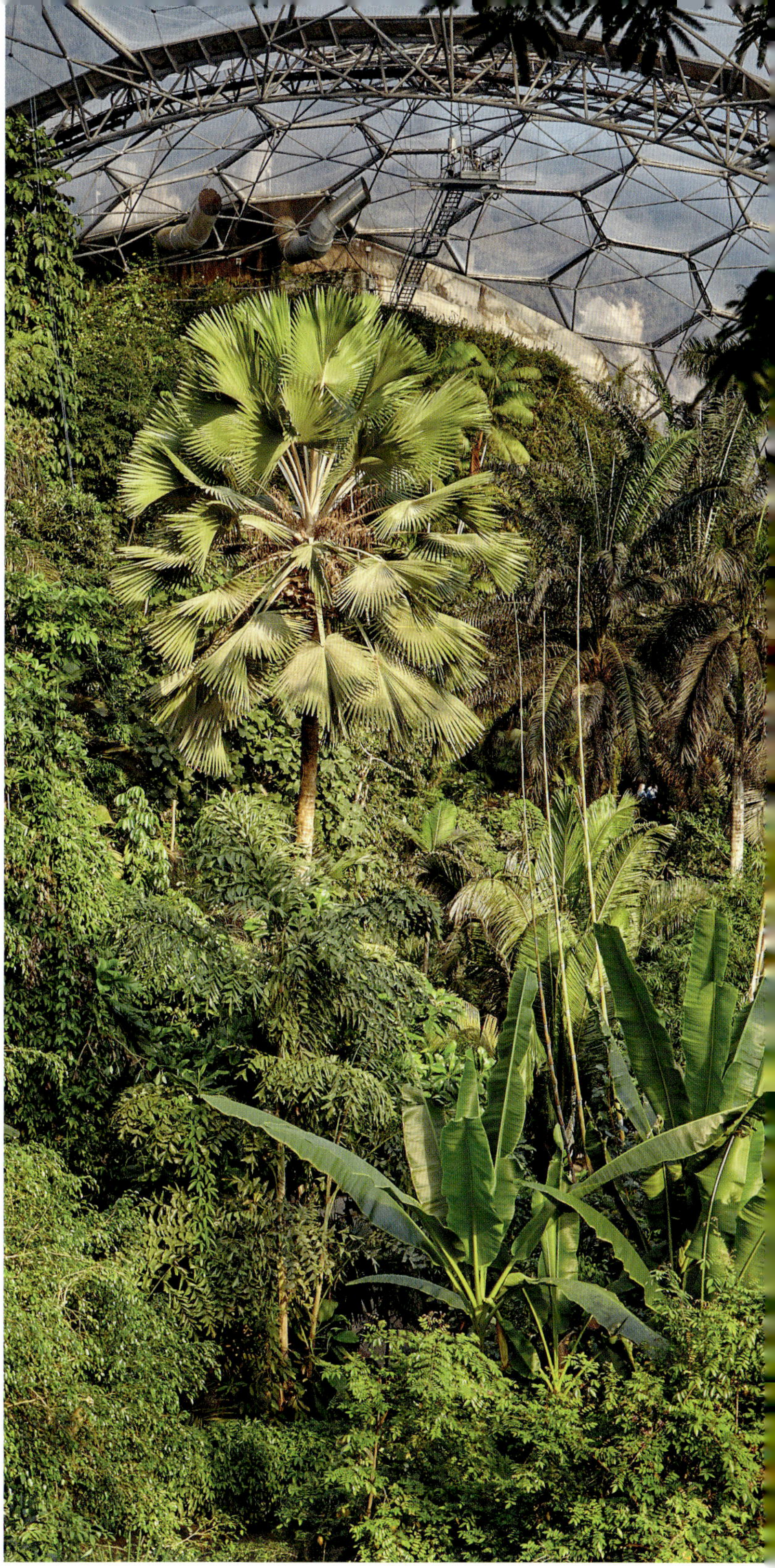

Above: A magnificent view inside the Rainforest Biome, seen from the canopy walkway, displays the tropical rainforest growing beneath the protective dome.

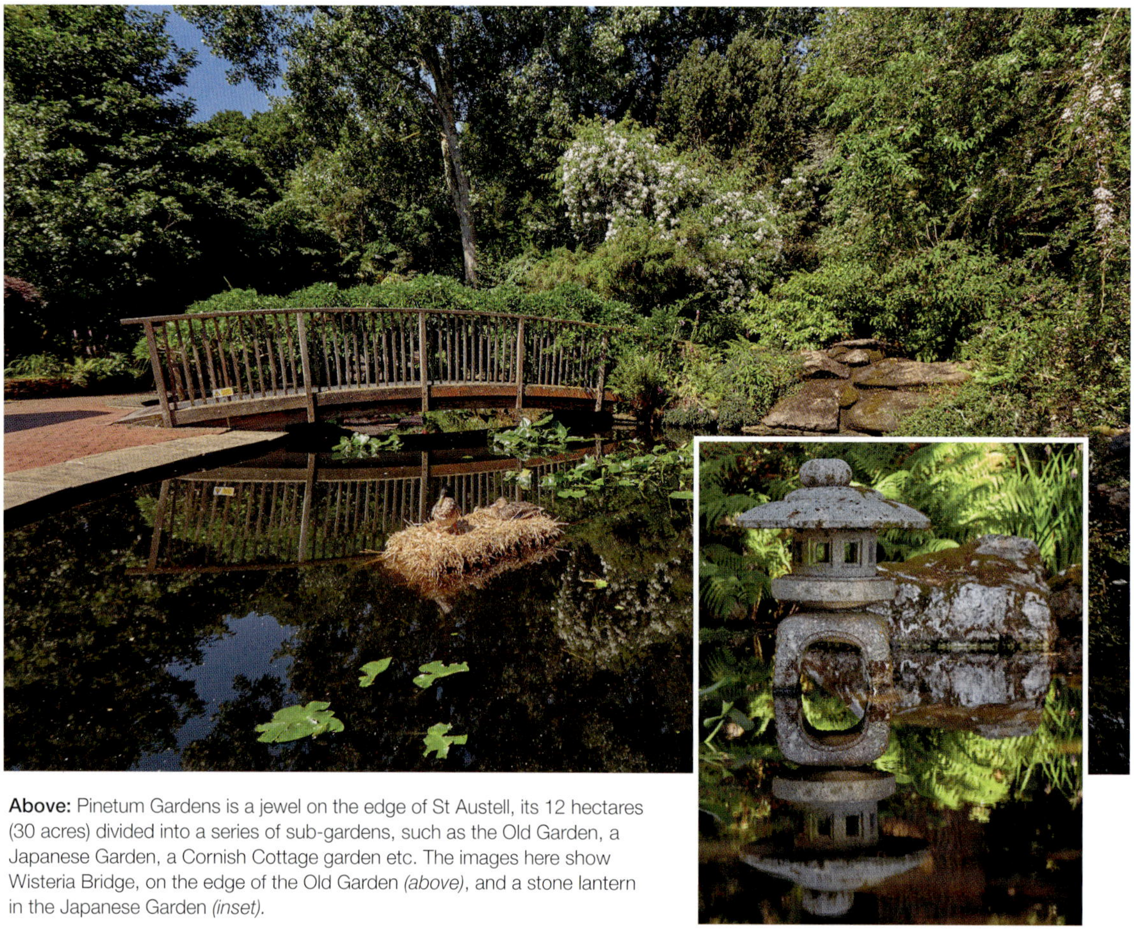

Beautiful Cornwall: A Portrait of a County

Above: Pinetum Gardens is a jewel on the edge of St Austell, its 12 hectares (30 acres) divided into a series of sub-gardens, such as the Old Garden, a Japanese Garden, a Cornish Cottage garden etc. The images here show Wisteria Bridge, on the edge of the Old Garden *(above)*, and a stone lantern in the Japanese Garden *(inset)*.

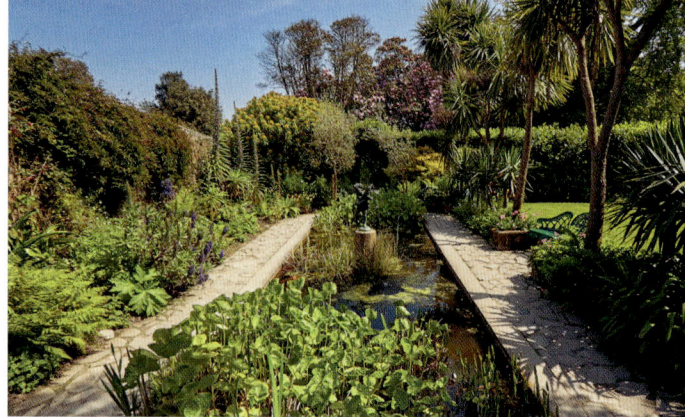

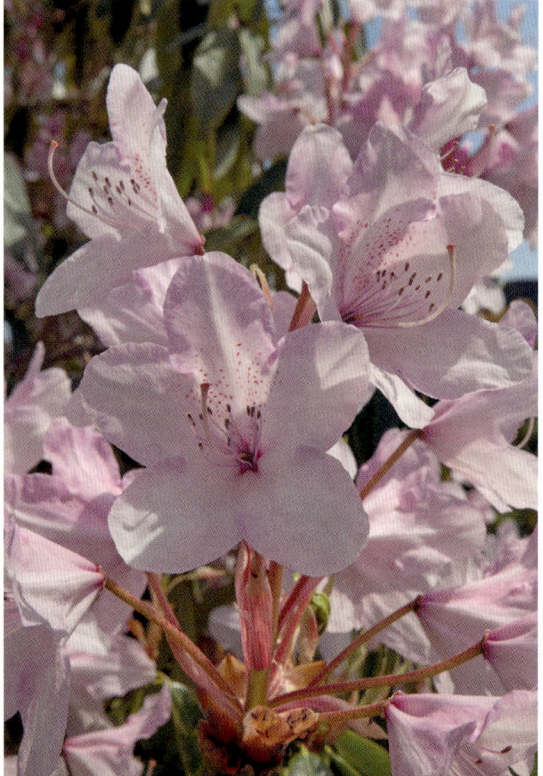

Left and Above: The rich mix of garden types found at the Lost Gardens of Heligan include the Sundial Garden *(above)*, with its lovely pond and border. As with many Cornish gardens, rhododendrons *(left)*, are common, adding a major splash of colour in spring.

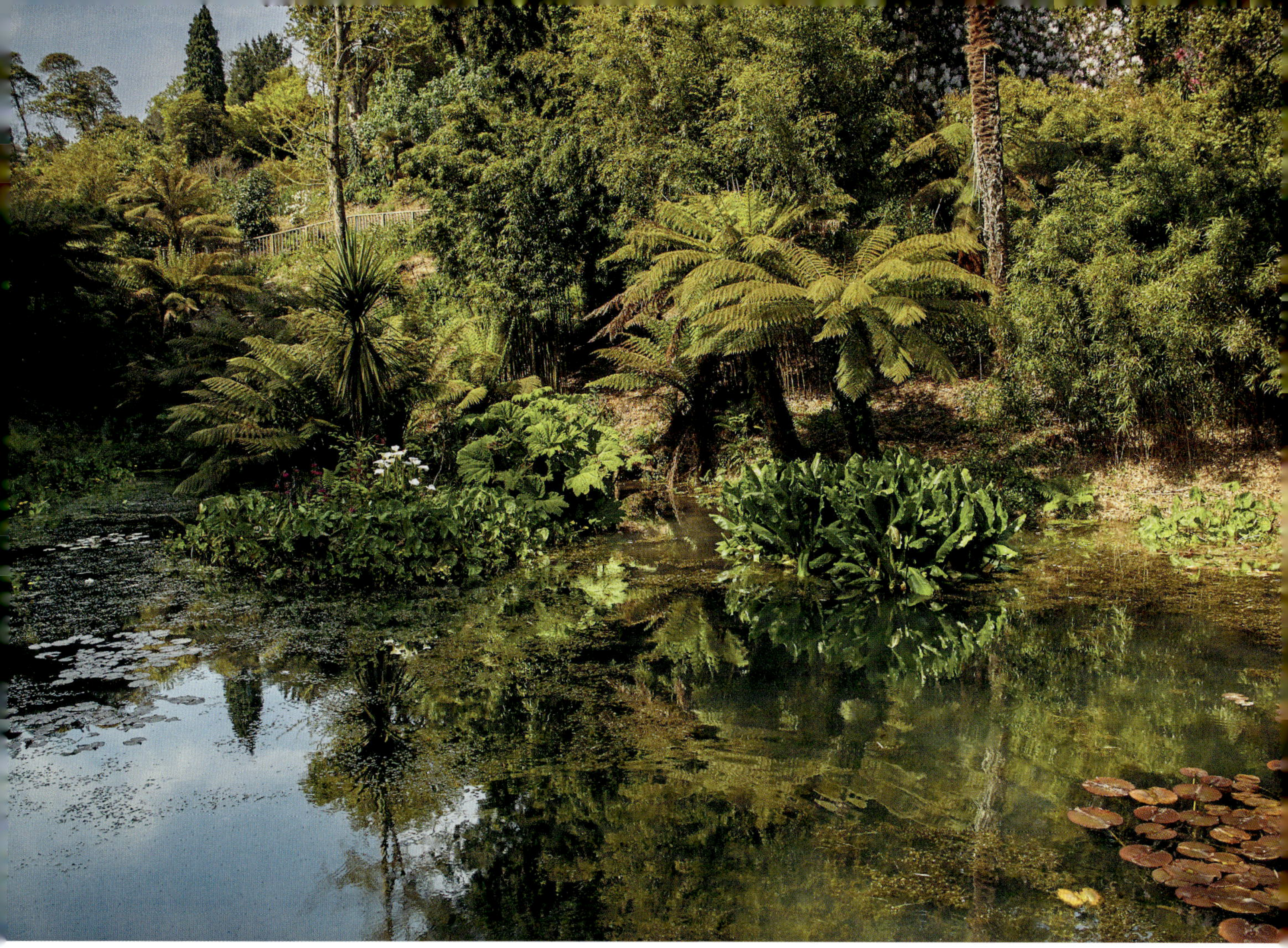

Above: Lying between St Austell and Mevigissey, the famously named Lost Gardens of Heligan are anything but lost today, their 80-plus hectares (200 acres) a major attraction. Among its many remarkable features is the Jungle, an area of dense vegetation set in a sheltered valley and filled with huge numbers of ferns and tree ferns, the latter brought back from Australia and New Zealand by Victorian plant hunters.

Right: A path winds its way around a huge rockery, as it descends from the hilltop Productive Gardens – site of walled vegetable gardens - down into the valley Jungle a short distance below.

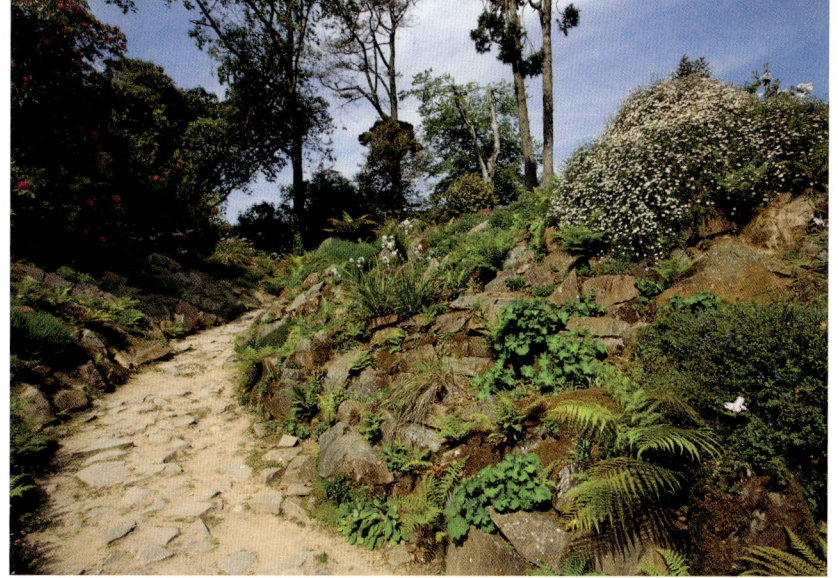

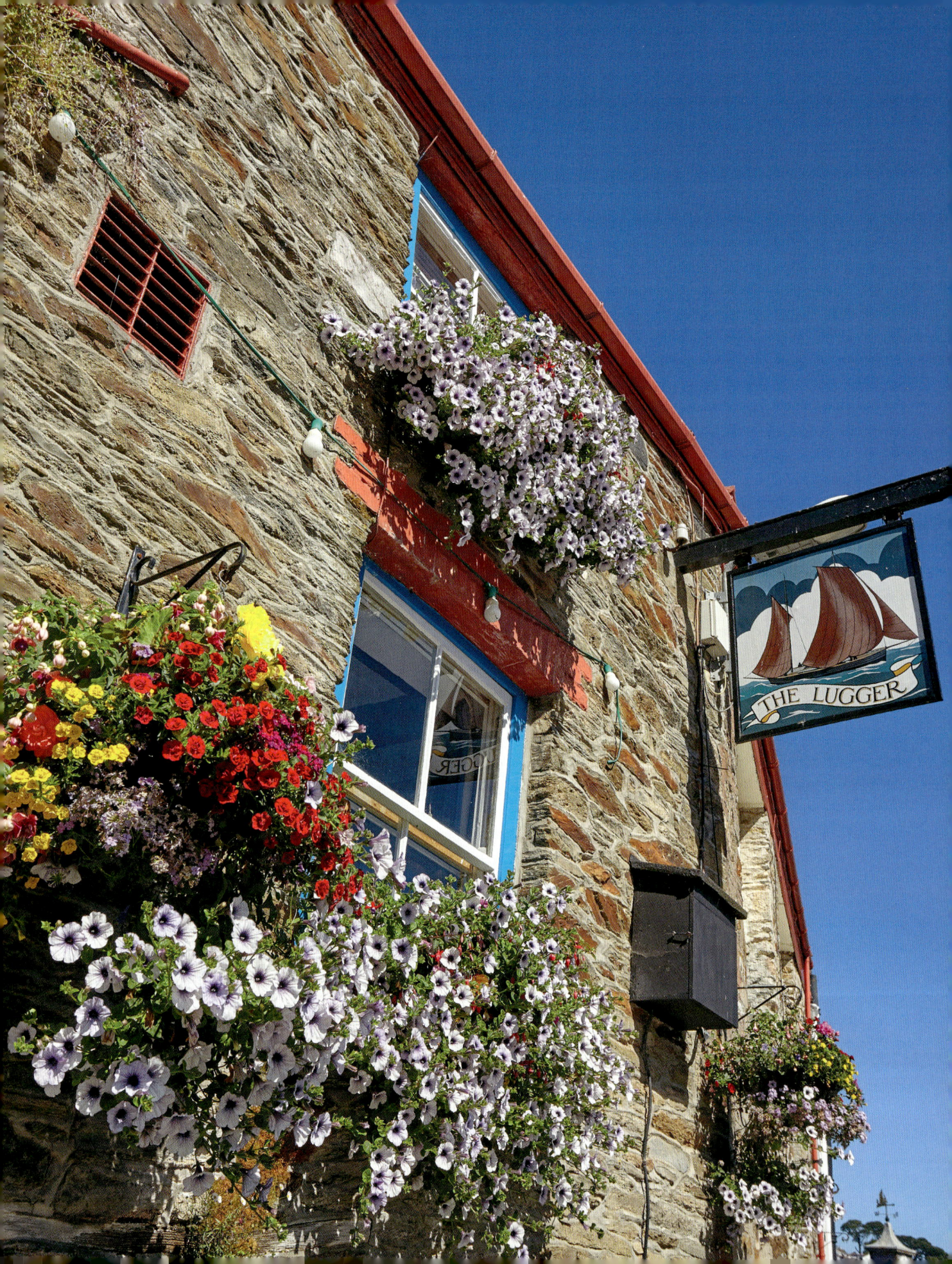

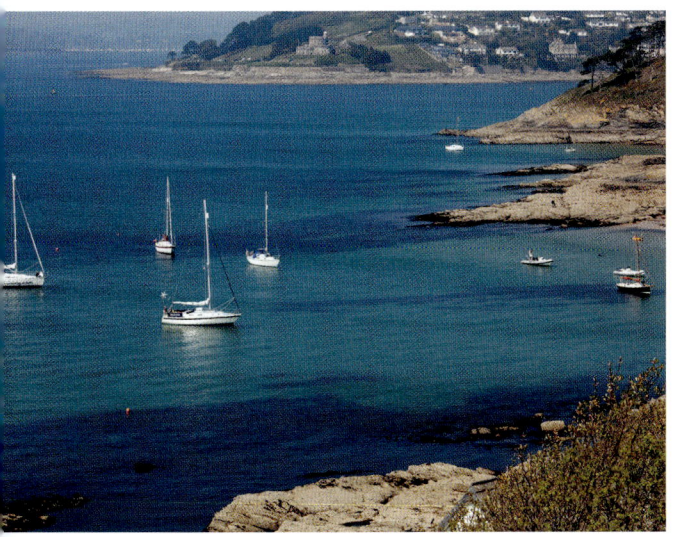

Above: Yachts moored in the deep blue waters of the River Fal's outermost mouth, close to St Anthony's Head. In the distance is St Mawes Castle and the town of St Mawes.

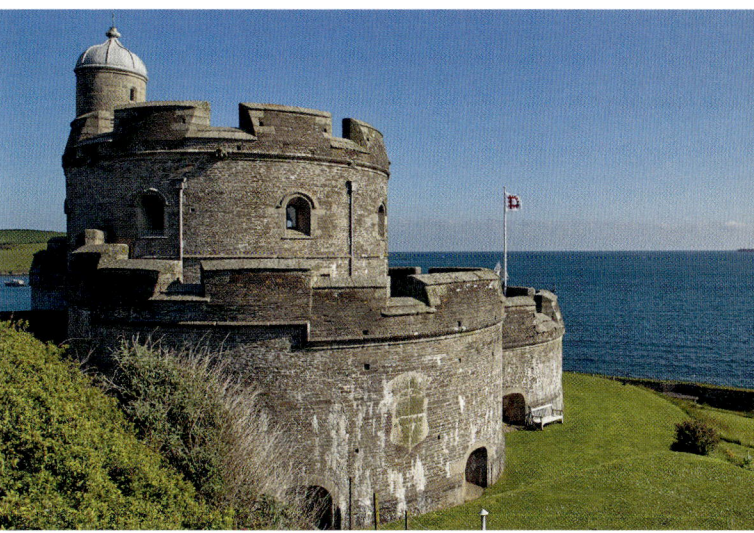

Above: St Mawes Castle, on the eastern shore of the River Fal's Carrick Roads, dates from the 16th century and the reign of King Henry VIII. Paired with Pendennis Castle on the opposite shore, it was built to defend the Fal from French or Spanish invasion.

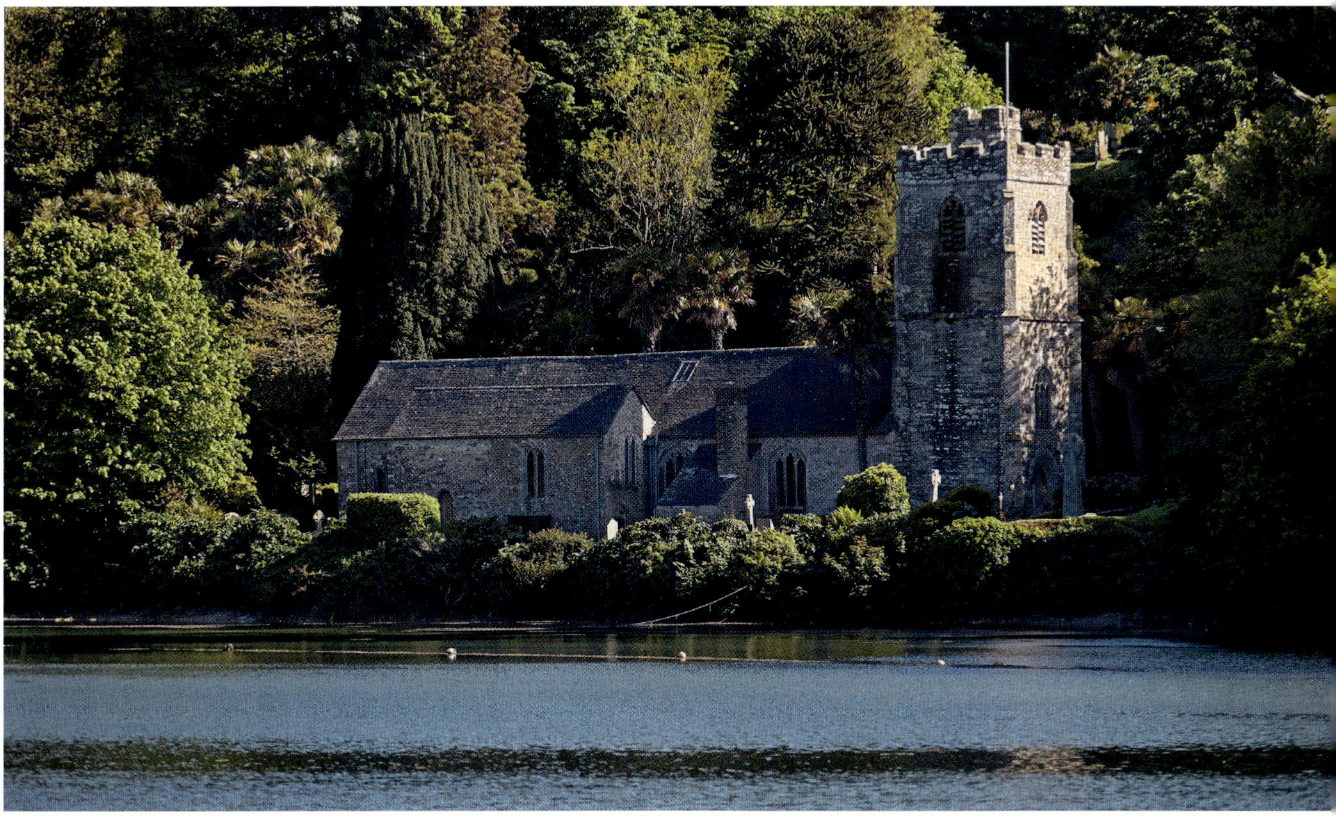

Left: The flower-covered walls of the Lugger Inn, a pub sitting beside the harbour at Polruan, on the eastern side of the Fowey estuary, opposite the town of Fowey.

Above: The beautiful 13th century church at St Just-in-Roseland, on the eastern shore of Carrick Roads, sits beside a quiet inlet, and is surrounded by its own verdant and peaceful garden.

Beautiful Cornwall: A Portrait of a County

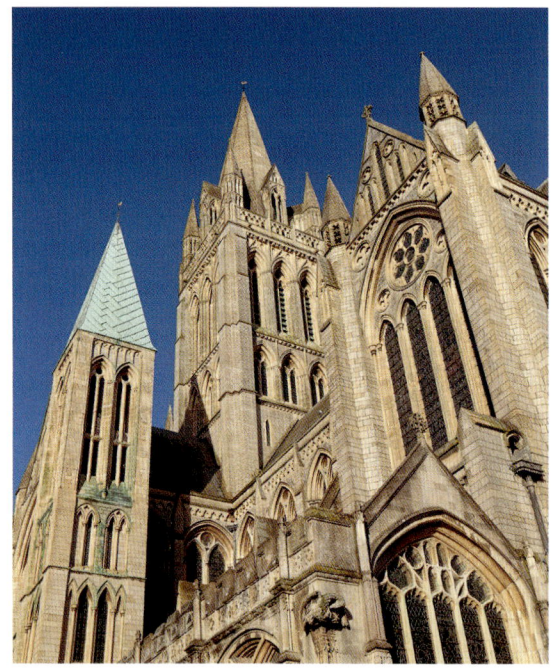

Above: The enormous spires of Truro Cathedral tower over this small city, Cornwall's capital. Built between 1880 and 1910, Truro Cathedral is relatively new, and was the first cathedral to have been built on a new site since 1220!

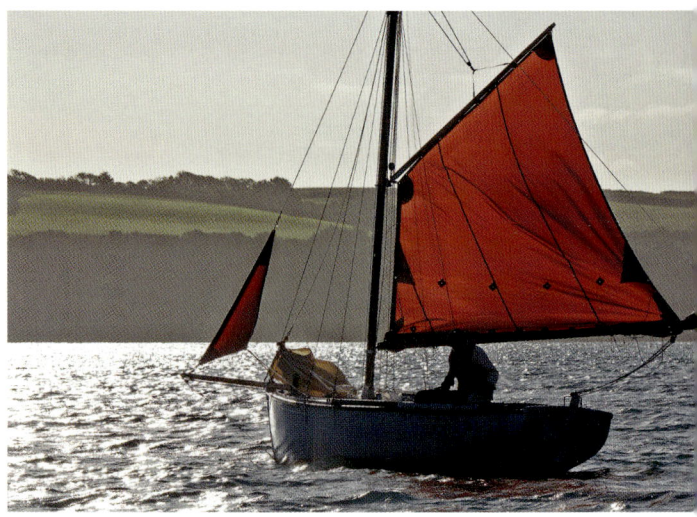

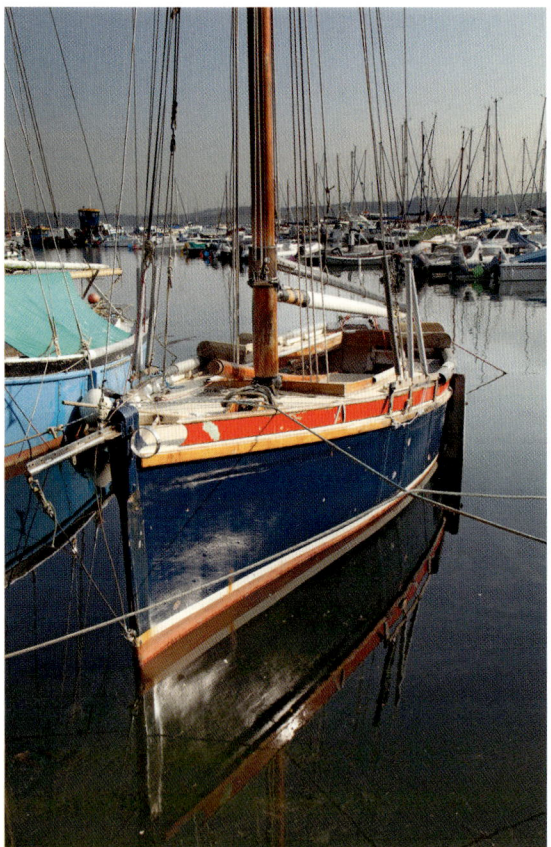

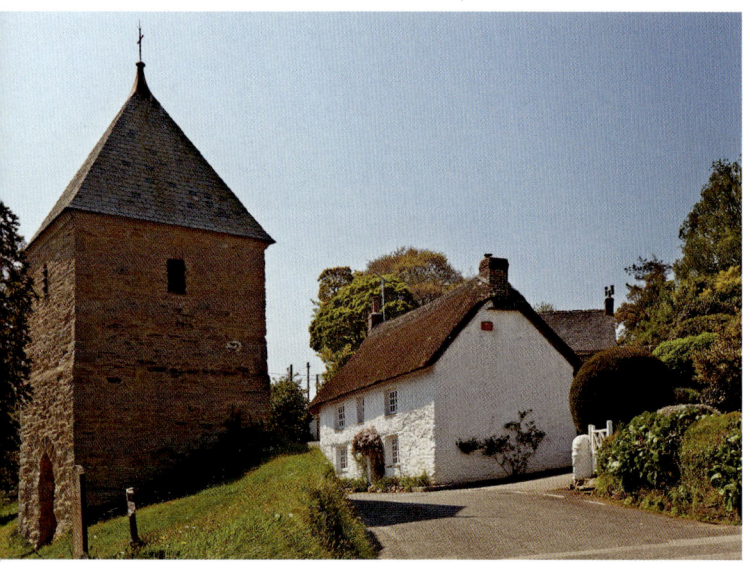

Above: The little village of Feock is typical of the settlements found in much of the quiet countryside around the Fal estuary. The tower belongs to that of St Feoca, the village church, unusually several metres away from the church itself.

Above and Top: Native oysters (rather different from the Pacific rock oysters we usually see) have to be dredged from the seabed below the low tide line. To conserve stocks of this now rather endangered oyster, dredging in the Fal is allowed only for a few old sail-powered boats, most of which are based in Mylor, and which can regularly be seen sailing across Carrick Roads as they work.

The South Coast

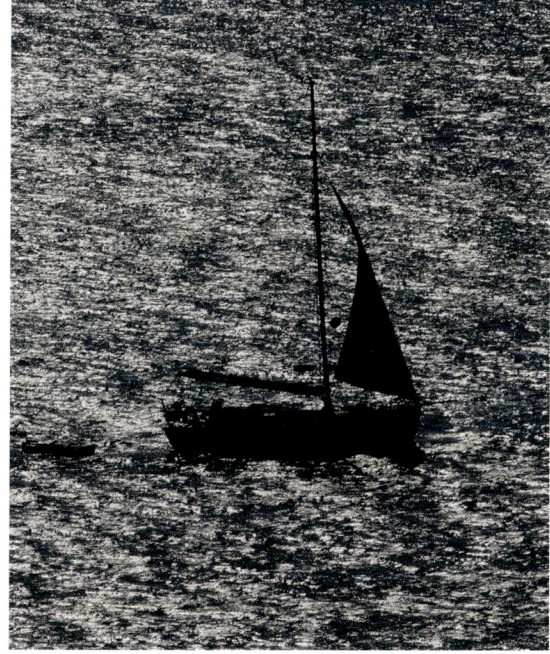

Above: Silhouetted against a low sun, a yacht sails under a headsail alone as it battles strong winds in Carrick Roads. The Fal estuary's sheltered waters are an important mecca for the southwest's yachts.

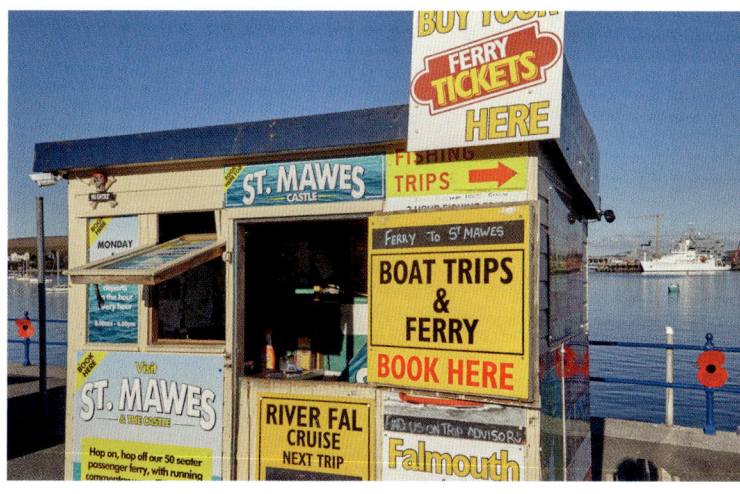

Above: A quayside booth in Falmouth, selling tickets for the many passenger ferries and sightseeing boats that regularly ply up and down the Fal estuary, as well as across to the nearby River Helford, popular outings for visitors.

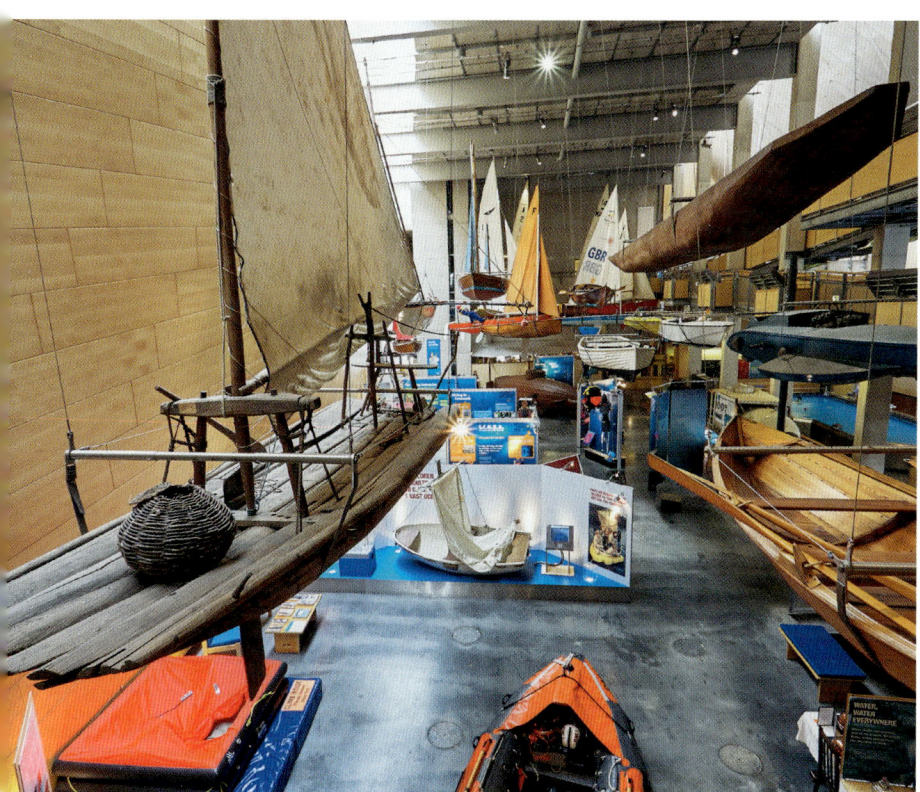

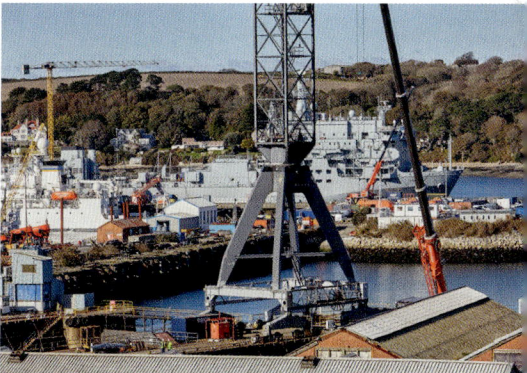

Above: Falmouth port is home to a series of large dry docks that are able to service quite a range of ocean-going ships, including vessels of the Royal Navy.

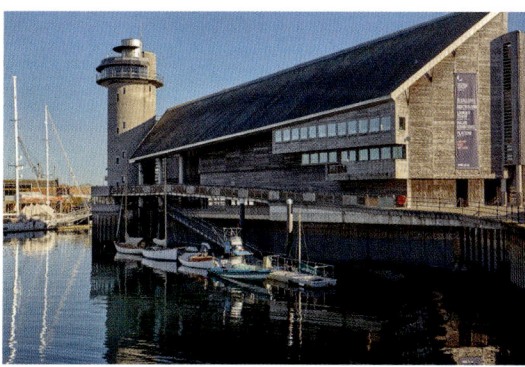

Above and Right: The modern Falmouth branch of the National Maritime Museum is in a purpose-built centre, standing beside the water on Discovery Quay. The museum is dedicated largely to small boats, with dinghies from all over the world displayed in quite inventive ways.

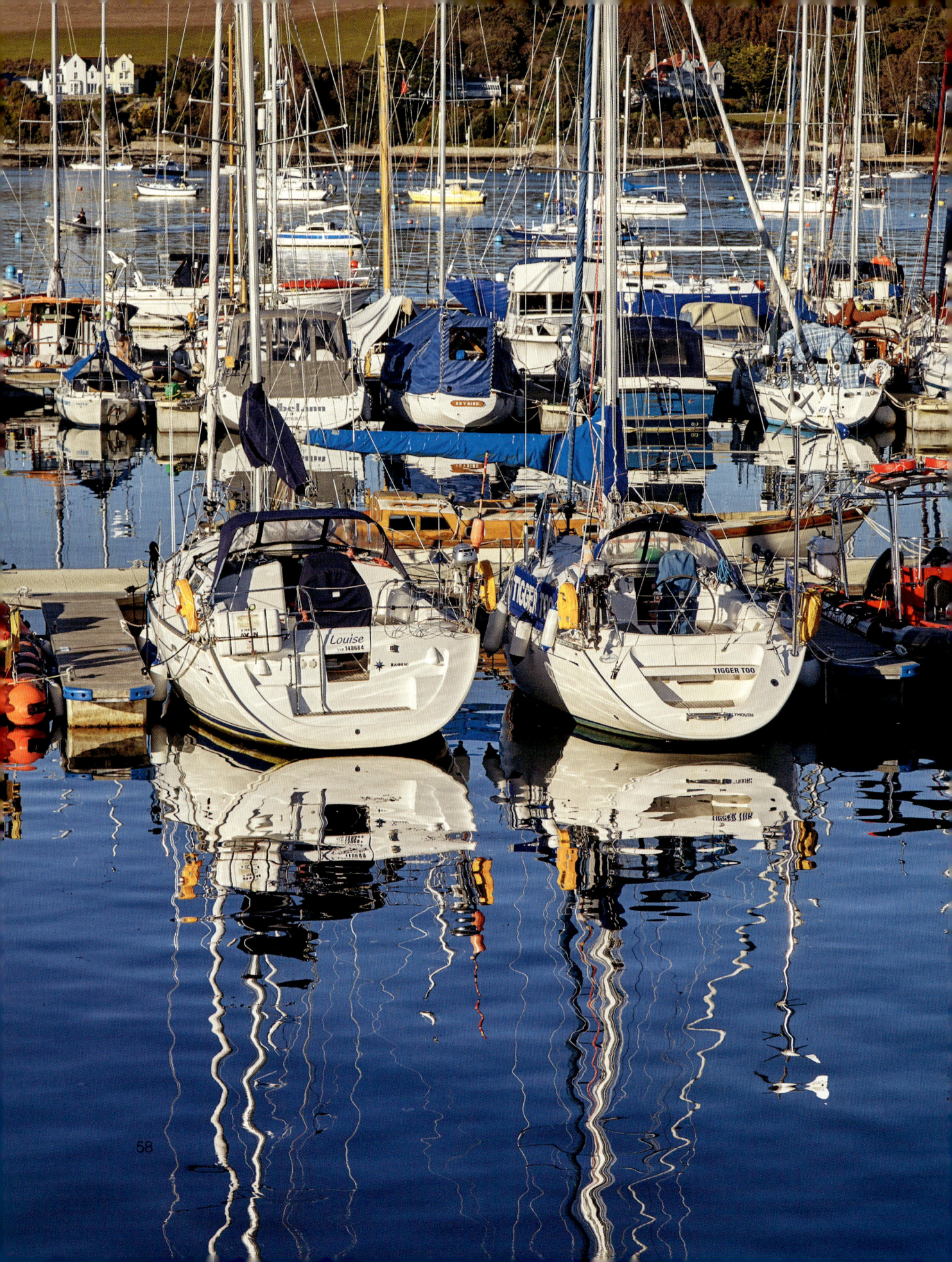

The South Coast

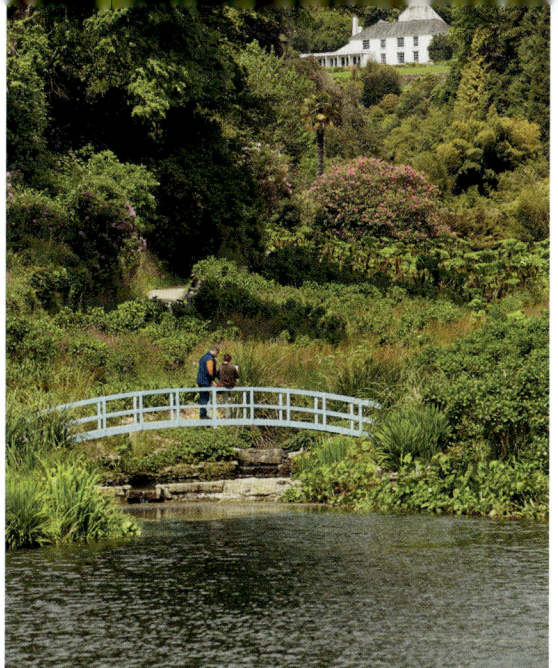

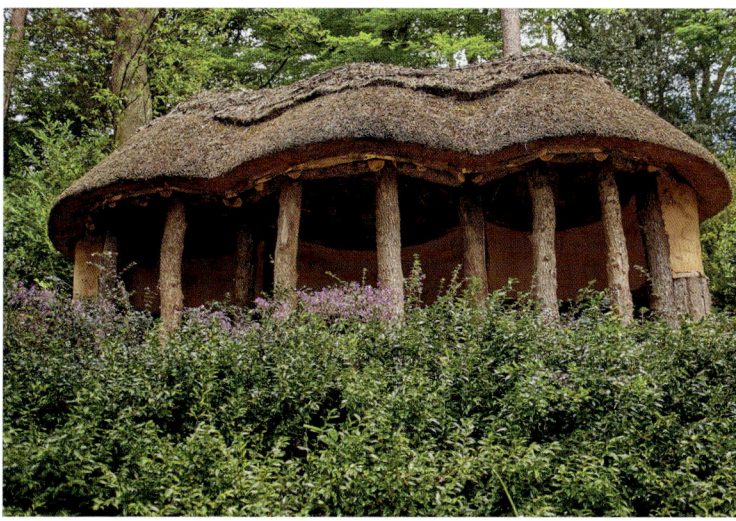

Above: Trebah Garden, sitting on the north shore of the Helford River, is yet another of Cornwall's fabulous gardens that benefit from the region's mild, damp climate. This scene shows the view from Mallard Pond up Rhododendron Valley to the estate's house.

Above: Alice's Seat is a modern recreation of the early 20th century original summerhouse, named after one of Trebah's owners. Its simple structure has cob walls and a thatched roof, and nestles among peaceful woodlands.

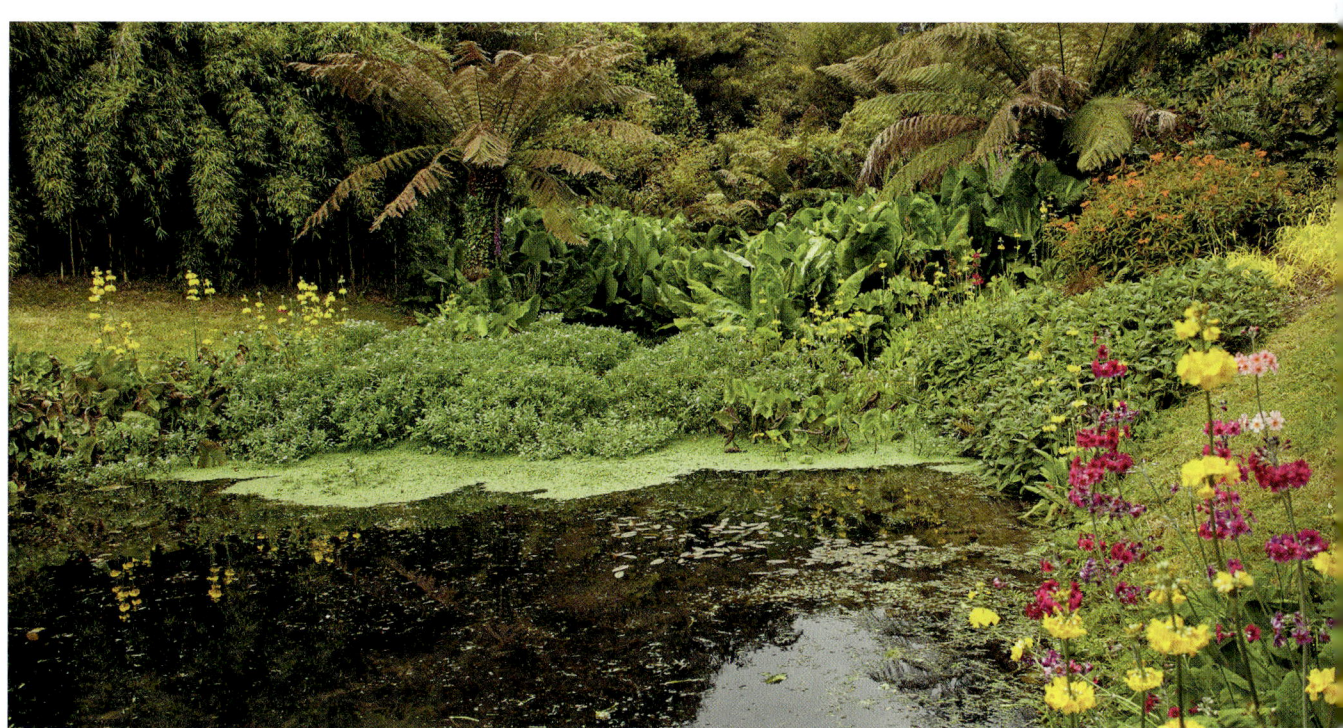

Above: One of Trebah's beautiful ponds, surrounded by dense vegetation that includes a number of very large tree ferns.

Left: Although the Fal's main yacht harbours are further up Carrick Roads at places like Mylor Harbour, Falmouth does have a number of well-used pontoons that become crowded with yachts, especially in summer.

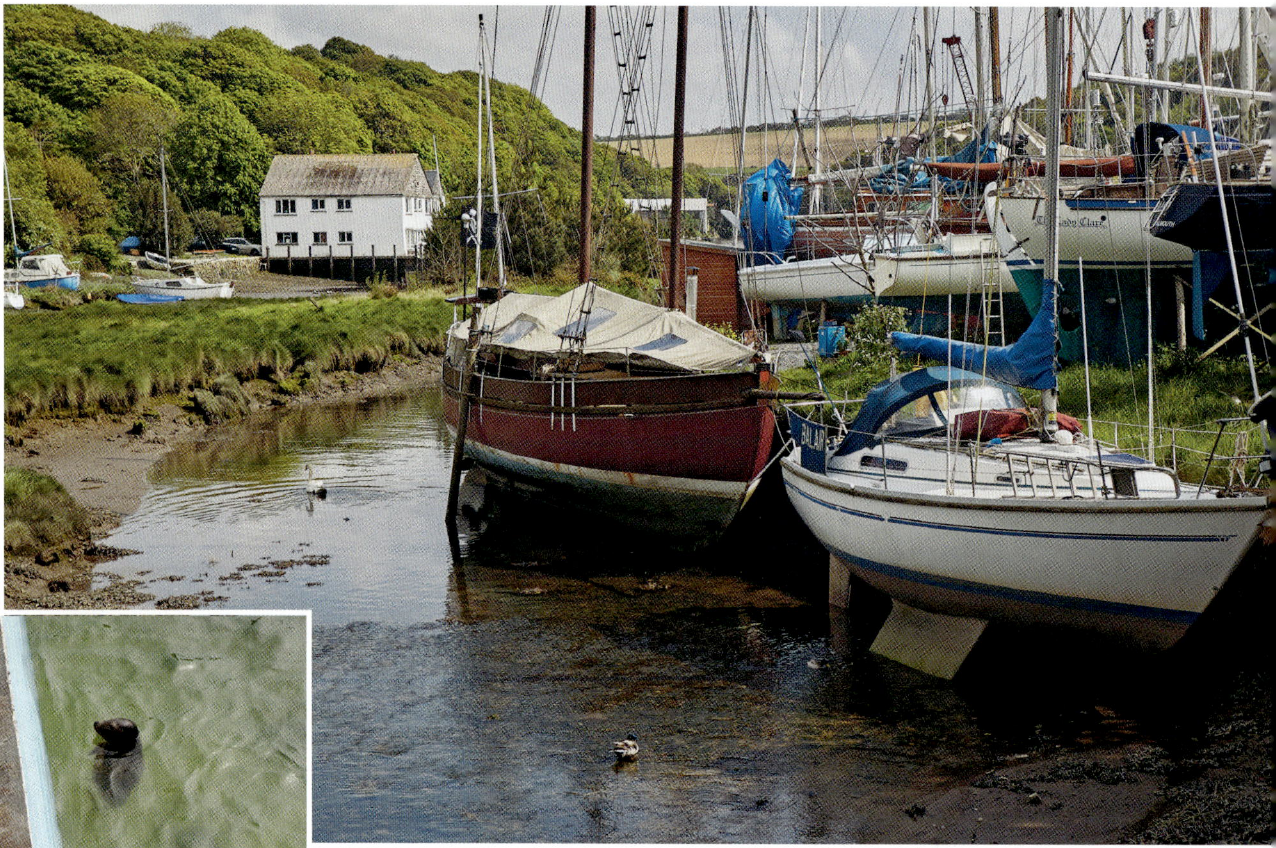

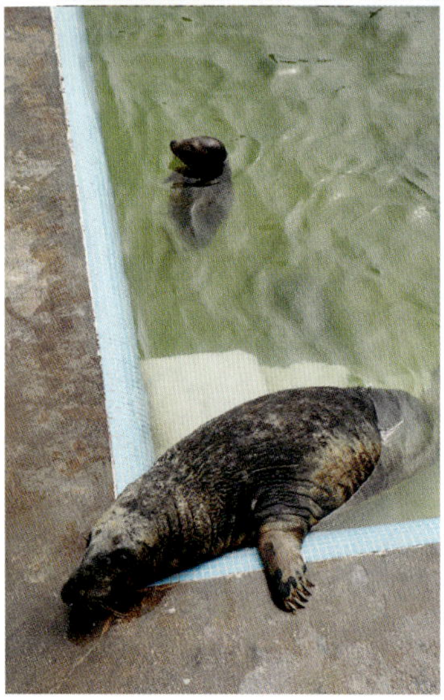

Beautiful Cornwall: A Portrait of a County

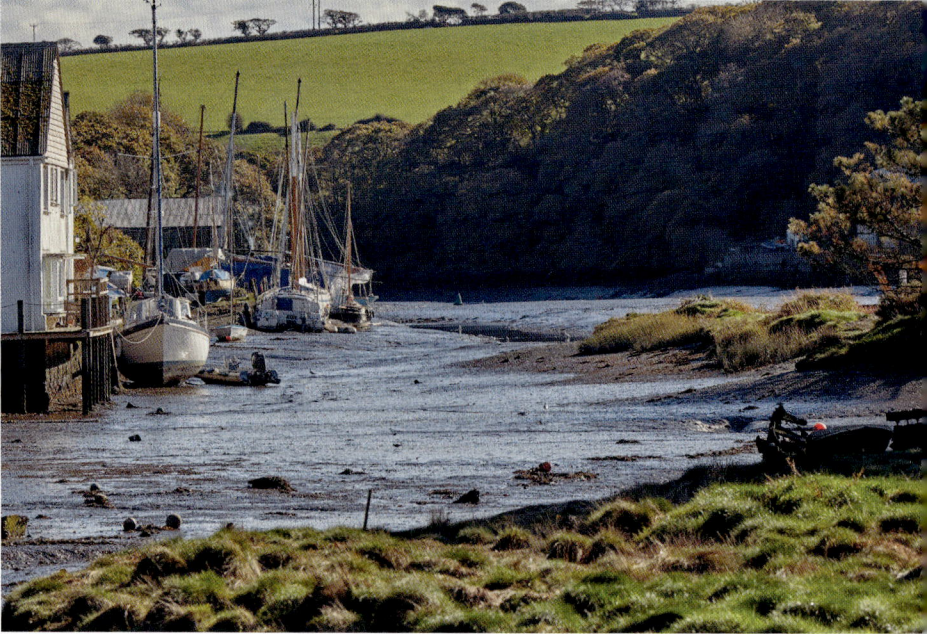

Above and Right: The Helford estuary pretty much empties out at low tide, leaving long expanses of mud banks across the valley floors. Despite this, a number of villages, especially Gweek, have important boat repair yards.

Inset: A grey seal basks on the side of a pool at the Cornish Seal Sanctuary in Gweek. This centre for sick and injured seals has given this tiny Helford River village a fame well beyond its size.

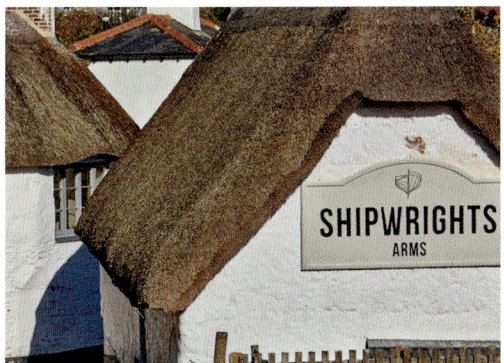

Above: The pretty village of Helford, on the southern shore of the Helford River, is a picturesque place of historic whitewashed cob-walled, thatch-roofed cottages.

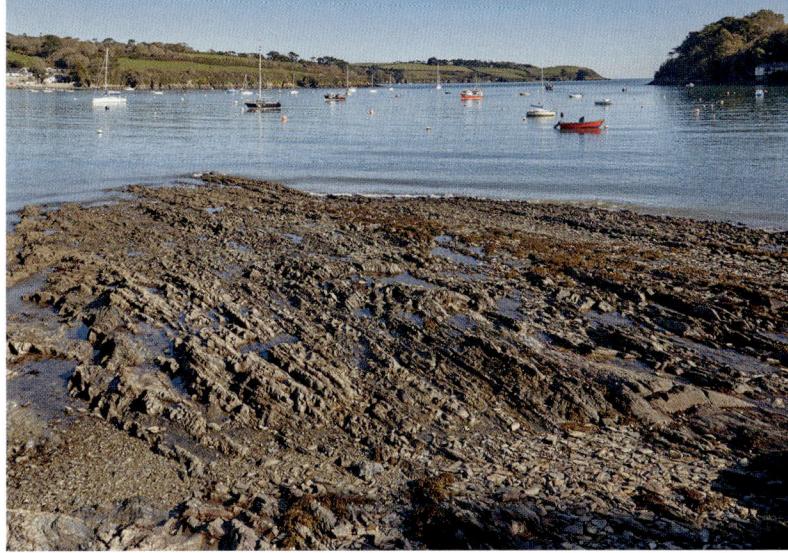

Above: A view eastwards towards the Helford's mouth and the sea, seen from the south shore of the estuary, near the village of Helford itself, reveals it to be a sheltered natural harbour filled with boat moorings.

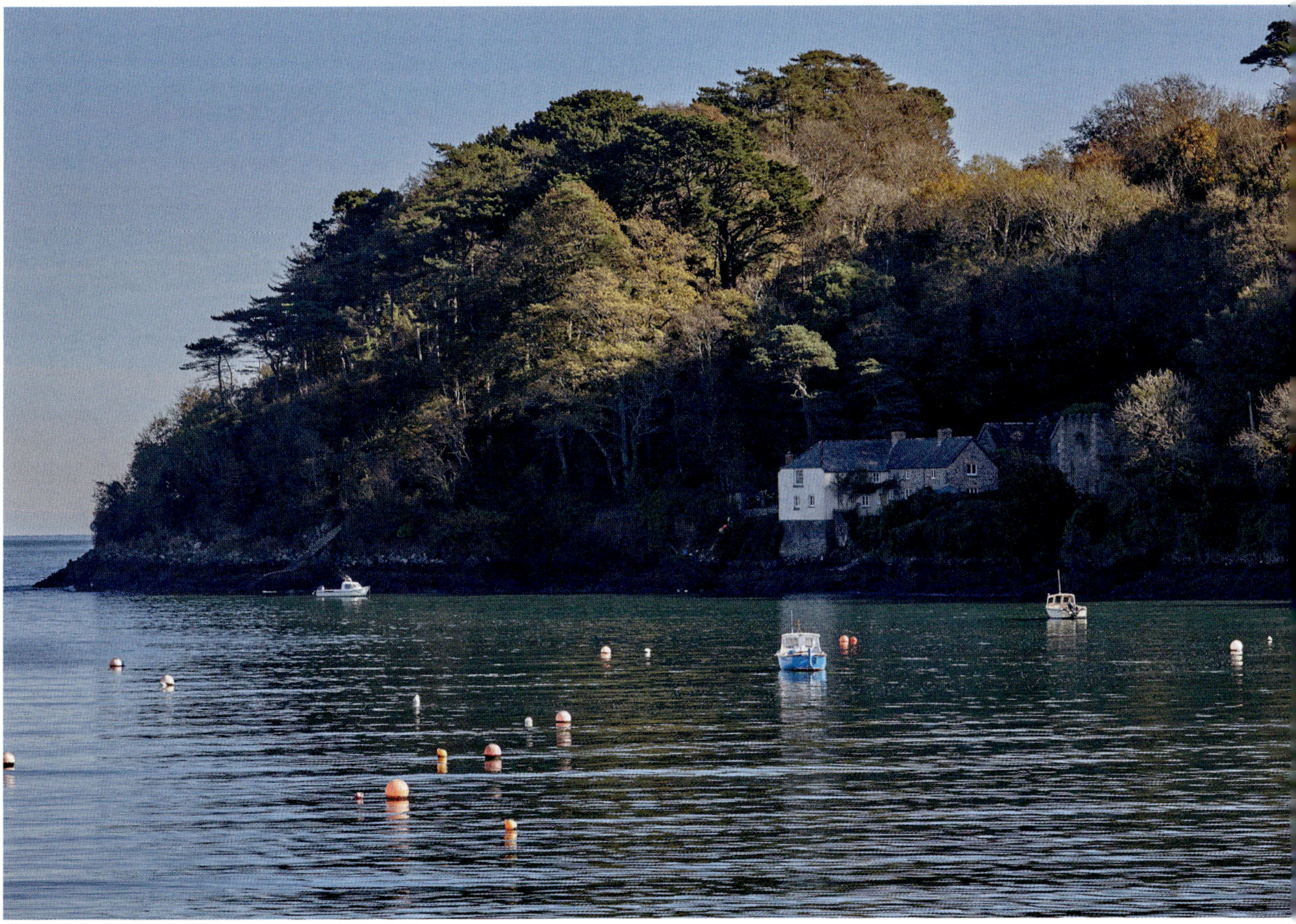

Above: A wooded headland partially lit by a low autumn sun, points into the Helford estuary from the south shore, a peaceful bucolic scene.

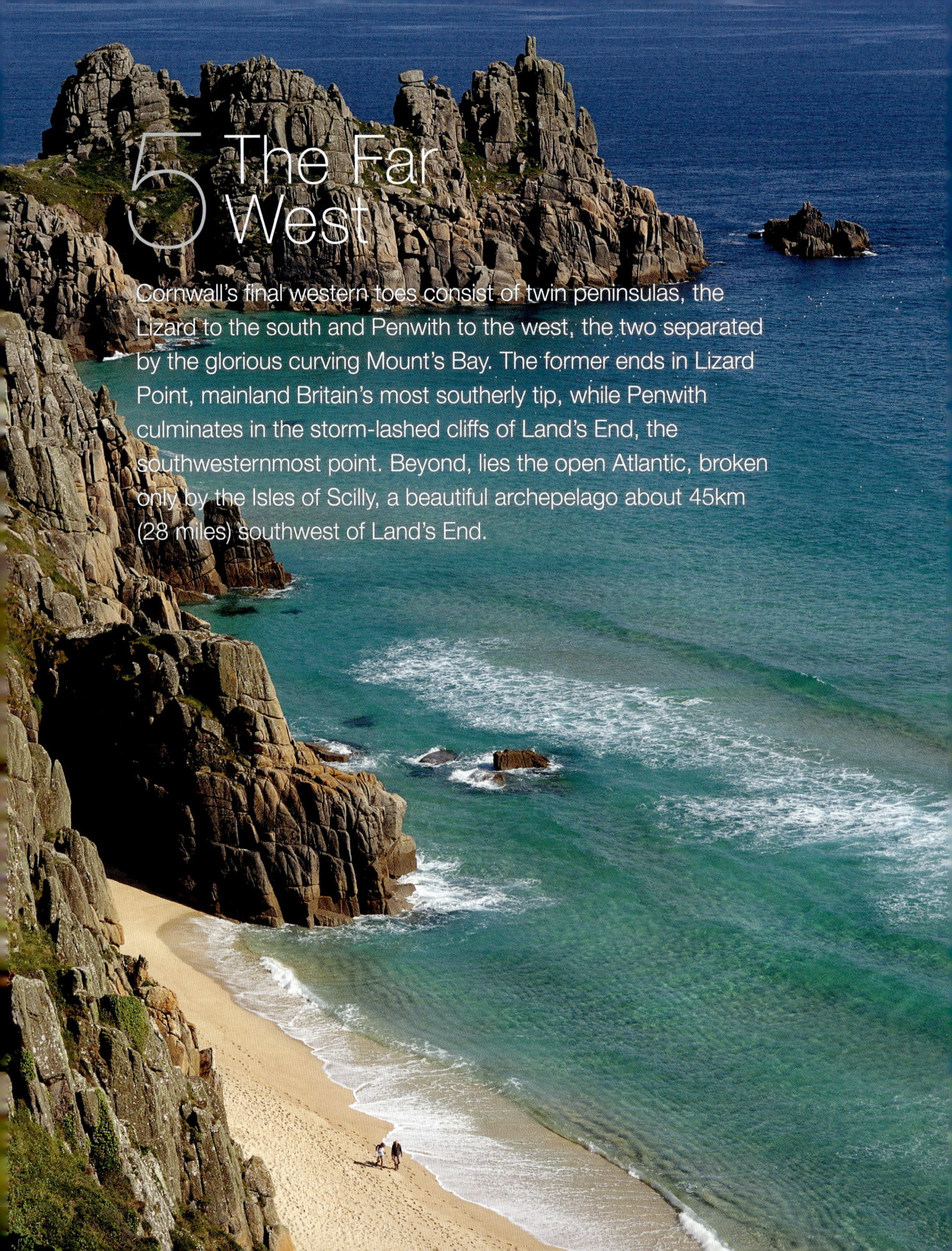

5 The Far West

Cornwall's final western toes consist of twin peninsulas, the Lizard to the south and Penwith to the west, the two separated by the glorious curving Mount's Bay. The former ends in Lizard Point, mainland Britain's most southerly tip, while Penwith culminates in the storm-lashed cliffs of Land's End, the southwesternmost point. Beyond, lies the open Atlantic, broken only by the Isles of Scilly, a beautiful archepelago about 45km (28 miles) southwest of Land's End.

The Far West

The region contains some of Cornwall's most spectacular and iconic coastal views, as well as a number of surfing beaches and fishing harbours. But it kicks off with an old industrial centre, that of Hayle, today most well known for its unbelievable beach, a 5km (3 miles) stretch of golden sands, backed by vast dunes.

To the west sits St Ives, a magnet for visitors in summer, home to an iconic harbour and several great beaches, including the surfing centre of Porthmeor. Its jumbled narrow lanes even manage to make space for Tate St Ives, its galleries a homage to some of Cornwall's greatest artists.

Over to the east, the Lizard hosts several fishing villages, most notably Coverack and Cadgwith, while Lizard Point itself is a good place to spot passing marine life. Nearby is spectacular Kynance Cove, another of Cornwall's iconic views, a sandy beach connecting together several offshore rocky islands.

The nearby town of Helston is a grey working town, but it bursts into colour every 8th May for its annual Flora Day, and in particular the Floral Dances (also called the Furry Dance), a series of colourful dances through the streets.

West of Helston is the hugely iconic castle-topped St Michael's Mount, lying a short distance off the beach at Marazion and connected to it by a tidal causeway. Nearby, Penzance is the 'capital' of the Penwith area, a not unattractive town, with another enviable location on the Mount's Bay shore. It becomes the centre of attention in June during its Golowan Festival, which culminates in its Mazey Day parades.

To the south, and conjoined with Penzance, is Newlyn, by far Cornwall's largest and busiest fishing port, while a short distance further on is Mousehole, a tiny fishing village impossibly quaint both by name and nature. At Mousehole the coast leaves the shelter of Mount's Bay and becomes increasingly rugged,

leading to the iconic cliff, sea and beach views at Logan Rock, Treen and Porthcurno. Further west are the magnificent granite buttresses of Gwennap Head, where the coast turns abruptly northwards, now facing the Atlantic and leading up to yet another icon, Land's End. To the north is Sennen, a small fishing cove and a spectacular beach, Penwith's main surfing venue.

From here the coast is dominated by high cliffs all the way to St Ives. This wild area was once a centre for tin mining, and the ruins still litter the landscape. At Pendeen is Geevor mine, one of the last to close and now a museum, while at Botallack are arguably Cornwall's most dramatic mine ruins, standing on rocks just a few feet above the foaming surf. They join a series of monuments to Penwith's bygone eras, the inland areas strewn with prehistoric remains that include Chysauster, a Neolithic village between Penzance and St Ives, and Lanyon and Chun Quoits, the remains of ancient burial chambers.

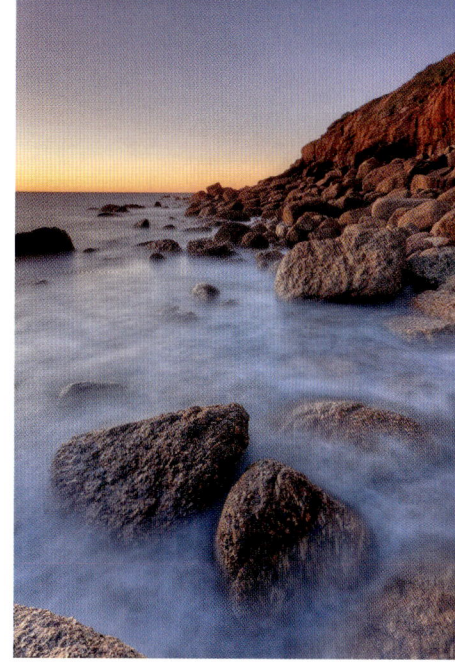

Finally, there are the Scillies. Hugely remote, only five of the 200 granite islands are inhabited, the remainder given over to wildlife and surf. Seals abound on its Western and Norrard Rocks, along with a host of marine birdlife. For the people of the islands, flower farming is one economic mainstay, the islands producing many of the UK's earliest daffodils. Tourism is the main livelihood, of course, the islands' many sandy beaches an attraction, along with Abbey Gardens, on the island of Tresco.

Left: One of west Cornwall's many iconic views, looking from the cliffs of Treen, along the sands of Pedn Vounder beach towards the rocky headland of Logan Rock.

Above Right: Shoreline granite boulders in the mouth of tiny Porthgwarra cove, near Land's End, seen at dawn.

Beautiful Cornwall: A Portrait of a County

Right: At Chynhalls Point, near Coverack on the Lizard peninsula, ponies are used to graze the vegetation and so maintain the headland's grassland and population of coastal flowers.

Below: The tiny cove of Cadgwith, just a few miles from Lizard Point, mainland Britain's most southerly point, still has a small but active fishing fleet.

Opposite: Beautiful Kynance Cove is a gem of a stretch of sand interspersed among stunning rocks, just a couple of miles from Lizard Point. The beach is visible only at low tide.

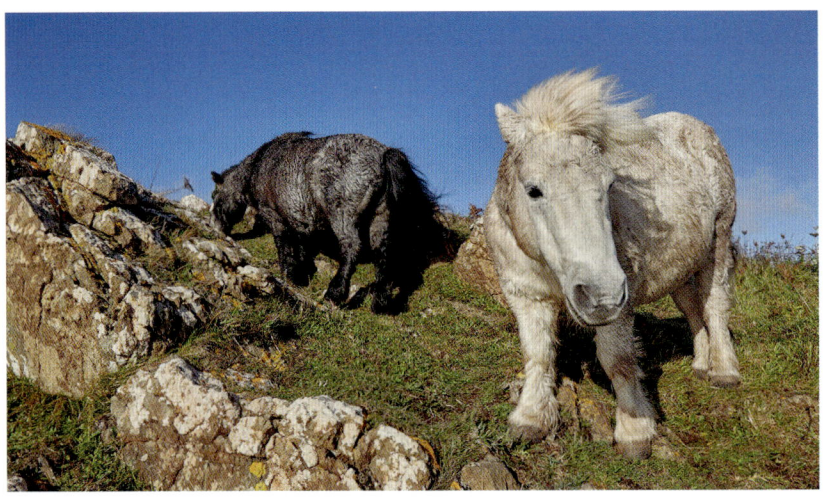

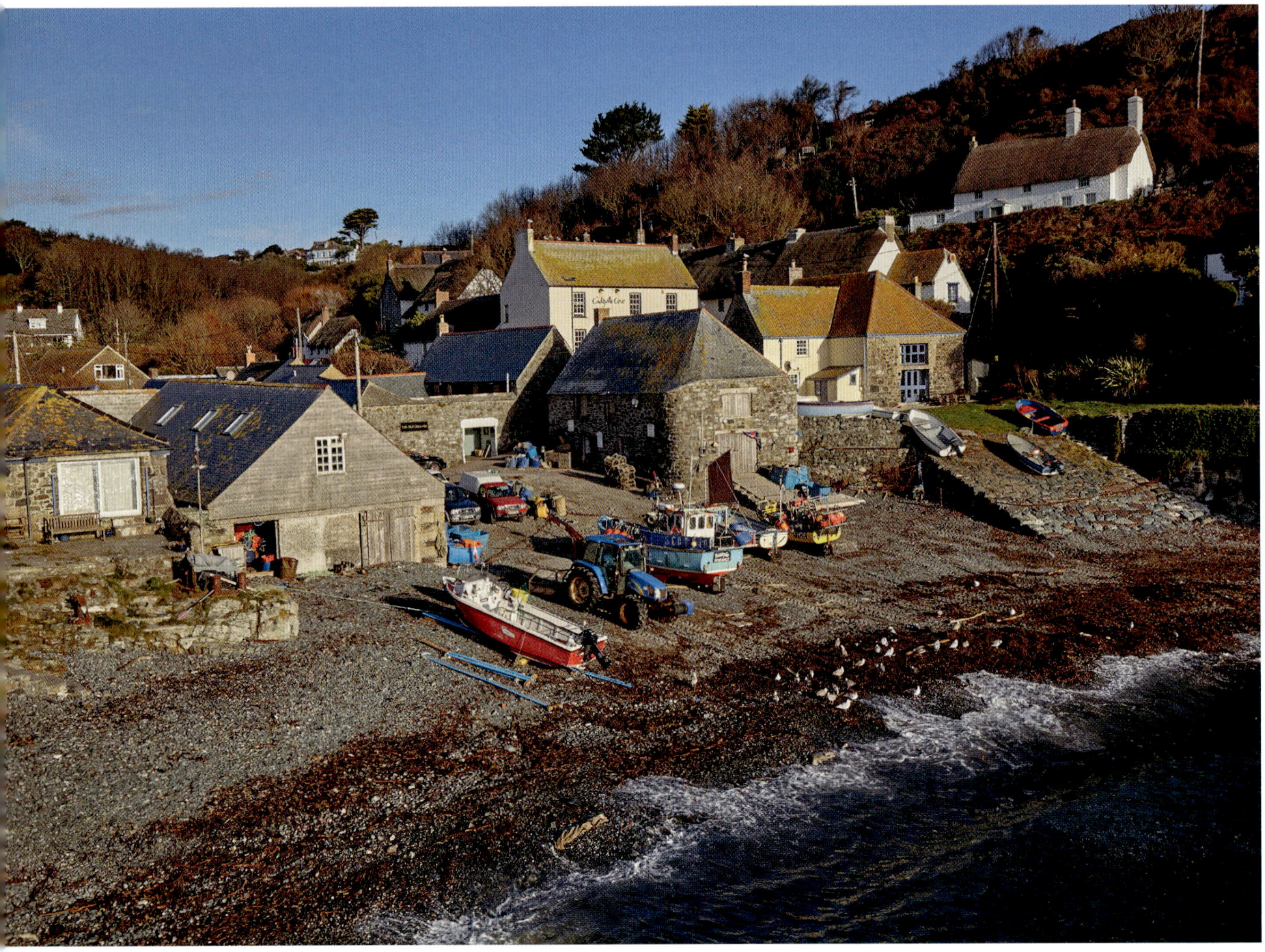

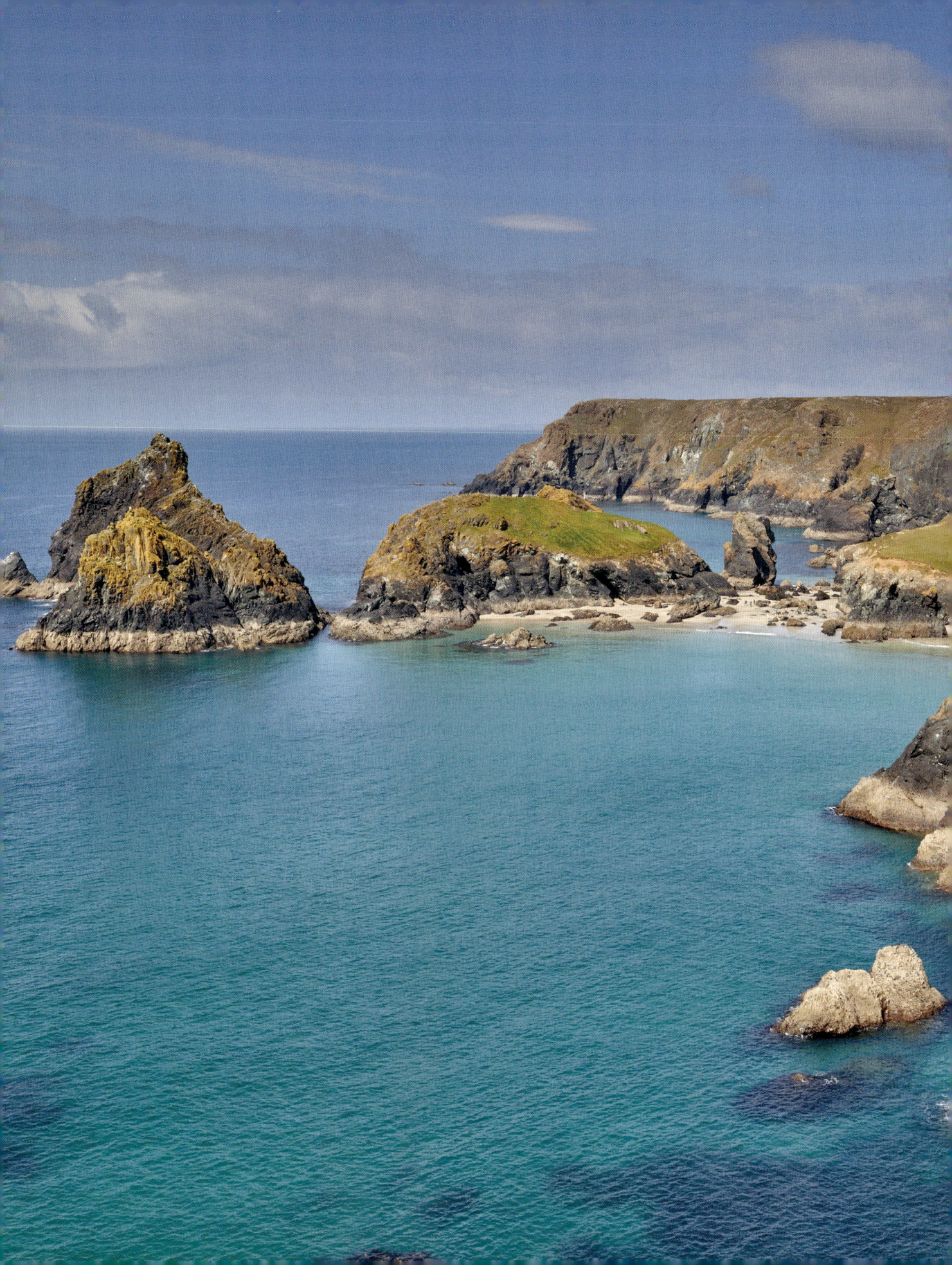

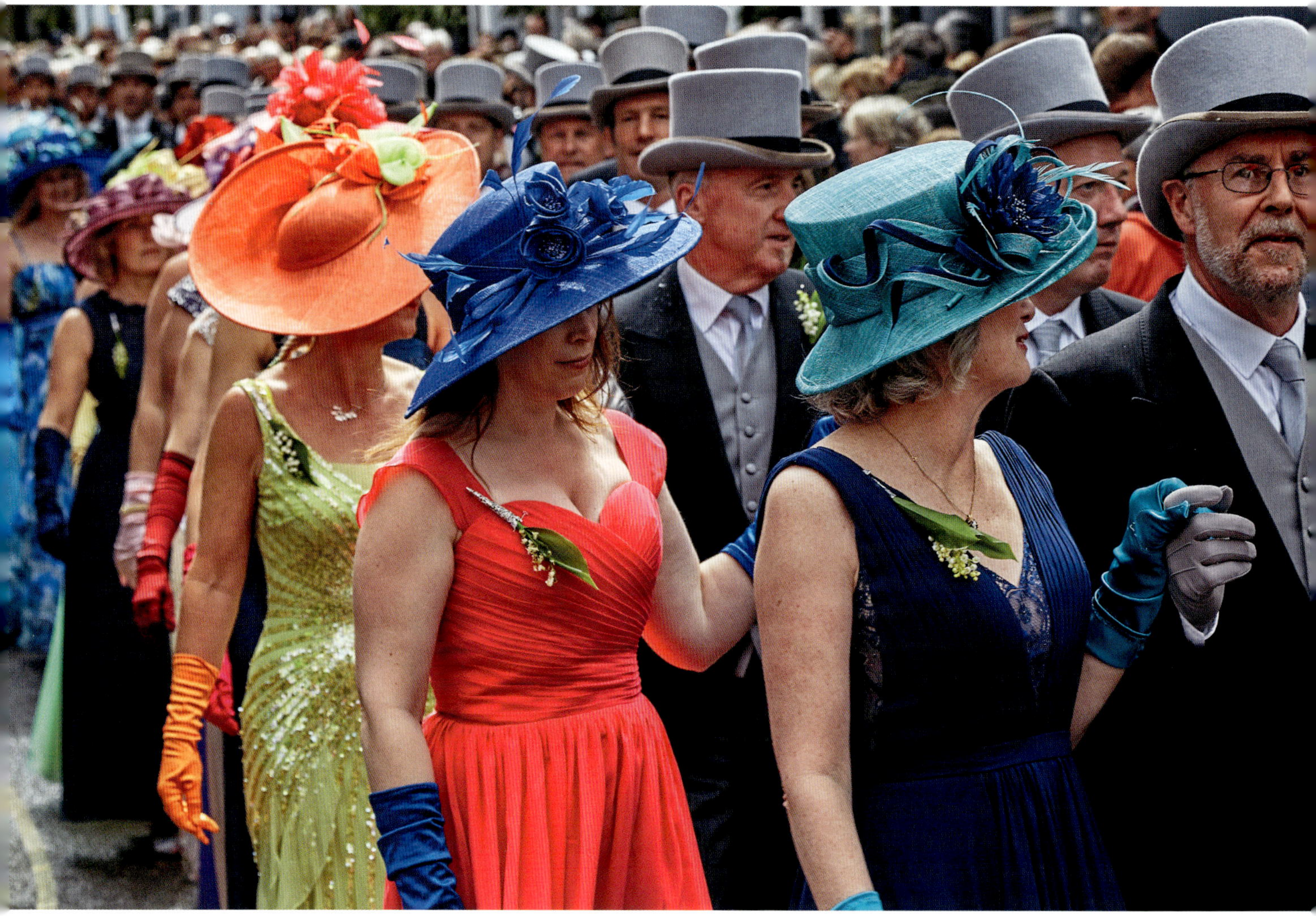

Beautiful Cornwall: A Portrait of a County

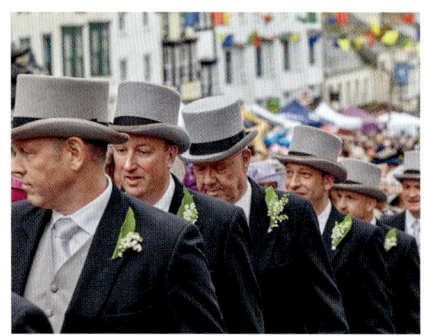
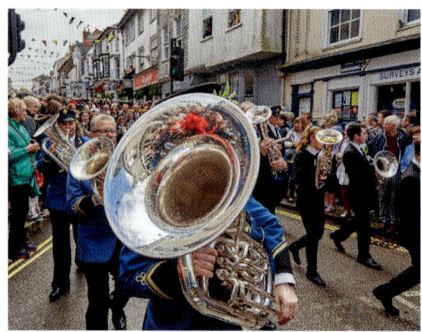
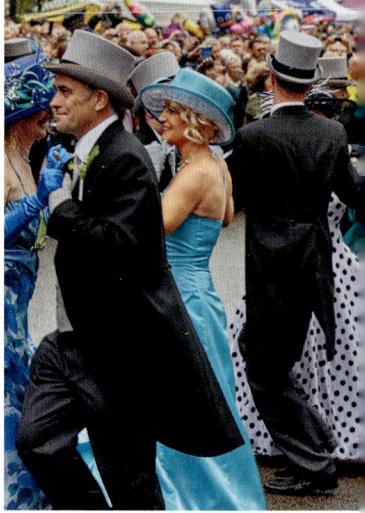

Above: The wonderfully quirky Flora Day, held every 8th May in Helston, consists of the town's citizens donning their finest clothes to dance through the town's streets, led by the Helston Town Band, to welcome in the spring. A series of dances are held throughout the day, known collectively as the Floral Dances, though often colloquially as simply the Furry Dance.

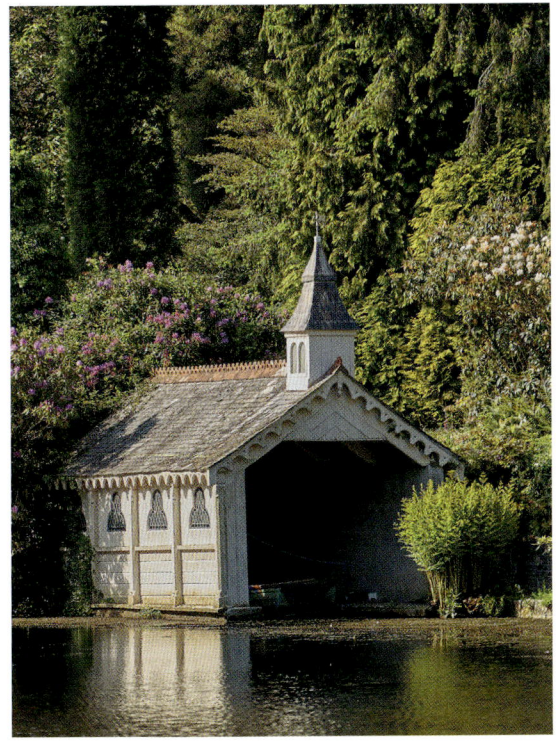
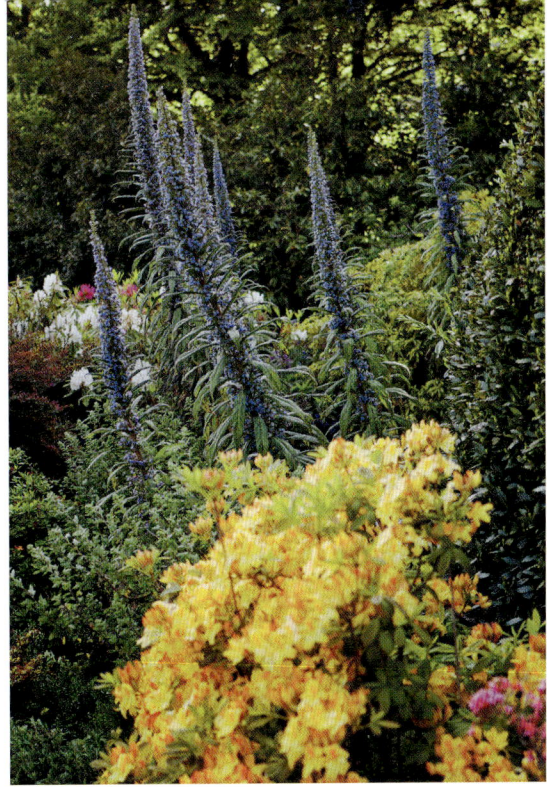

Above and Left: In a county filled with some of Britain's finest and most famous gardens, Trevarno, just outside Helston, is sometimes rather overlooked. It is however, a really quite beautiful place, its lake and the wooden lakeside boathouse among the main features.

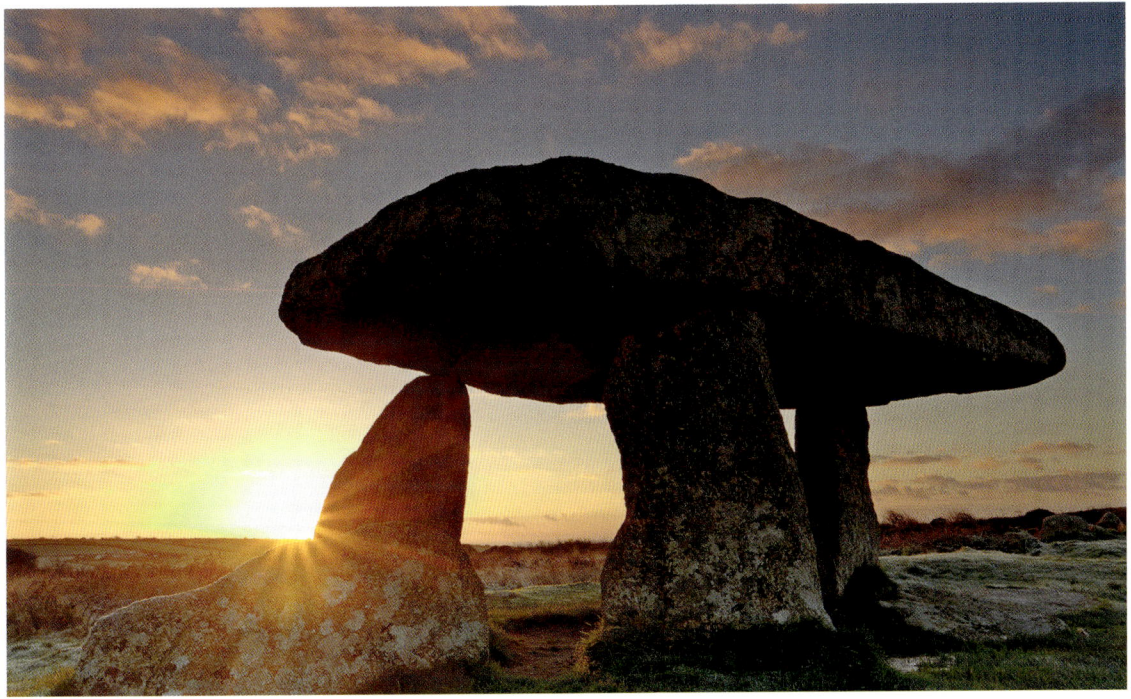

Above: Yet another sunrise lights up the 5000-year-old Lanyon Quoit, four giant granite slabs, all that remains of a burial chamber in the hills near Penzance.

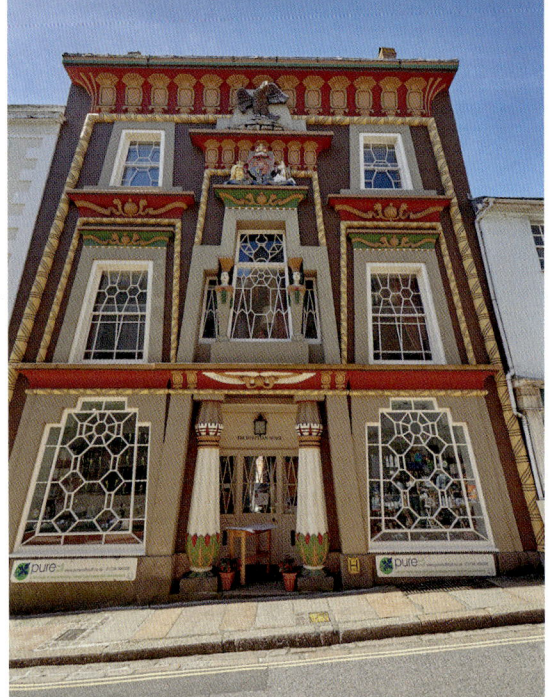

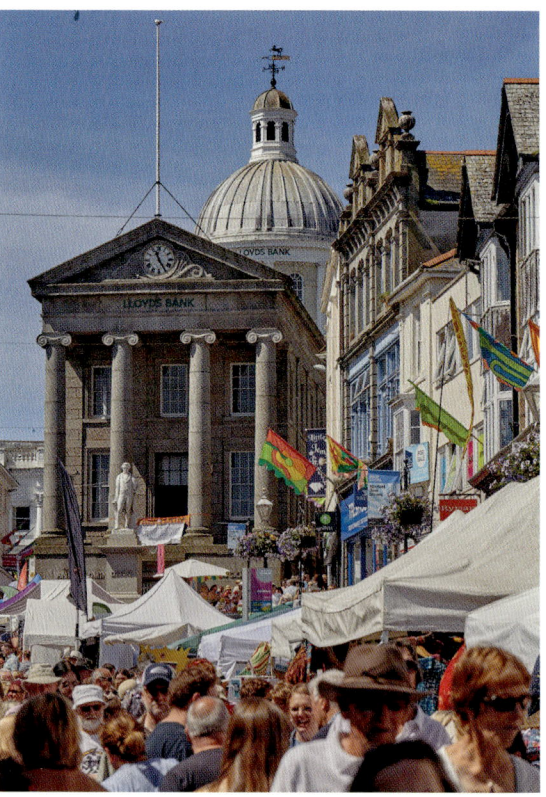

Above: The spectacular Egyptian House, today owned by the National Trust, is a remarkable statement among the otherwise rather grey stone Georgian buildings of Chapel Street, in the heart of Penzance.

Below: Fishing boats in the harbour at Newlyn, by some margin Cornwall's largest and busiest fishing port, with over 600 boats landing about 40 different species of seafood daily.

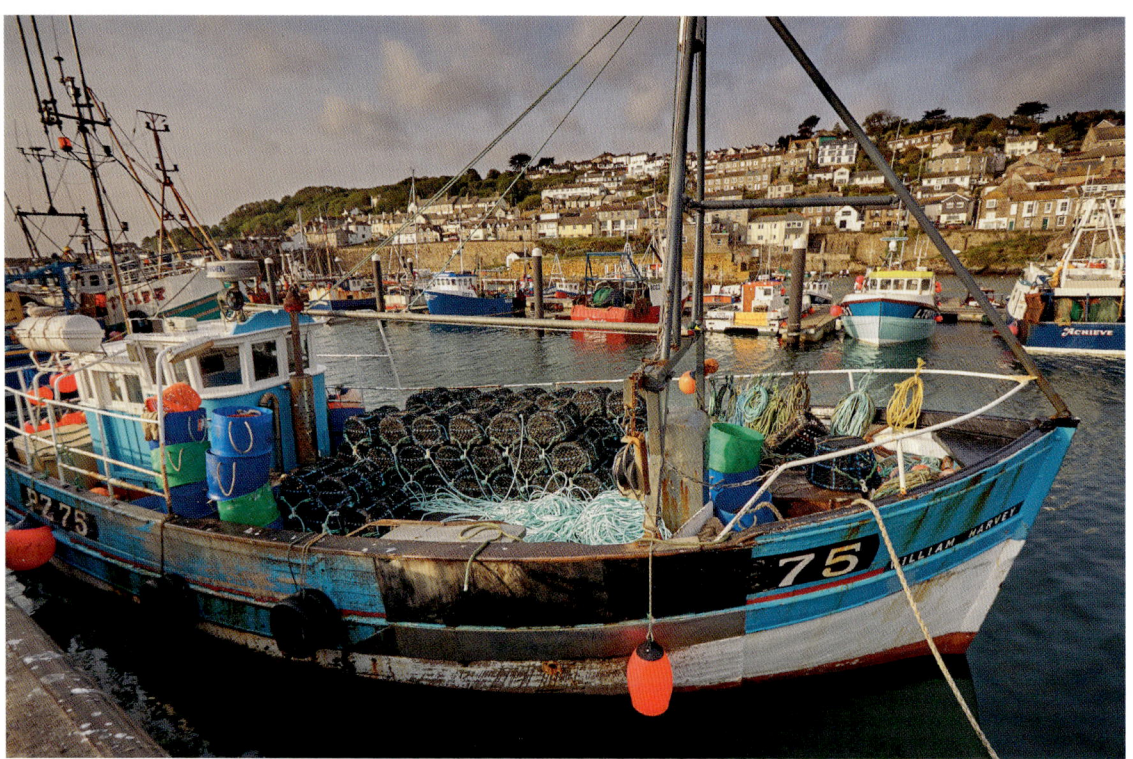

Left: Every June the streets of Penzance come alive, not to say absolutely packed, with the mid-summer Mazey Day parades of the annual Golowan Festival, a recently resurrected event that had died out in the 19th century.

Right: A low-tide view of the historic and interestingly named fishing village of Mousehole, so named (it is said) for the tiny entrance to its harbour.

Below: The famous outdoor Minack Theatre, climbs steeply up the cliffs at Porthcurno, carved out of those cliffs' very rocks.

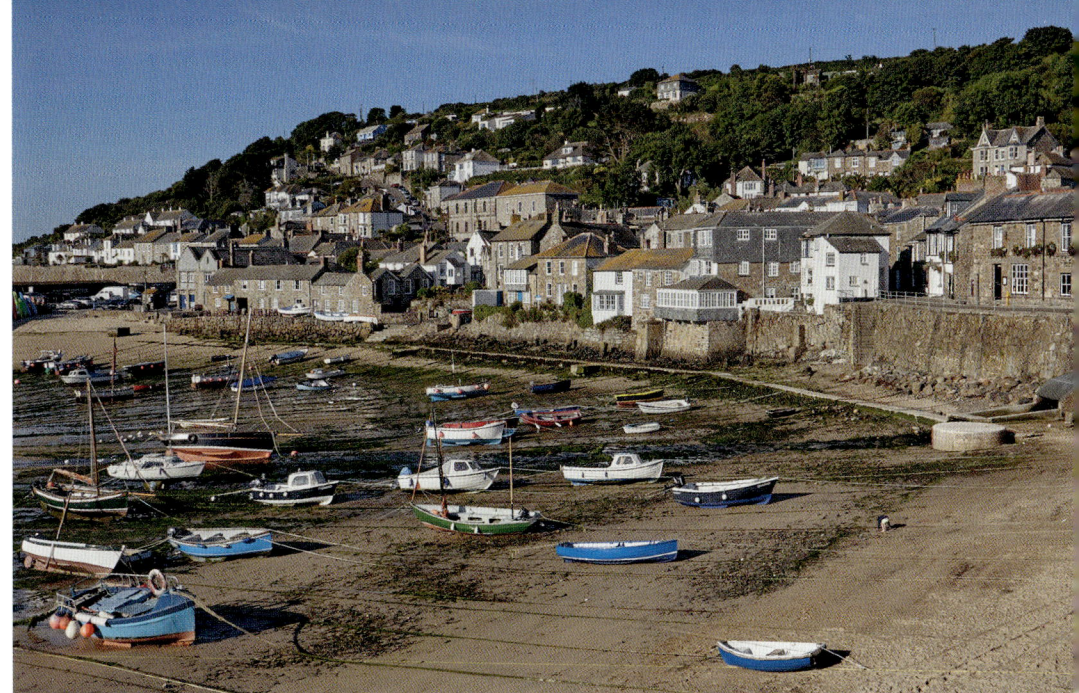

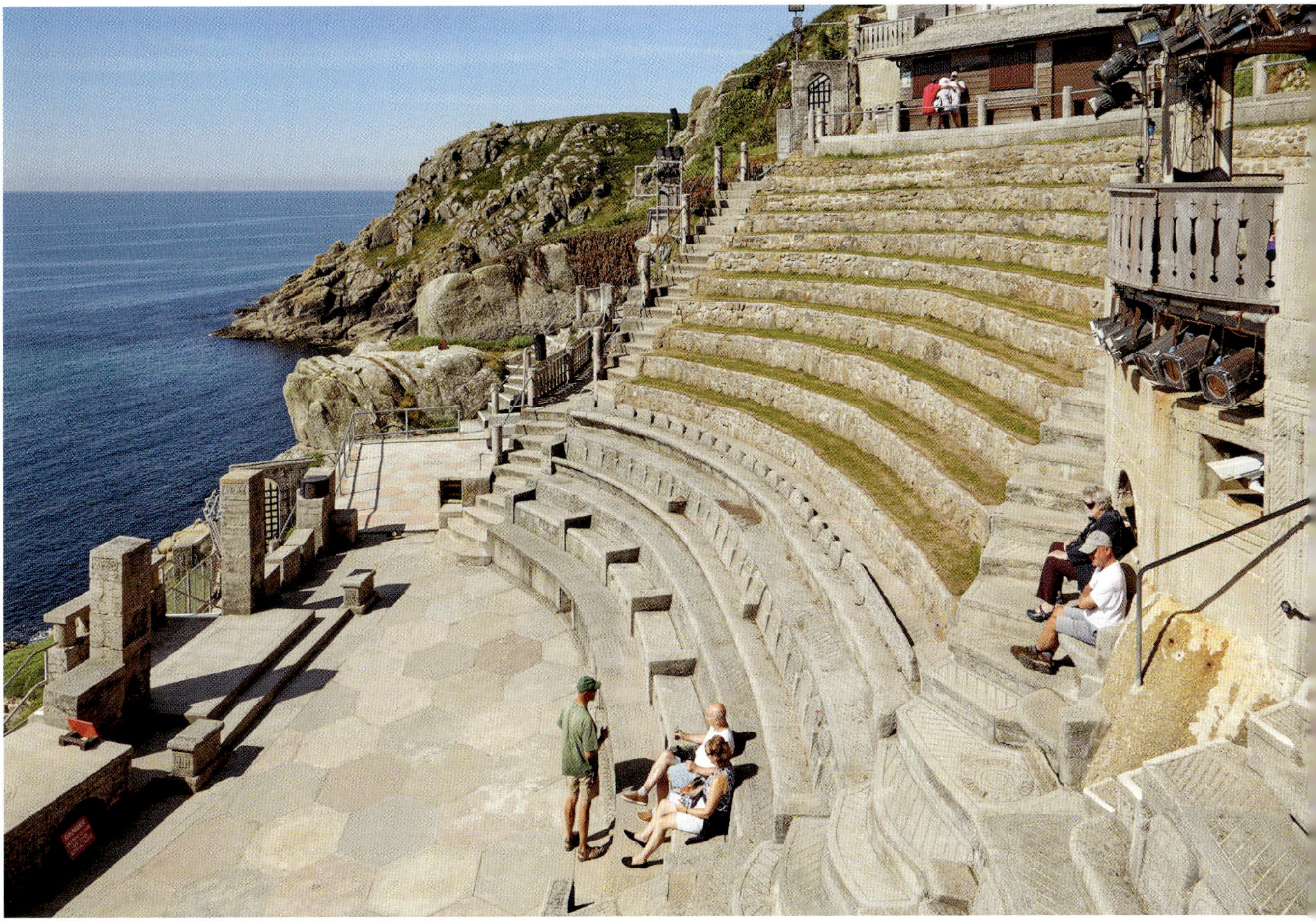

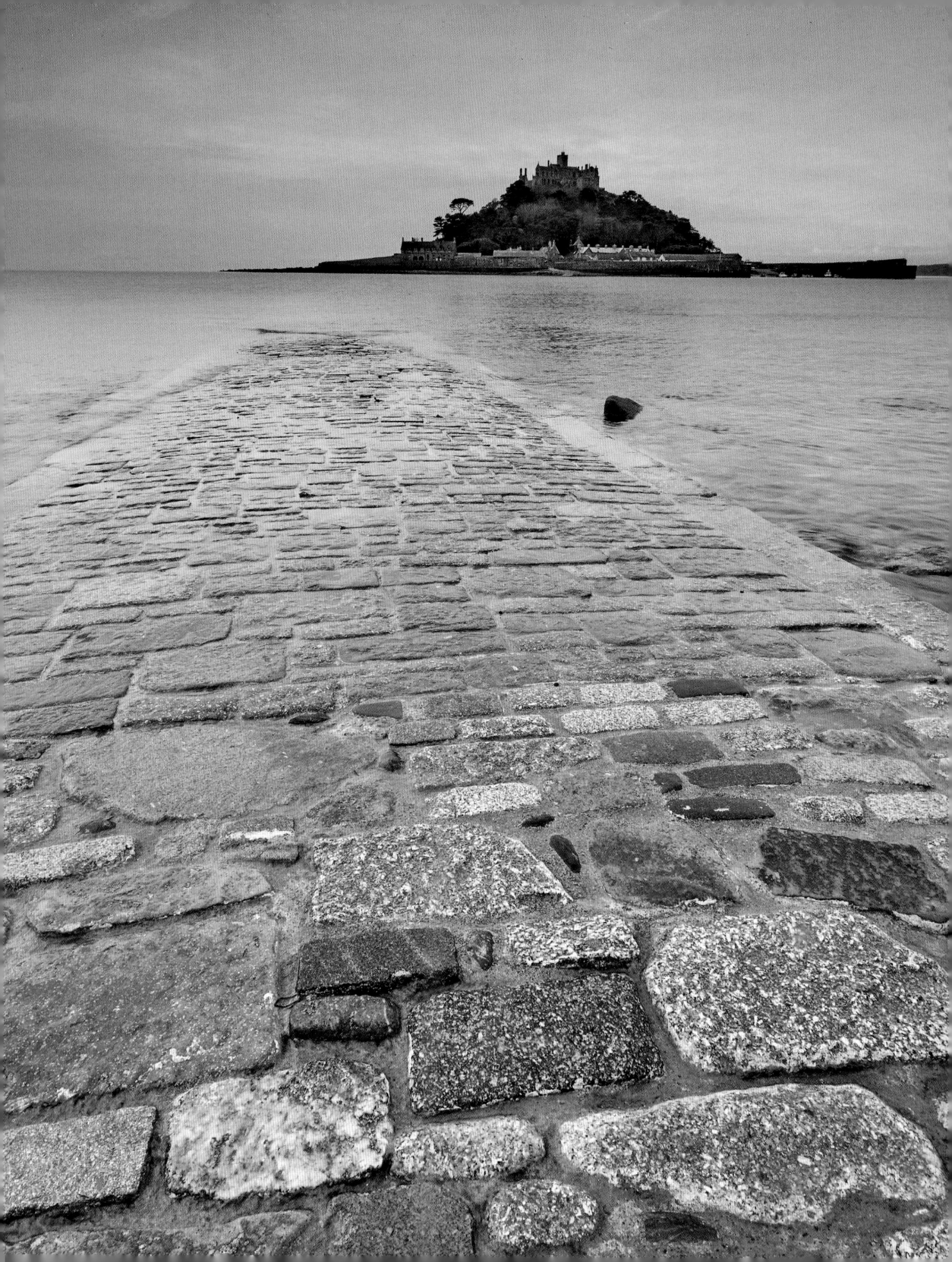

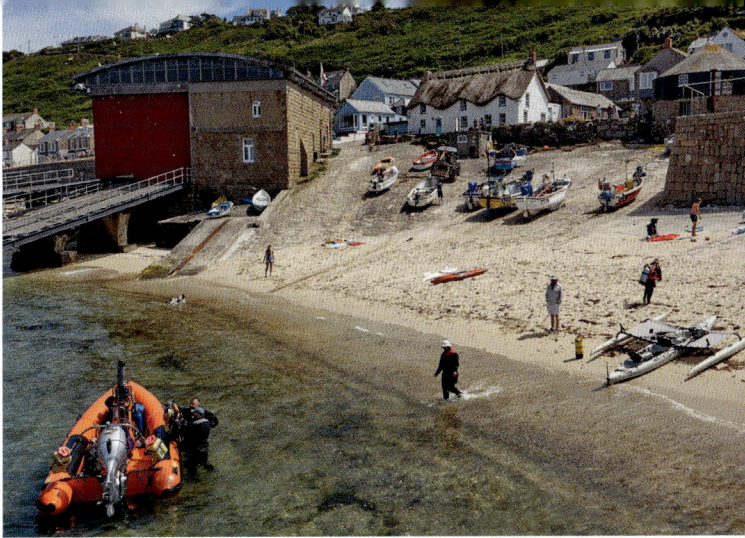

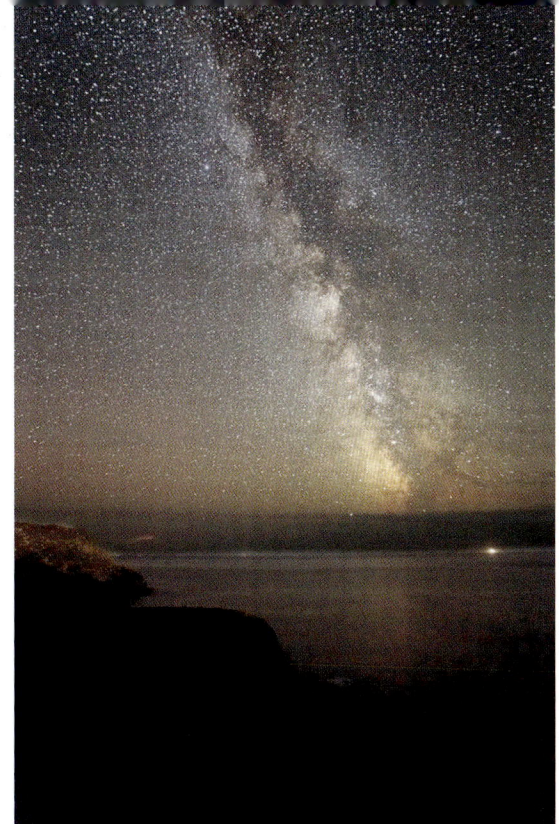

Opposite: An iconic sunrise view of St Michael's Mount, with its causeway just emerging from the sea as the tide slowly ebbs.

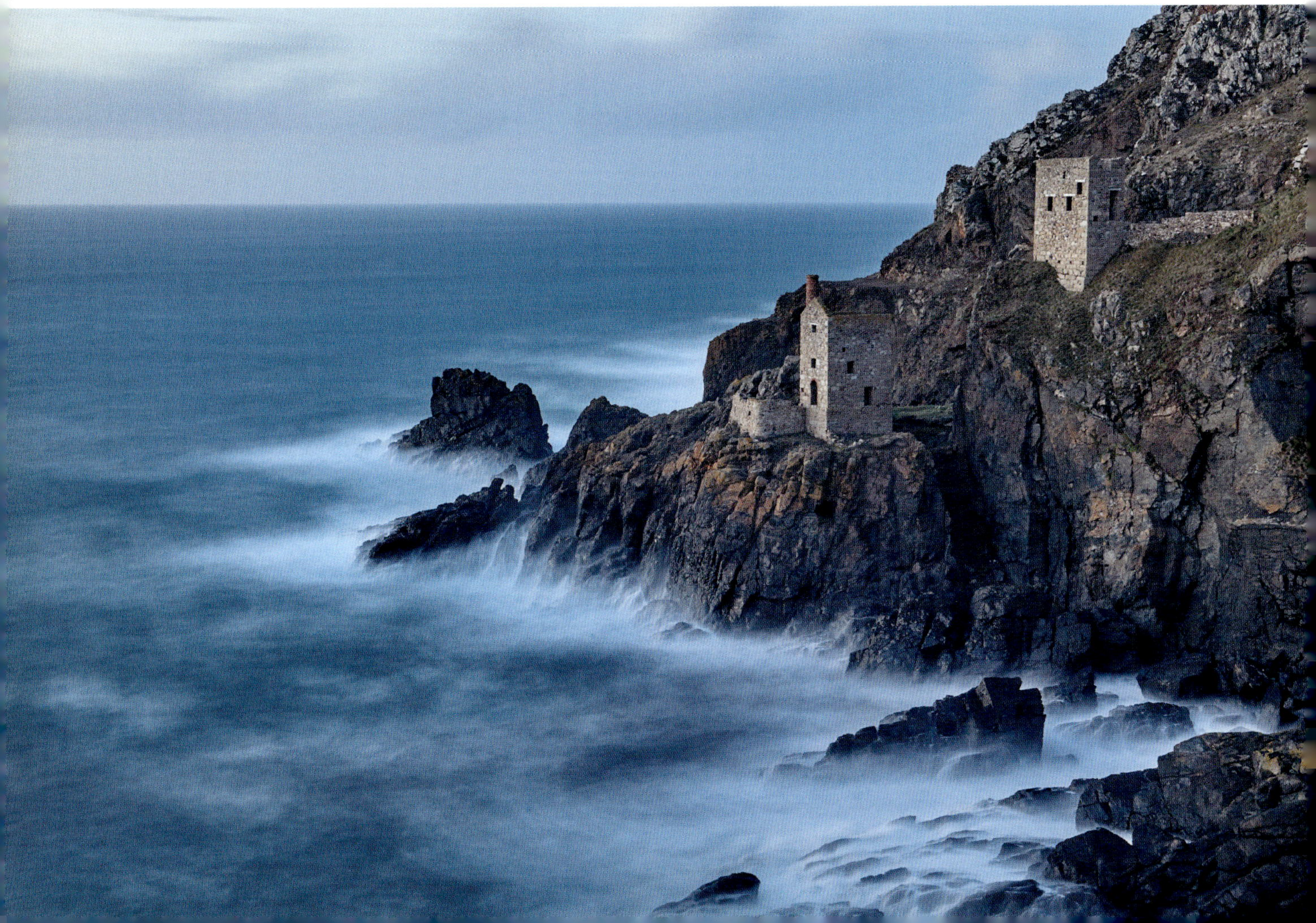

Left: The night sky seen from Land's End, with the Milky Way arcing across the sky from the southwest horizon. With good dark skies across many parts of west Cornwall, this is a fantastic place to see the night sky.

Above: The lifeboat station and sandy fishing harbour at Sennen Cove, the nearest village to Land's End. To the east stretches its spectacular beach, one of west Cornwall's most well known surfing venues.

Below: In a county strewn with well-known mine ruins, the cliffside remains of Botallack make this arguably the most iconic of all, encapsulating both the endeavour and harshness of Cornwall's historic economy and life.

Beautiful Cornwall: A Portrait of a County

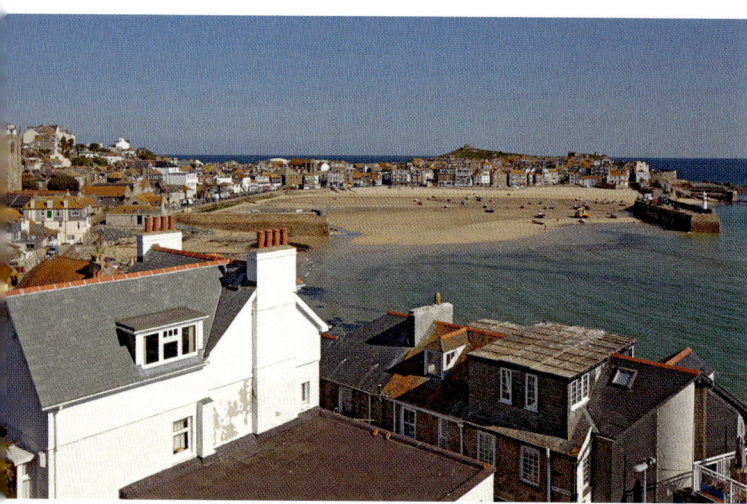

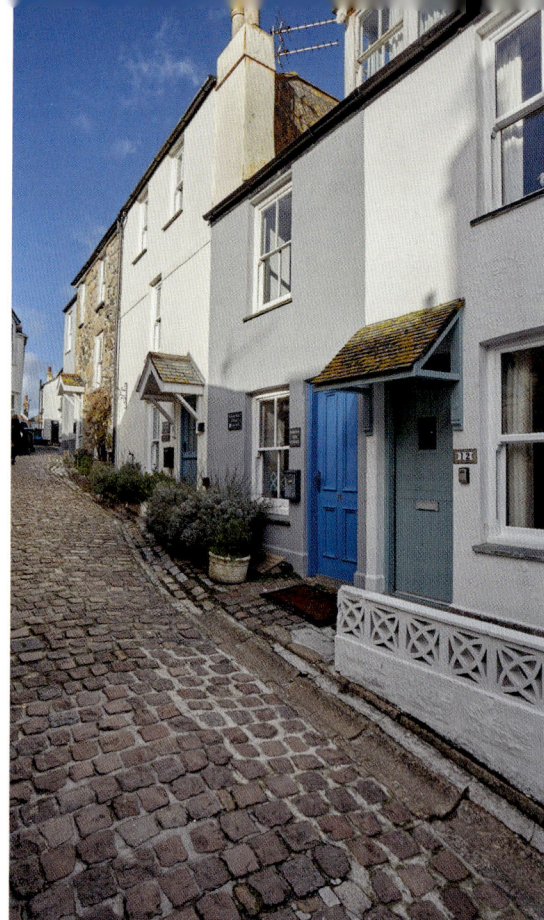

Above: Yet another of west Cornwall's famous views, that of the harbour at St Ives, seen at low tide.

Right: The historic part of St Ives is filled with tiny cobbled lanes, lined with an assortment of old cottages, these days mostly rented out as holiday homes.

Below: A modern reconstruction of a traditional lug-rigged sailing fishing boat, sits on the sands of St Ives' harbour at low tide.

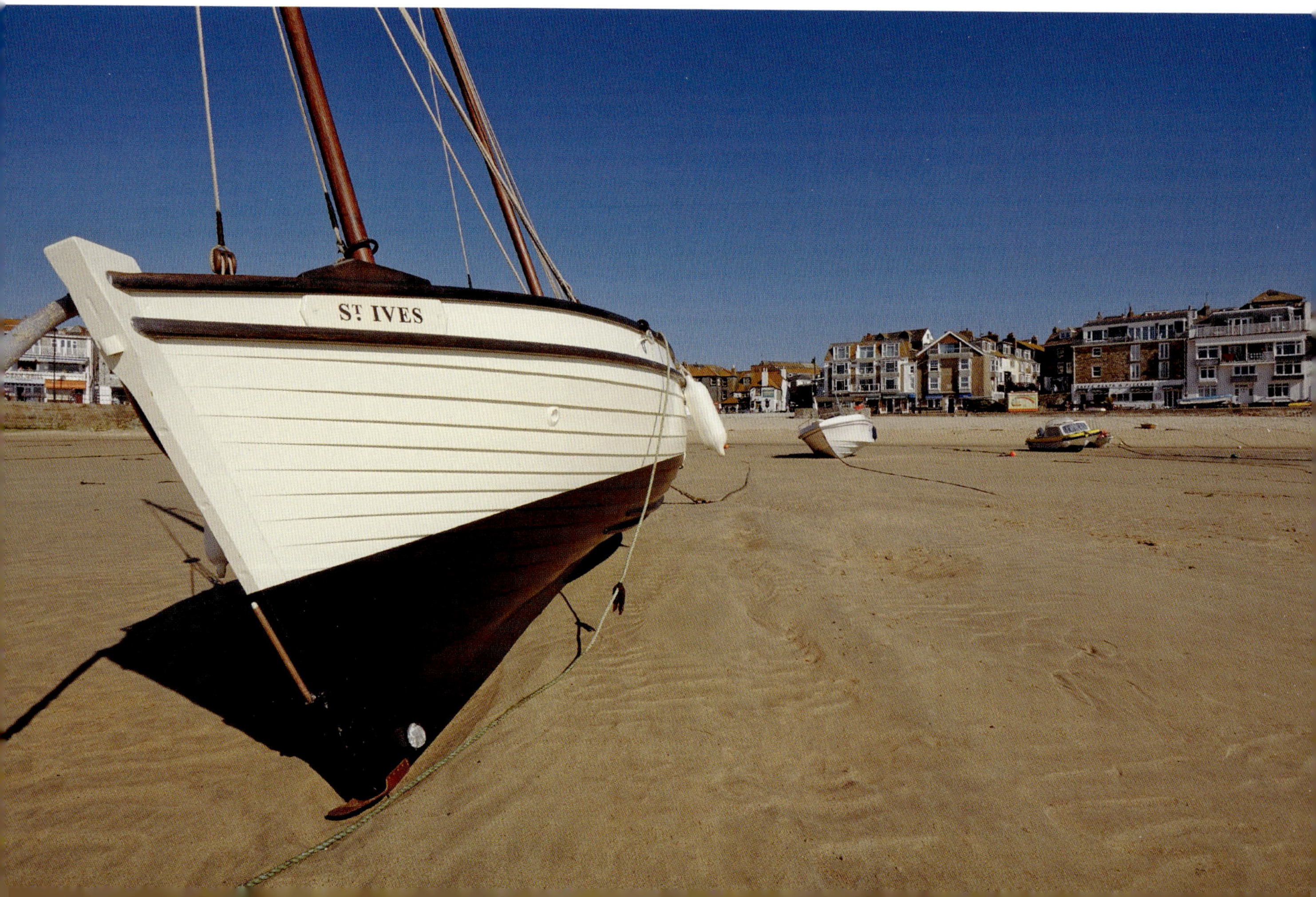

The Far West

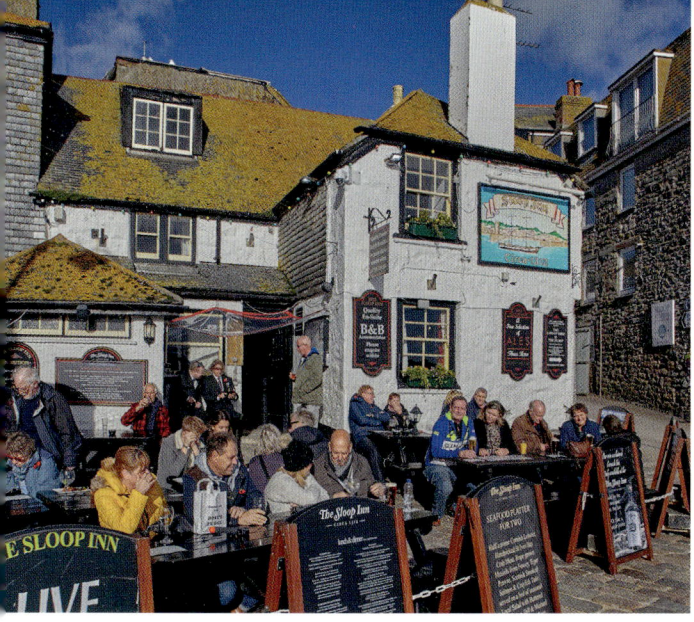
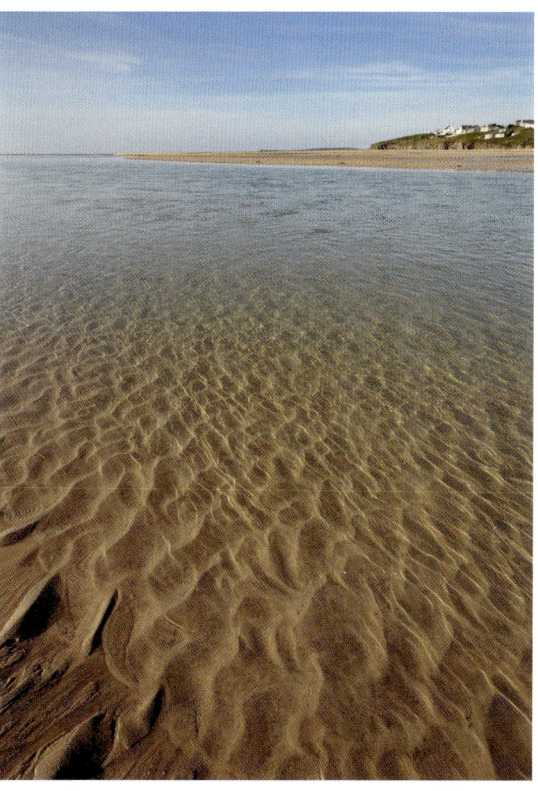

Above: The well known Sloop Inn is one of St Ives' oldest buildings, sitting beside the harbour, and for many hundreds of years providing valued refreshment to a constant stream of both visitors and fishermen.

Right: West Cornwall's only significant river, the Hayle River, reaches the sea at Lelant, between Hayle and St Ives, its clear, shallow waters flowing across a vast beach in its final few hundred metres.

Below: The magnificent beach that runs between Hayle and Godrevy Point, three miles (5 km) of golden sands, backed by a vast area of sand dunes that are now largely protected as a string of nature reserves.

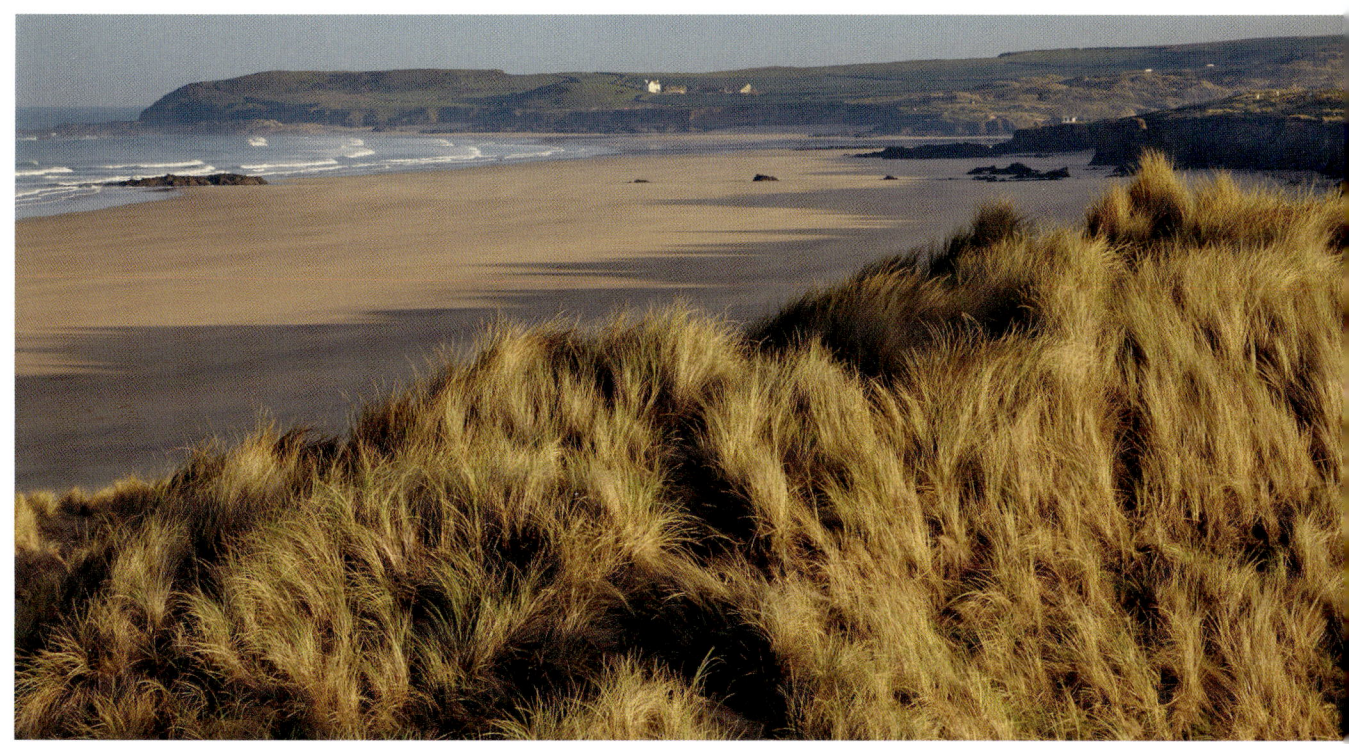

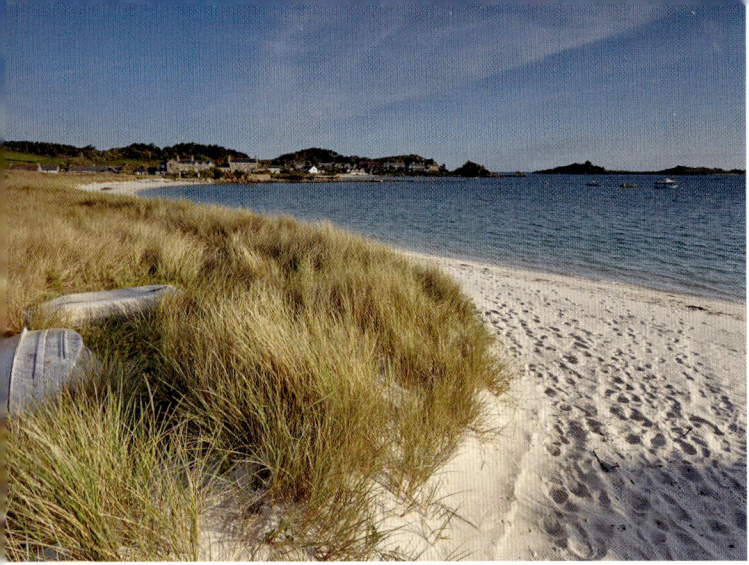

Above: Dunes and a sandy beach at Block House Point, with a view towards the village of Old Grimsby, on the eastern shore of Tresco, one the five inhabited islands in the Isles of Scilly.

Below: Silhouettes at dusk, in New Grimsby Harbour, the channel that separates Tresco and the island of Bryher. Cromwell's Castle, on the right, guards the northern entrance to the channel.

Right: The Gaia statue in the magnificent Abbey Gardens, a stunning garden that is the only outdoor home in the UK to an array of Mediterranean and Canary Island plants.

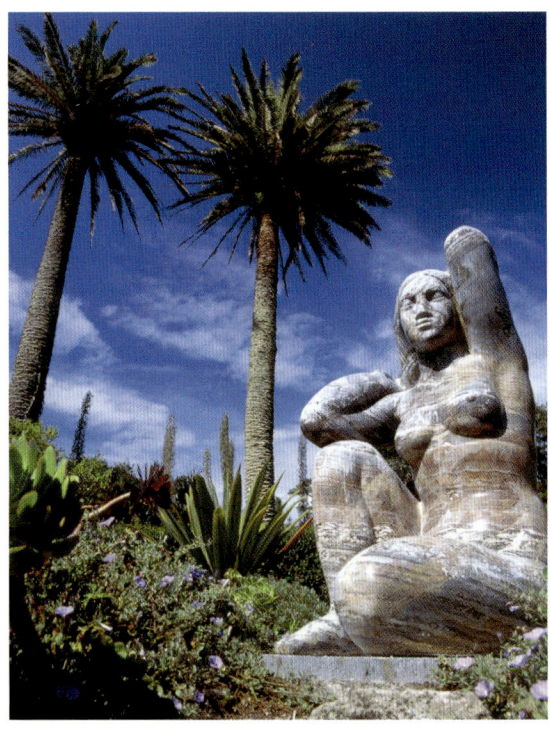

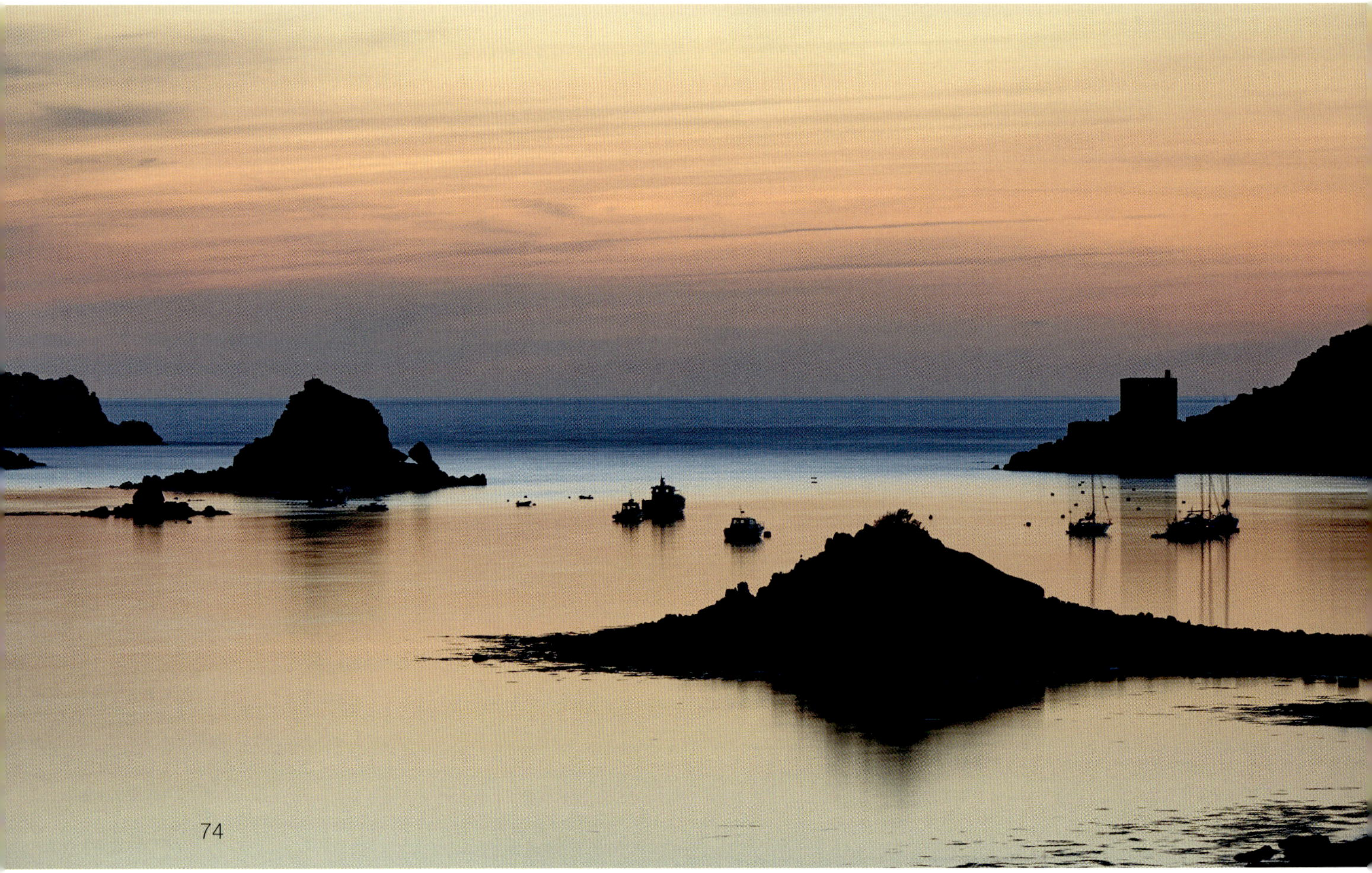

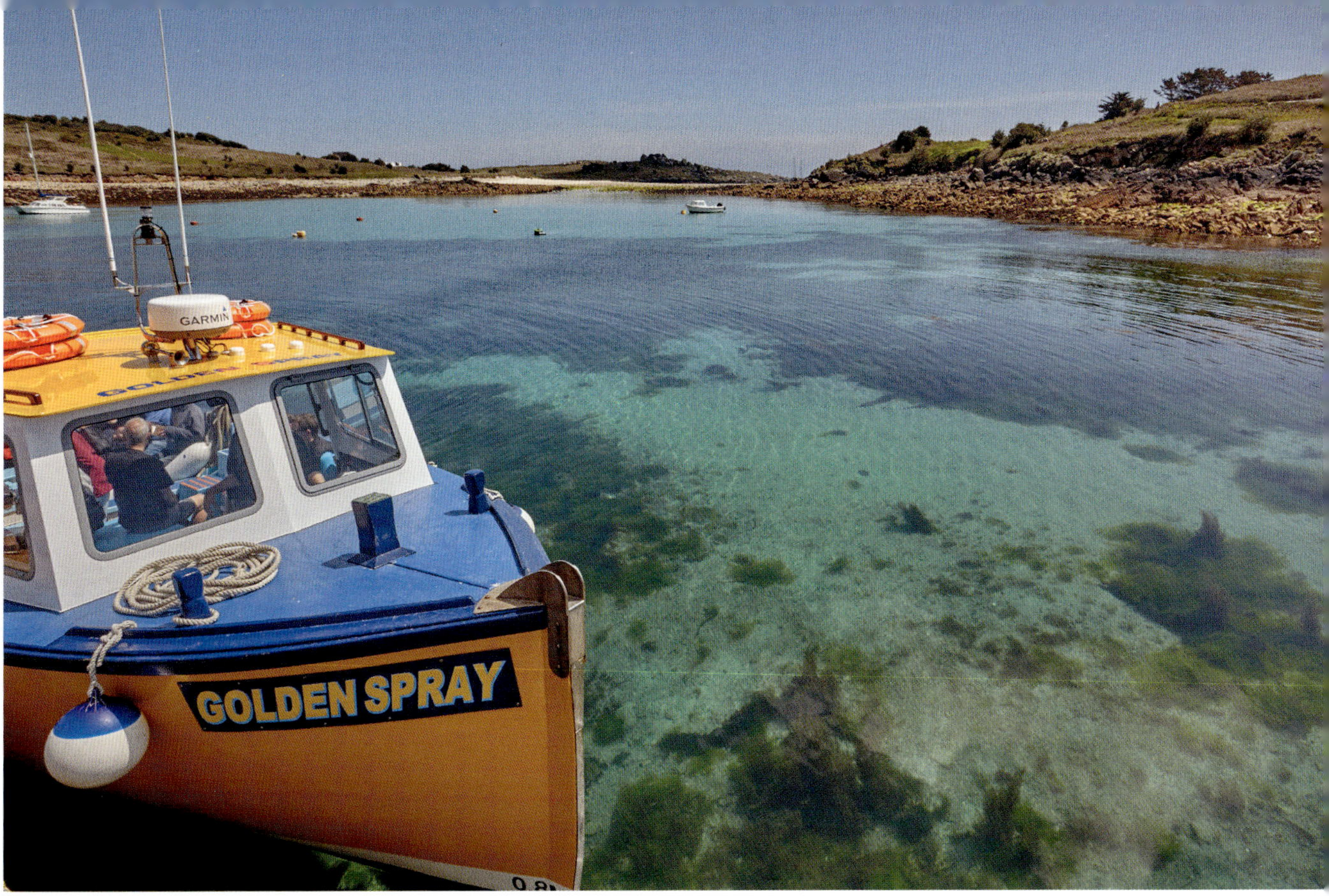

Above: Clear turquoise waters in Porth Conger, the harbour at the northern end of St Agnes, one of the smallest of the Scillies' inhabited islands.

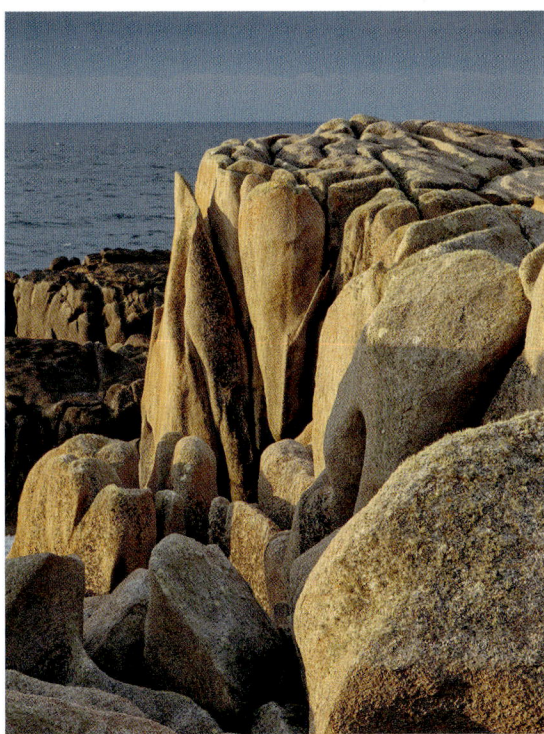

Above: Huge granite blocks mark the outer limit of Outer Head, the southernmost point of St Mary's, the Scillies' main island.

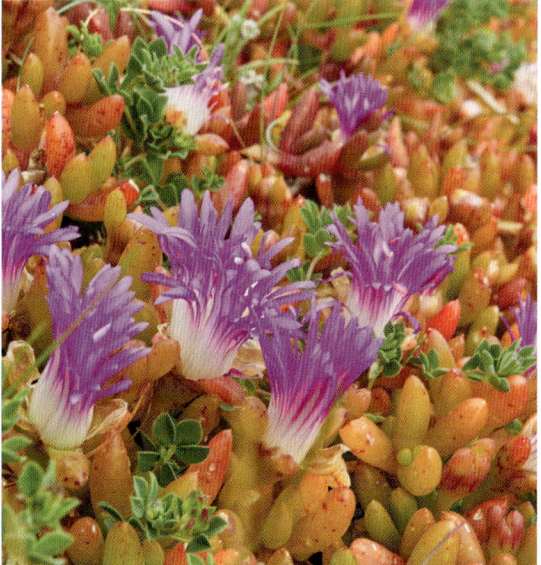

Above: Vibrant flowers of the Hottentot fig, a South African plant that has taken hold in the Scillies, and is now growing wild across the islands; here seen at Porth Hellick, on the east coast of St Mary's.

Beautiful Cornwall: A Portrait of a County

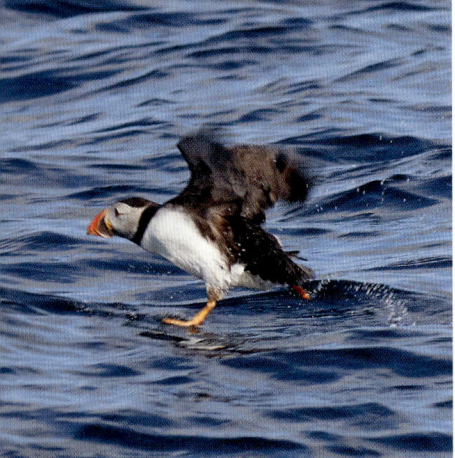
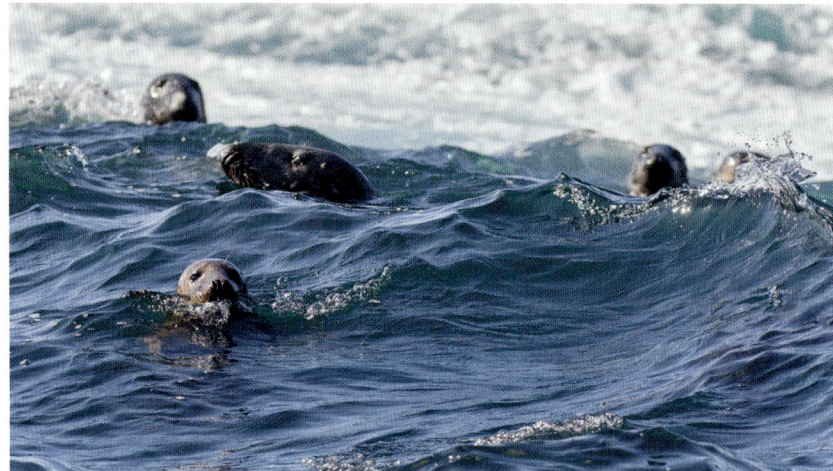
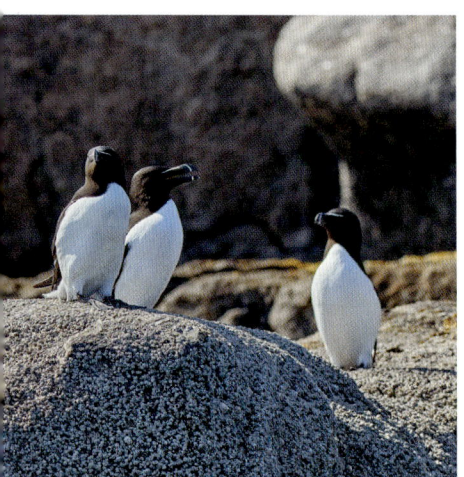

Top Left: A puffin coming into land on the water just off Mincarlo, one of the islets in the Norrard Rocks, on the Scillies' western edge.

Middle Left: Razorbills in the Western Rocks, the westernmost tip of the Scillies, where they commonly breed during spring and early summer.

Below Left: Oystercatchers on the beach in Pentle Bay, on Tresco. Though normally a very shy bird, in the Scillies they are often much more approachable than their cousins in mainland UK.

Above: Grey seals are perhaps the most common marine wildlife in the Scillies, especially in the Western Rocks, where they can be seen on and around the rocks and islets throughout the year.

Below: A dusk view of Hugh Town, the Scillies' only town, sitting on the southwest coast of St Mary's, seen from the village of Porthloo, to the north.

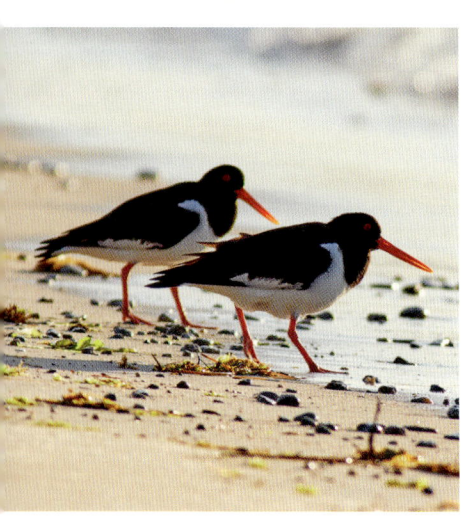
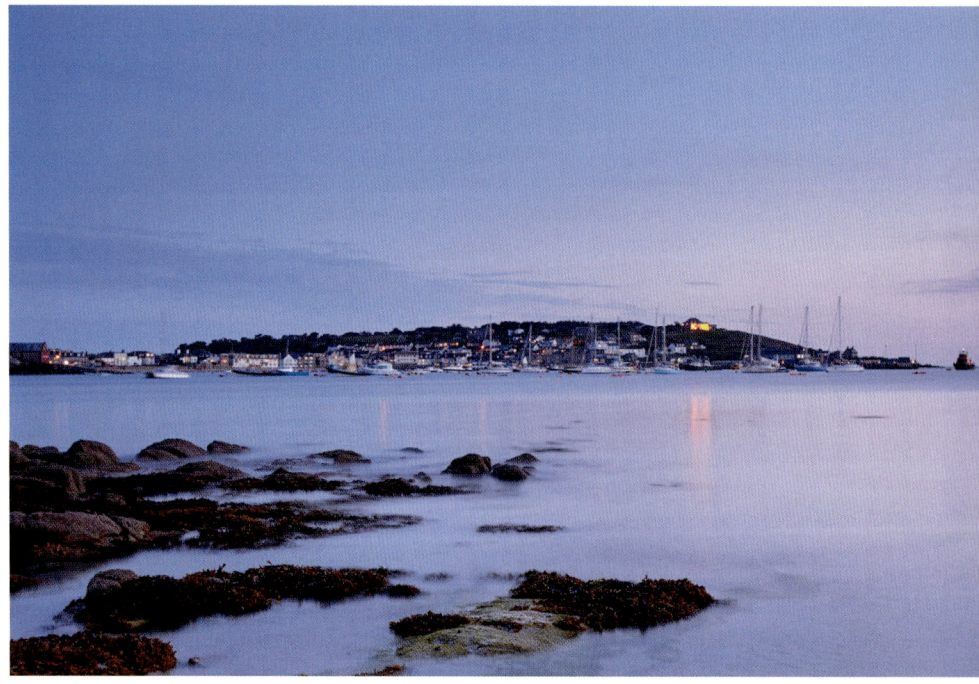

The Far West

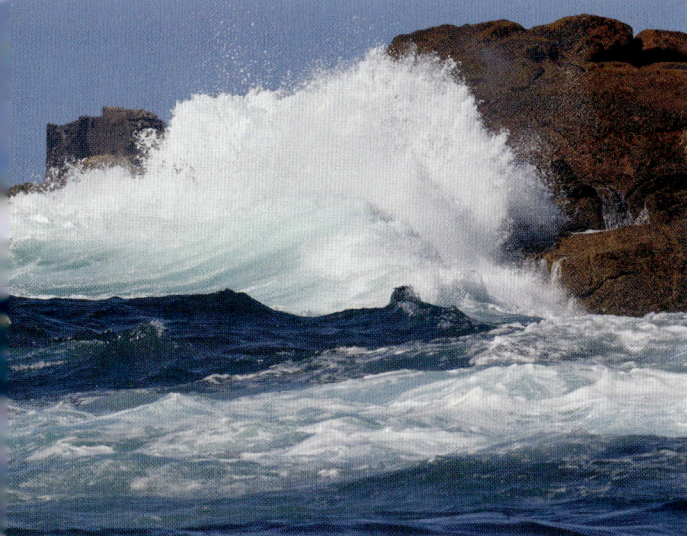
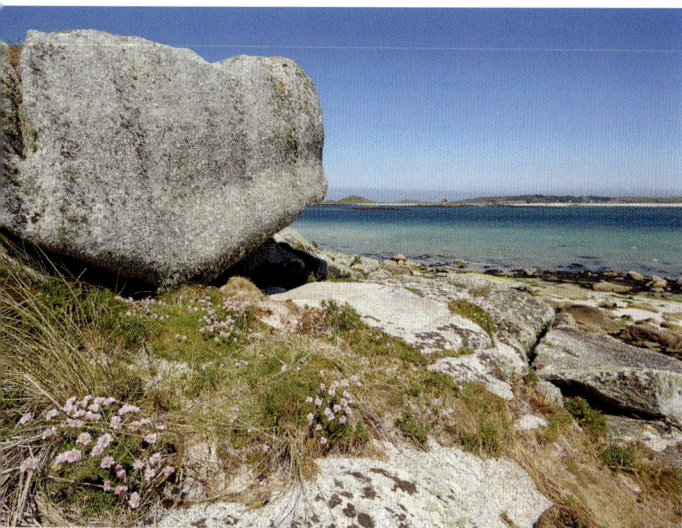
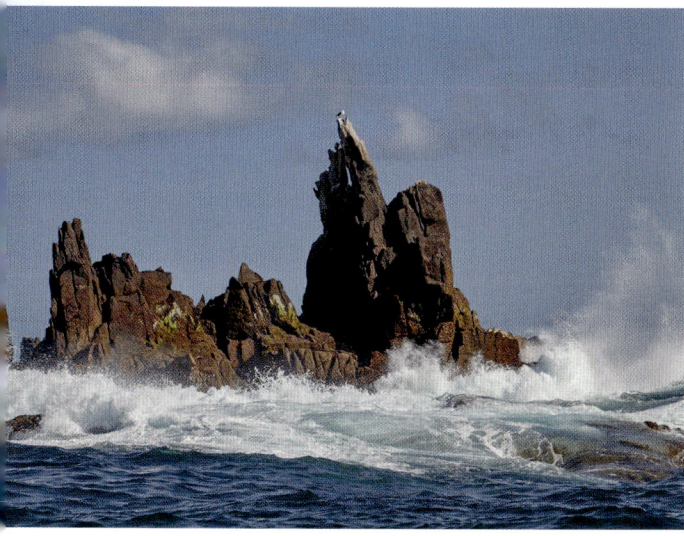
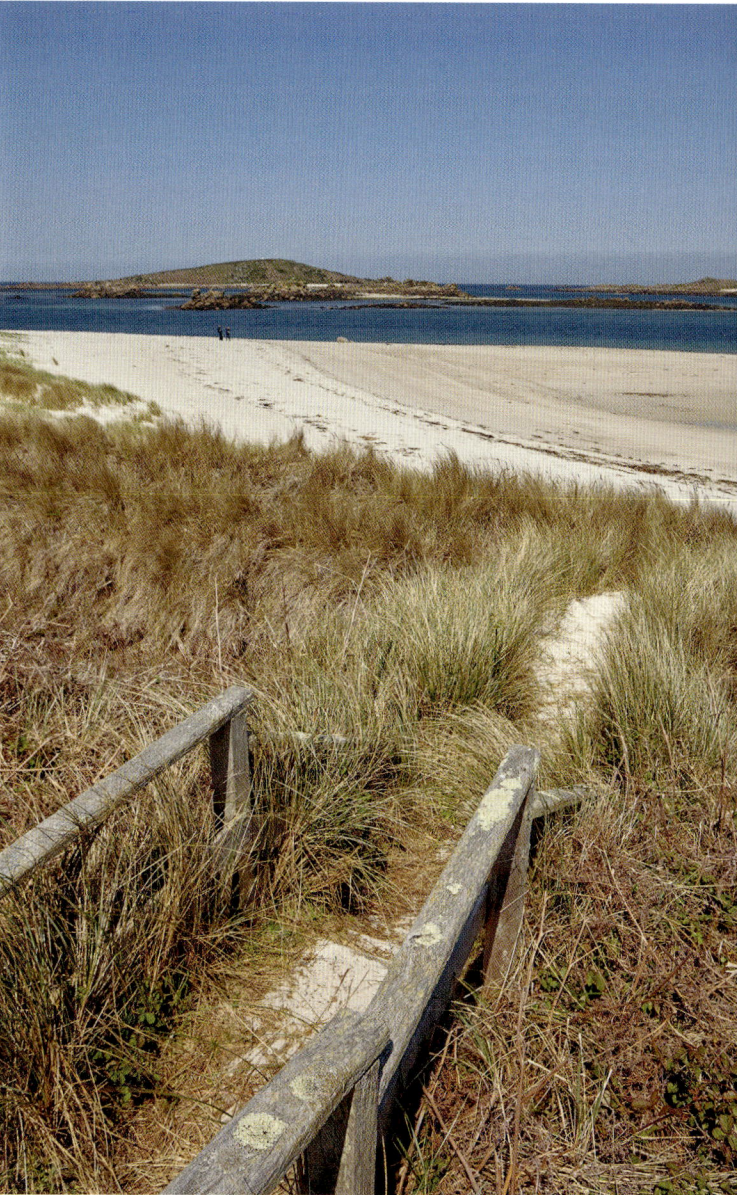

Top Left: Even on a calm day the Atlantic swell crashes onto the rocks of appropriately named Hell Bay, on the northwest shore of Bryher.

Middle Left: Granite boulders and sea pink (or thrift), typify the shore along much of Pentle Bay, on Tresco's east shore.

Bottom Left: Atlantic surf pounds granite rocks on the island of Annet, a nature reserve protected for its breeding populations of marine birds, and which is permanently closed to visitors.

Above Right: The wonderful sandy beach that lines Pentle Bay, on Tresco's east shore, with a view looking out towards the Eastern Isles, on the Scillies' eastern edge.

Resources

Here are some contact details that will give more information about a variety of aspects of Cornwall.

Local government

www.cornwall.gov.uk
The Cornwall local government website, covering the whole of Cornwall, excluding the Isles of Scilly

www.scilly.gov.uk
The local governent website for the Isles of Scilly

Tourism promotion

www.visitcornwall.com
The Cornwall Tourist Board

www.cornwall-online.co.uk
Cornwall tourism promotion and accommodation listings

www.visitislesofscilly.com
The Isles of Scilly Tourist Board

www.islesofscilly-travel.co.uk
Ferry and flight bookings for the Scillies

http://penzance.co.uk
Information about Penzance

www.stives-cornwall.co.uk
Information about St Ives, from the St Ives Tourism Association

www.visitnewquay.org
Newquay tourism information

www.falmouth.co.uk
Falmouth tourism information

www.visittruro.org.uk
The Truro Tourist Board

www.padstowlive.com
Padstow tourism information

www.visitbude.info
Bude Area Tourist Board

www.staustellbay.co.uk
St Austell Bay Tourist Board

www.fowey.co.uk
Fowey tourism information

https://visitlaunceston.co.uk
Launceston tourism information

General

www.edenproject.com
The Eden Project

Protected areas and conservation

www.cornishmining.org.uk
Cornwall and West Devon Mining Landscape World Heritage Site

https://cornwall-landscape.org
Cornwall National Landscape (formerly the Cornwall Area of Outstanding Natural Beauty

www.cornwallwildlifetrust.org.uk
Cornwall Wildlife Trust

www.cornwall-ifca.gov.uk/
Inshore Fisheries and Conservation Authority, Cornwall

https://group.rspb.org.uk/kernow
The Cornwall branch of the Royal Society for the Protection of Birds

www.nationaltrust.org.uk
National Trust

Festivals and other annual events

https://padstowobbyoss.wordpress.com/
Obby Oss Festival (Padstow)

https://helstonfloraday.org.uk
Helston Floral Dance (Helston)

https://golowanfestival.org
Golowan Festival (Penzance)

www.royalcornwallshow.org
Royal Cornwall Show (Wadebridge)

https://camelfordshow.co.uk
Camelford Agricultural Show (Camelford)

https://boardmasters.com
Boardmasters (Newquay)

https://falmouthweek.co.uk
Falmouth Week (Falmouth)

https://tunesinthepark.com
Port Eliot Festival (St Germans)

www.wpgc.uk
World Pilot Gig Championships (Isles of Scilly)

This is just a taste of some of the events taking place annually in Cornwall; there are many more that we don't have space to list here!

Index

Entries in **bold** refer to a photograph.

A
Abbey Garden 63, **74**
adder 7
agriculture 13
agricultural show(s) 13, **35**
Annet **77**
Area of Outstanding Natural Beauty
    Cornwall 7
Arthur, King 10, 31, **33**, **39**
Athelstan, King 4
Atlantic 2, **3**, 4, 5, **15**, **42-43**, 63

B
badger 7
beach(es) 3, 5, **14**, 14, **41**, **45**, 47, 63, **73**
Bedruthan Steps **3**, **30**, 31, **41**
Block House Point **74**
bluebell 7
Boardmasters **14**, 31, **44**
Bodmin 31
Bodmin Moor **4**, 4, 7, 10, 13, 17, **31**, 31, **39**, 40
Boscastle **6**, 31, **32**
Botallack **10**, 63, **71**
Bryher **74**, **77**
Bronze Age 10
Brown Willy **4**, 4, 31, **39**
Bude 4, 5, 30, 31, **32**
butterfly 7
    blue 7
    painted lady 7
    pearl-bordered fritillary 7
    tortoiseshell 7
    wall brown 7
buzzard

C
Cadgwith 63, **64**
Cadsonbury 17, **22**, **25**
Callington 17
Calstock 17, **23**
Camborne 11, 12
Camelford **35**
    Agricultural Show **35**
Cardinham Woods **5**, 31, **40**
Carn Galver **10**
Carrick Roads **46**, 47, **55**, **56**, **57**
castle 10, **11**, **21**, **33**, **47**, **74**
cattle **13**, 13, **35**, **55**
Cawsand **27**
Celtic 3, **8**
Charlestown 47, **49**
china clay 12
chough 7
Chun Quoit 63
Chynhalls Point **64**
Chysauster 63
cliff 3, **4**, 5, **6**, 6, 14, **32**, **65**, **71**
coast path 15
conservation 7

Constantine Bay **8**, 31,
Cornish Metals 11
Cornish Riviera 31
cormorant 7
Cornish
    language 3, 9
    nationalist party 8
    traditions 3, 8
Cornish Seal Sanctuary 47, **60**
Cornwall and West Devon Mining Landscape World Heritage Site 11
Cornwall National Landscape 7
Cotehele **24**
Coverack 63, **64**
crab 12-13
Crackington Haven **32**
Cromwell's Castle **74**
curlew 7

D
Dartmoor 17, 31
deer 7
Delabole 13
Devon 4, 16, 17
Doc Martin 31, **33**
Dodman Point 47
Dolly Pentreath 9
dolmen 10, **11**
dolphin 7
Dozmary Pool **39**
dune 5, 14, 31, **45**, 63
dunlin 7

E
Eastern Isles **77**
Eden Project **13**, 13, **47**, **50**
    Mediterranean Biome **50**, **51**
    Rainforest Biome **50**, **51**
English Channel 4, **29**, 46
estuary 4-5, **16**, 17, **18**, **25**, **28**, 31, **34**, **35**, **46**, 47, **48**, **55**, **56**, **57**, **58**, **61**, **73**

F
falcon, peregrine 7
Falmouth 5, 13, 47, **57**, **58**
farm animal **13**, **35**
farming 13
festival 8-9, **9**, 31, **36**, 63, **66**
fishing 3, **12**, 12, 15, **46**, **54**, **56**, 63, **64**, 68, 69
Fistral beach 3, **14**, 31, **44**
Fowey 47, **48**, **49**
Freathy cliff **26**
fulmar **7**, 7

G
Gaelic 3, 9
Gaia statue **74**

gannet 7
Geevor mine 11, 63
Glendurgan Garden 47
Godrevy **73**
godwit 7
Golitha Falls 31, **40**
Golowan 9, 63, **68**
Gorran Haven 47
gorse 6
granite **4**, **5**, 31, **77**
grape **13**, **34**
guillemot 7
gull 7
Gunnislake 17, **22**
Gweek 47, **60**
Gwennap Head **2**, **5**, 63

H
haddock 13
hake 13
Hamoaze, The 16, **17**, 17, **18**
hang-gliding **41**
hare 7
Hayle 5, 63, **73**
heath, Cornish **6**, 7
heather 6, 7
    bell 7
Helford **61**
Heligan, Lost Gardens of 47, **52**, **53**
Hell Bay **77**
Helston 63, **66**, **67**
    Flora Day **9**, 9, 63, **66**
    Floral/Furry Dance **9**, 9, 63, **66**
Hepworth, Barbara 15
heron 7
Holywell Bay **42-43**
horse **39**, **64**
Hottentot fig **75**
Hugh Town **76**
Hurlers, The **38**

I
Industrial Revolution 3, 11

JK
Kernow 9
kestrel **7**, 7
Kingsand **27**
Kit Hill 17
Kynance Cove 63, **65**

L
Land's End 5, 10, 62, **63**, **71**
language, Cornish 3, 9
Lanyon Quoit 63, **67**
Launceston 17
    Castle 17, **21**
Leach, Bernard 15
Lelant 73
lizard 7
Lizard, The 5, 7, 62, 63, **64**, **65**
Logan Rock 5, **62**, 63, **70**
Looe 12, 17, **19**

M
Marazion **62**, 63
Mazey Day 9, 63, **68**

Mebyon Kernow 8
Men-an-tol **11**
Merry Maidens **11**
Mevagissey 12, **15**, 15, 47, **54**
Millbrook Lake 17, **28**
Minack Theatre **69**
Mincarlo **76**
mining
    copper 3, 10-11, 12
    tin **2**, 3, **10**, 10-11, 12, 63, **71**, **80**
monkfish 13
moor **4**, 4, 7, 8, 10, 13, 17, **39**
Mt Edgcumbe Country Park 17, **28**, **29**
Mount's Bay **62**, 62, 63
Mousehole 8, 9, 15, 63, **69**
Mylor Harbour **46**, 47, **56**

N
National Maritime Museum, Cornwall **57**
National Trust 7
New Grimsby **74**
Newlyn 12, 12, 15, 63, **68**
    School 15
Newquay 3, 13, **14**, 30, 31, **37**, **44**
Norrard Rocks 63, **76**

O
Obby Oss 8, **9**, 31, **36**
Old Grimsby **74**
orchid, Southern Marsh 7
otter 7
Outer Head **75**
oyster, native **46**, **56**
oystercatcher **76**

P
Padstow 3, 5, 12, 30, 31, **34**, **35**, **36**
Pedn Vounder **14**, **62**
Penberth **12**, **69**
Pendeen 11, 63
Penlee Point 17, **27**
pennywort, wall **6**
Pentire Point **34**
Pentle Bay **5**, **76**, **77**
Penwith 5, 10, 62, 63
Penzance 9, 63, **68**
Perranporth 31
pilchard 12
Pinetum Gardens 47, **52**
plaice 13
Plymouth 4
    Sound 16, **27**, **29**
pochard 7
Poldark **45**
pollack 13
Polperro **15**,15,17, **19**, **20**, **21**
Polruan **54**
Polzeath 31
pony **39**, **64**
Porth Conger **75**
Porthcurno **4**, **14**, 63
Porthgwarra **63**
Porthmeor beach **63**

Porth Nanven **80**
Port Isaac 31, **33**
puffin 7, **76**

QR
rabbit 7
Rame Head 17, **27**, **29**
    Peninsula 17, **28**
Ramsar site 7
razorbill **7**, 7, **76**
Redruth 12
redshank 7
Restormel Castle **47**
rhododendron **52**
Rick Stein 31
River
    Camel 5, 31, **34**, **35**
    Fal 5, **46**, 47, **55**, **56**, **57**
    Fowey 5, 31, **40**, 47, **48**
    Hayle **73**
    Helford 5, 47, **60**, **61**
    Looe 5, 31
    Lynher 4, **16**, 16, 17, **25**, 31
    Tamar 4, 5, 16, **17**, 17, **18**, **22**, **23**, **24**
    Rough Tor **4**, 4, 31, 31, **39**

S
sailing **46**, **56**, **57**
St Agnes
    in north Cornwall **2**, 31, **41**, **80**
    in the Scillies **75**
St Anthony **55**
St Austell 12, 47
St Ives 3, 10, 12, 15, 63, **72**, **73**
    School 15
    Tate 15, 63
St German's **25**
St John's Lake 17, **28**
St Just-in-Roseland **8**, **55**
St Mary's **75**, **76**
St Mawes 47, **55**
St Michael's Mount 5, **70**, 63
St Piran, flag of 3, 8
Saltash 19
Sandy Mouth **15**, 31, **45**
sardine 13
scallop 13
Scilly, Isles of 4, **5**, 5, 7, 62, 63, **74-77**
sea campion 7
seafood 3, 14, 15
sea holly **6**
seal 7
    common (harbour) 7
    grey **7**, 7, **60**, **76**
sea pink 6, 6, **32**, **77**
Sennen Cove 5, 63, **71**, **79**
shag **7**, 7
shark, basking 7
sheep **13**, 13, **35**
shellfish 5
shoveler 7
Sites of Special Scientific Interest 7
Sloop Inn **73**
solar farm 13

sole, lemon 13
South Crofty mine 11
Stepper Point **35**
stone circle 10, **11**, **38**
Strongbow Exploration 11
Summerleaze beach **32**
surfing 5, **8**, **14**, 14-15, 31, **37**, **44**, 63

T
Tamar Bridges **18**
thrift **6**, 6, **32**, **77**
Tintagel 10, **11**, 31, **33**
Tom Bawcock's Eve 8
tourism 14-15, 63
Trebah Garden 47, **59**
Treen 5, **62**, 63
trefoil, bird's-foot 6
Tresco **5**, 63, **74**, **76**, **77**
Trevarno Garden **67**
Trevibban Mill vineyard **13**, **34**
Trevithick, Richard 11
Trevose Head 31
Truro 47, **56**
    Cathedral 47, **56**
turbot 13
turnstone 7

U
University of Cornwall 13
Upton Towan **73**

V
vetch, yellow kidney **6**, 6
vineyard **13**, **34**

W
Wadebridge 13, 31
waterfall 31, **40**
Watergate Bay 31
Western Rocks 63, **76**
Wheal Coates **80**
White Alps 12
Whitsand Bay 16, **17**, **26**
Widemouth Bay 31
wigeon 7
wildlife 6, **7**, 6-7
windfarm 13, **13**, **34**
wind turbine **13**, 13
wood anemone 7
woodland **5**, 6, 7, **22**, 31, **40**
World Heritage Site 11

XYZ

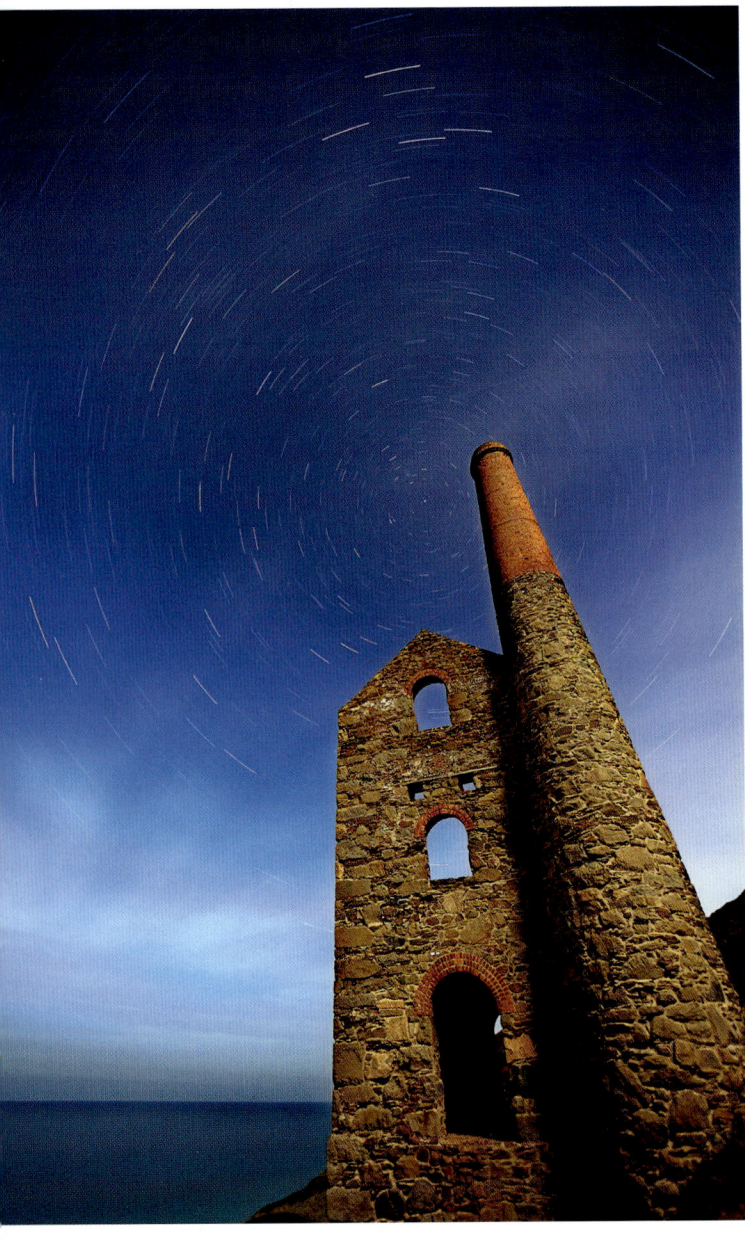

The 2019 first edition is published by Aquaterra Publishing

5 Canons Close
Bishopsteignton
Teignmouth
Devon
TQ14 9RU
Great Britain

www.aquaterrapublishing.co.uk

This second edition is published in 2024 by Aquaterra Publishing.

Copyright © 2024 in text Nigel Hicks.

The author asserts his moral rights to be identified as the author of this work.

Copyright © 2024 in photographs Nigel Hicks.

Copyright © 2024 in cartography Aquaterra Publishing.

All rights reserved. No part of this publication may be reproduced, stored in a retrieval system or transmitted in any form or by any means, electronic, mechanical, photocopying, recording or otherwise, without the prior written permission of the publishers and copyright holders.

Great care has been taken to maintain the accuracy of the information contained in this work. However, neither the publishers nor the author can be held responsible for any consequences arising from the use of the information contained therein.

ISBN: 978-09927970-6-5

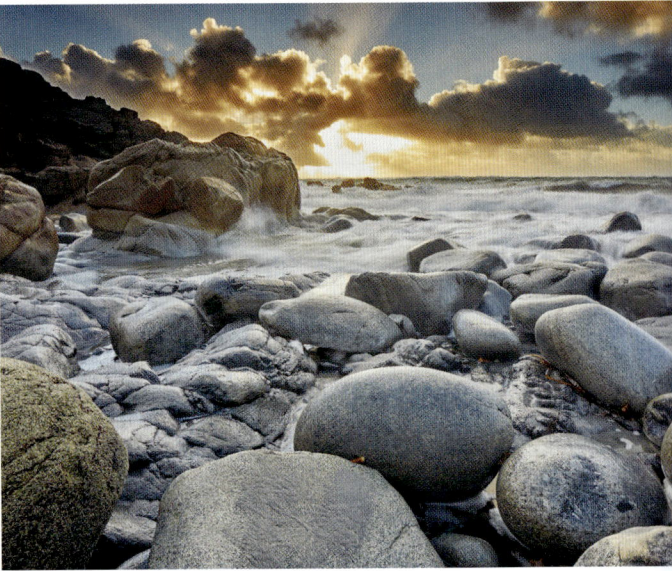

Above: The ruins of Wheal Coates mine, on the cliffs near St Agnes, photographed at night and showing the trails of stars as they rotate around the Pole Star, lying just left of the chimney.

Right: As the sun sets over the Atlantic, surf rolls in over shoreline boulders, at Porth Nanven, near St Just.

Previous page: Fishing boats drawn up on the slipway at Sennen Cove, with the lifeboat station behind.

Front cover image: The dunes of Holywell Bay bathed in golden early morning sunlight.

Text and Cover design:
Topics – The Creative Partnership, Exeter, Devon, Great Britain
www.topicsdesign.co.uk

Printed by:
W&G Baird Ltd.
www.wgbaird.com